How Decisions in Life are Shaping L

PURPOSE

Impact, Influence & Positive Transformation

22 Authentic and Bold Stories
by a Global Collective of Leadership Consultants

Curated by Eve Simon

Copyright © 2020
Authors, see Contents
hello@purpose-book.com

Printed and Published by:
BoD – Books on Demand, Norderstedt

Editing: Various Editors
For authenticity, stories written by authors from the UK have been edited in British English, all others in American English.

Consulting and Design by Fempress Media, Germany

ISBN: 9783748107262

All rights reserved; no part of this publication may be reproduced or transmitted by any means, electronic, mechanical, photocopying or otherwise, without the prior permission of the publisher.

Contents

Introduction: The Spark — 9

Making The Most Out Of This Book — 13

My Journey Towards My True Self
Agneta Dieden – Sweden — 15

Author Of Your Own Life Story
Abby Barton – United Kingdom — 27

Moving From Legal Grounds To Solid Ground
Andrew Cohn – United States — 37

Sunflower
Ann-Sofie Ellefors – Sweden / Luxembourg — 45

Evolution Of Me
Artur Chernikau – Latvia — 55

A Call To Adventure
Carl Lindeborg – Sweden — 65

Discovering My Gifts
Dr. Erika Maria Kleestorfer – Austria — 79

Leaders: The Shamans Of A New Paradigm
Eve Simon – Germany / United States — 91

The Road Home
Fredrik Lyhagen – Czech Republic / Sweden — 103

My Path To Purpose: A Series Of Dots
Graham Bird – United Kingdom — 113

I Did It!
Hans Veenman – The Netherlands 123

Dare To Be Happy
Jean-Christophe Normand – France 135

Invent Yourself, Then Reinvent Yourself
Karin Verhaest – Belgium 145

Where There Is A Will There´s A Way
Kristina Zumpolle Flodin – The Netherlands / Sweden 155

Lead With Your Heart
Lasse Wrennmark – Sweden 165

Two Good Reasons
Marion Bourgeois – Germany 173

A Drawing Of A Tree
Michele Scott – United Kingdom / South Africa 187

The Magic Of Life-Changing Encounters
Mikaela Nyström – Finland 195

The Calling Of The Heart
Monika Jankowska – Poland 203

From Cell To Soul
Shuntian Yao – China 213

River Of Life
Simone Alz – Germany 221

Be The Change
Xavier Bertrand – France 231

Conclusion by Cyril Legrand 243

A Higher Cause 251

Acknowledgment 253

Introduction
The Spark

There's a saying that 7 people around the world have the same brilliant idea at the same time. Only those who are crazy enough and brave enough to act on this spark while including others in the process are innovative enough to bring their ideas to reality. This was certainly the case in the creation of this book.

I was inspired to bring people around the world together to share their deep authentic stories about how purpose became their driver in life and business.

My vision was to create a book that empowers, encourages and invites leaders – and by leaders I mean everyone, not just by position but by mindset - to look beyond the obvious, to drive change for the greater good and, last but not least, live an authentic and self-actualized life.

There was no question about who I wanted to do this with: my colleagues and friends of the Oxford Leadership community. I'm grateful beyond words that many of them said yes to my crazy idea and started creating with me.

The book you are holding in your hands is not meant to be a lecturing book nor a sales pitch. Rather, it's a collection of authentic, bold and often vulnerable personal stories – all with an individual perspective and experience.

Herein you'll find 22 stories – some you may relate to more than others. Perhaps some of the stories will inspire you to reflect in ways that are surprising. Our intention was to move you through the sharing of our individual personal stories – regardless of the direction in which it takes you.

The book might help you find answers to questions you may have such as:

- What impact can a purpose have on me and society?
- Why do purpose-driven companies perform better?
- Where does purpose come from?

- How does purpose influence my life?
- How do I even find my purpose?
- Why do we as leaders need to reflect on purpose anyway?

You might feel inspired and uplifted. You may even find answers to questions you never considered before.

What unites us within the Oxford Leadership community is that we don't think of ourselves as working for a ‚company' just to earn a paycheck – rather, a purpose to be aligned with. We all share a common purpose at Oxford Leadership to ‚Transform Leaders for Good'. And even though we are all independent, this is what brought us together through the years for clients all over the world.

Throughout our personal development and growth journeys, we've all experienced the power to start within. Self-mastery of emotions, thoughts, vision, values, barriers, and purpose is the key to greater impact. This is what the world needs - leaders who become conscious and alive to powerfully use their influence to make an impact for the greater good – for the people they lead and the society they touch.

Staying true to your purpose and bringing a vision into the world isn't always easy. Sometimes you need to lean in even further, face the shadows, describe an outcome you don't even know yet, or convince people beyond some present context.

My vision became our vision and thus came alive. I am deeply grateful for every contribution … for every one of the dearest authors, muses, vision givers and storytellers who said yes and went the extra mile to put their purpose into writing.

Ecosystems such as the one from Oxford Leadership are more likely to survive the future – because they share, contribute, support, expand, adapt and cherish their relationships. They fly freely - connected by a deeper purpose. Isn't this the superpower of the 21st century?

I believe in the collective – with each individual making the whole complete. The world will be healthier with individuals and companies who are driven by a purpose higher than themselves. Leaders are not those who are defined by their titles but rather by a mindset that will challenge the status quo to create new solutions. I believe business is the driving force for creating a society where everyone can thrive. Purpose is giving us an innate superpower to go this extra mile, not for personal benefit but for the greater good.

May you gain great insights inspired by our stories and the love between the lines.

In gratitude,

Eve Simon
Curator of the PURPOSE book

Making The Most Out Of This Book

As you dive into the following twenty-two chapters, we suggest you take some time in-between reading to reflect on your own journey toward your unique purpose. Above all, we hope you will get inspired by our authors' stories.

Please consider the following six questions to learn more about what brings meaning to you in order to live a life in which your purpose can have more impact:

1. What are you most passionate about?

2. What would others say is your unique contribution?

3. What do you most enjoy doing when you tap into skills or talents that come naturally to you?

4. What did you love doing as a child before anyone had an opinion about it?

5. What would you do if you had no fear?

6. When you reflect upon your experiences and the competencies you have, what has life prepared you to give?

Life is a journey, and purpose ignites the path. Our awareness and the decisions we make influence how wisely we use our time on earth.

Enjoy!

My Journey Towards My True Self

by Agneta Dieden

In 2011, I was recommended a three-day leadership program, the Self Managing Leadership, run by Oxford Leadership. I was very reluctant. Looking at the framework for the course, I could see that part of the process was defining an inner compass with values, purpose, and a vision - working with barriers. With a bit of arrogance, I thought I had done all that and it was part of my work as a coach.

The program immediately broke my hesitation and pulled me in. This was different from all the other leadership programs I attended. In three days it provided a solid process that enabled depth and clarity. Context setting with storytelling invited reflection. When we finished, I walked up to the trainer, who happened to be Brian Bacon, the founder of Oxford Leadership, and said "I found my purpose. This is what I want to do. I want to deliver these programs."

I met with other colleagues of Oxford Leadership and found something new. I found diversity, people from different countries with different backgrounds and personalities whose self-awareness was bigger than their ego. People who were not driven by money but by love for what they can give and contribute to in leadership and business. I put my own business on a pause button and started to deliver and design programs for Oxford Leadership. For the first time in my professional life, I felt belonging. I found my tribe.

Since then, almost nine years have passed. I have focused all my energy on Oxford Leadership, building business, designing and delivering programs as a facilitator and coach. It has been quite a ride.

I am mentored by my wholehearted colleagues. We give each other constant feedback and in addition to the evaluations we get from the groups, it can be quite tough. If we don´t grow and evolve, we cannot bring that quality to our groups. We give of our whole selves and if we are not authentic, people sense it.

If I step into the overachiever and over-prepare, I lose my heart and soul. I need to dare to be vulnerable and true and at the same time have focus. What works for me is to have a clear intention, presence and then let go. Every time is different and that is the beauty of the programs we deliver at Oxford Leadership. It´s blissful to be a catalyst for people connecting to their purpose and to do what I´m passionate about. It is the grace I called for during a vision quest to Death Valley in 2008.

One thing I have learned through my purpose journey is the impact of setting an intention. I set my daily intention early in the morning and it affects the outcome of the day. I set my intention before I step into a meeting and it affects the outcome. The intention is about what quality I want to bring and how things are going to work out. When I set the intention of "effortlessly," meaning no struggle, and open up to the possibility of everything working out seamlessly, it somehow does. I have not stopped being surprised by the magic and simplicity that setting intention brings to life.

Starting the journey toward my true self

A dragonfly lands on my chest.
I see its trembling wings with the colors that the light brings forward.
What does it want to say to me?

It says life is fragile and we shall take good care of it. Each of us brings meaning to life. You do not need to be big and strong to start a journey. I´m sitting in the April afternoon sun gathering light after the long, dark Swedish winter. Yes, I have done an inner journey, many journeys. It has been strenuous, at times painful, but enormously enriching.

I will share some of my experiences from an open and personal point of view, starting at the age of 16 until now, my late 50s. Everyone´s journey is different. In essence, we all search for meaning and we all have a history that shaped us. We bring meaning to life and it is done by being true to ourselves, using our gifts and experiences in a meaningful way. Most of us grow up and try to fit in and then at some point some of us, including myself, start to reflect upon who we really are. Who am I really? And the journey starts towards something that feels truer.

Swedish economist and former United Nations Secretary-General Dag Hammarskjöld once said, "The longest journey is the journey inwards." Sometimes I have wondered Does it never end? The answer is no. It´s eternal. I take myself to new levels of awareness, to something which is more in alignment with my inner core. There is no one recipe for this. It's a quest that continues through life. It's like peeling the skin of an onion and discovering a new layer underneath. Once you start peeling, you cannot put the skin back. Instead, you peel the next layer, and then the next, and you see and understand more. That does not always make life easier. Being truer to myself involves making conscious choices and those choices can bring me outside my comfort zone. The reward is happiness coming from a greater sense of belonging and meaning.

An existential crisis: Who am I in all this?

I'm in the dining room of my childhood home working on embroidery homework from school. Embroidery requires focused attention. I'm 16 years old and my mind easily drifts away in all kinds of thoughts.

My parents have guests coming over and while passing the dining room they greet me. One of them looks me in the eyes and says, "So, you are 16 now. I remember it's not always easy to be that age." His eyes are kind and a bit sad. I'm instantly connected to the sadness inside me. Yes, I find life challenging, trying to understand my role in the world. What is life about? Who am I in all this? Why do I have this feeling of not belonging?

I grew up in a middle-class family. Both my parents were hard-working people. Careful about how they spent their money, my father moved up the social ladder in order to make a better living. The internalized message I have from my father is, life is hard work. And from my mother, It's the importance of fitting into society, and good enough is exceeding expectations. These messages contributed to the struggles and the successes I had in my life. It took some time before I became aware of how living these beliefs took me away from love and joy. Life became hard work and doing the right thing was something seen from the outside. It took therapy, meditation, travels, a deep dive into different spiritual practices, and inspirational, caring colleagues in order to break the patterns created from these beliefs.

I had my first existential crises as a 16-year-old. An existential crisis can be a window of opportunity. Either we open the window and leave some habits behind in order for something new to enter, or we close it until the next crisis comes. I chose to open it a bit.

I needed to find something to address the confusion inside. Watching the world from the eyes of a 16-year-old, I felt as if I was detached from the feeling of belonging in a group which I assumed everyone else was experiencing. What came my way was TM, transcendental meditation, which uses a silent mantra as a meditation technique. I was starting to dip my toe into the spiritual realm where being present with the unknown and the silence on the inside brought me calmness and trust. Life is beautiful the way it is. It might not be the way I want it to be, and I might not understand in the moment why certain things happen. Later in life, when I connect the dots, it will all come out fine.

Imperfection creates happiness. Not perfection.

The only thing that is perfect in life is the beauty of nature. Finding peace on the inside through the chattering mind helped me to see this. It´s not that the chatter stopped. I don´t think it ever will. By noticing it, I became better and better at coming back to what really mattered. It helped me find my inner center. Today when I meditate, I also feel love and enormous gratitude for what life brings. This feeling brings light into my day.

Loneliness: Where do I belong?

I now understand the difference between belonging and fitting into society´s norms. What I was trying to do was to accommodate to norms, to push myself into a form that was not truly mine. I achieved good grades at school, went to UCSC (University of California Santa Cruz) for a year, took my master´s in Science, MSc, in Sweden and started to work in sales as an account manager at IBM.

I achieved my sales quotas and made it to the 100% club. I could walk around with a 100% needle and join rewarding conventions abroad. On the outside it looked good, still, I had this insecure and fake feeling.

Working at IBM at the age of 26, I got the feedback from a colleague that he perceived me as secure, confident and successful. On the inside, I felt like I was not good enough, like a fraud trying to play an imposter role.

I could not pinpoint exactly what this was about since I did meet expectations. Real belonging happens when we are in touch with our authentic selves. Somehow, I had a taste of the authenticity, the real me, and I knew there was something more than the over-achieving person I had become. My approach to getting there was by pushing myself harder instead of letting go of my own inner critic who always push more. Letting go is trusting that good enough will do and help will come if needed. It is paradoxical how the effect of letting go can bring success rather than trying to control life. However, I did not understand that quite yet. Letting go also is leaving space for miracles and the unexpected in life.

Become who you are

At the age of 38, I had two sons, aged 7 and 4. I left IBM after nine years. In my last position at IBM, I was part of the management team of IBM Financial Services where we focused on financing IBM solutions. I had felt a pull towards the area of human resources.

During my maternity leave, I started to study psychology at the University of Stockholm and that opened possibilities for a career change. I was now working for an international executive search firm as one of the few female partners globally. My husband and I were juggling double careers and the wish to be emotionally present with our kids as much as possible.

We had a high school girl picking them up from day care. My golden moment of the day was to come home in time to read them a good night story. Lying in our big bed with a child on each side. I still miss those moments of bliss when everything around me stopped and I was embraced by their love and curiosity.

Studying psychology was interesting, but not what I was searching for in terms of my purpose. I wanted something deeper, something that brought me closer to understand myself from the inside out. With kids and a husband and a demanding job, my life became like a project, organized in detail. I lost touch with myself.

Life was pulling me towards my second existential crisis when I received a copy of Become Who You Are by Piero Ferrucci. Piero´s teachings stem from psychosynthesis. He was a student of Roberto Assagioli, who developed psychosynthesis, a discipline known as psychology with a soul. I felt it was something special. I had an urge to do something that broke my habitual patterns. I decided right then to study it. I did not even need to read the book.

It happened to be a four-year therapist training curriculum. It ran into weekend studying, so I could still do my job as an executive search consultant. My main reason to join the training was to learn more about myself. Five years later, after being in therapy with three different therapists, trying to outsmart the first one, finding the second one too soft, and sort of giving up on the third one, I had better self-awareness. I still felt as if there was something blocking me. I realized: I´m not my mind, I´m not my feelings, I´m not my body, I´m so much more."

A step into the unknown: What is the more?

This period in my life was disruptive. The psychosynthesis training and the therapy started a process in myself. Being a person who throws myself into work wholeheartedly with passion and commitment, I was not recognizing myself. I was not happy and had lost my energy. One day I found myself crying. It was a burnout reaction, the doctor called it stress-related depression. I saw it as a kind of spiritual break down. I was not aligned with my true self and my entire body was revolting against me. The cost of conforming and sticking to the fact that I had a wonderful life with good pay, a great husband and lovely kids, did not work any longer. I had to start from a clean slate.

After six years of enjoying my work, it feels heavier and heavier to walk in through the door of the firm. Entering the office, I meet one of my partner colleagues. He looks at me and asks, "How are you, Agneta?" I give my usual answer with a bit of a strained smile, "Good, thanks." He looks at me again and asks, "How are you really?"

That question takes me off guard and I hear myself answer, "You know what? I think I´m going to quit!" It´s not the answer he expects to get. We walk into my office and seat ourselves in my comfortable armchairs. I feel totally convinced. I am going to quit.

Energy bubbled up inside me. It happened to be my birthday and I was leaving life as a search consultant behind and stepping into the unknown.

When you stand up for your truth, you might get a bloody nose. For most people, it´s crazy to quit a good job without knowing anything about the next step. People questioned my choice. There is something about going against the mainstream that creates reactions. It did not take courage to decide to leave my job, yet afterward, I can see that it was an act of courage. Courage comes from the French word coeur which means heart. I was following my heart. I did not know how I was going to earn my living but I believed in myself. I always managed through dedicated work, persistence, and discipline. These qualities were my allies.

I moved away from the insecure overachiever at IBM. Through studies of psychology and therapy, I peeled off some layers of patterns that did not serve me. I was ready for a new chapter, a chapter that would bring me closer to my purpose. It was a lot to deal with – unworthiness, fear of failure and feelings of not belonging. I increased my self-awareness. There was still more to do on self-love and I felt a pull to continue to explore within contexts that were out of the ordinary.

When we speak about purpose at Oxford Leadership, we use the model of the harmonic triangle where the three corners are Self, Others, and Truth. The explanation is that when we connect to our "truth," our purpose, we want to give from that place. When we give unconditionally to others, we get something back in return. Somehow, synchronicities or meaningful coincidences, came my way.

I´m back at the Psychosynthesis Academy in Stockholm where I did my training. I´m there for a seminar. Diana Whitmore, one of the founders of the Psychosynthesis Trust in London is visiting Stockholm. She takes us into a visualization, "Remember the time you decided to become a therapist." I hear her words and my whole inside reacts. I never decided to become a therapist. My purpose is something else. I walk up to Diana afterward and tell her that. I´m too results-oriented. She looks at me, smiles, and says "Maybe coaching? My husband is John Whitmore. He has introduced the GROW model in coaching and has a training in two weeks."

The gift of synchronicity showed up. Two weeks later, I´m sitting in another circle at a college outside London. Someone pulls out of the coaching training and I get the seat. Coaching assignments start to present themselves. Previous search clients call, and I find myself coaching people in a friend's paint studio. I listened to my inner voice telling me I should move on and I was on a new path.

Searching for my true self

At age 44 I started building my own coaching business which was a challenge in itself. Coaching was not yet mainstream and I had to justify and explain when initiating sales calls. It was a struggle. I found an office to share with some other people and slowly business started to build. Since I was a partner of the search firm, I had some money. I could survive by making a lot less than I ever made. I was on a deeper quest for purpose and connection both inside and outside and tried different things in parallel to my job. My quest took me to India, Peru, and Death Valley.

India and Osho

I had friends who went to the Osho center in Pune, India and came back feeling grateful and happy. I decided to try it out over a three-week Christmas break and signed up for an artistic painting class. Our teacher sparkled. When she felt we became too addicted to form, she walked by and splashed some color on our painting. Always smiling, she said things like, "Wow, what is emerging now?" It was amazing.

Letting go of control. I can see even more today how I can benefit from practicing this attitude in many situations. Being in the moment, being curious about how human beings, like a piece of precious art, can unfold. The Osho guru thing, however, was not for me. I learned that I had to treat myself gently and break the rules if they go against my inner well-being. That is self-love. I did not follow the rituals of the Osho center. I did my painting and went my own way. It was a good lesson for me since I have a tendency to conform too much in order to secure belonging.

Peru and the Shamans

I'm hiking a five-day trail to the Choquequirao Ruins in the Sacred Valley of the Incas near Cusco at 3000 meters above the sea level. We are a group of fifteen people walking with three wisdom keepers, shamans. We are walking one step at a time, one breath at a time. The air is thin and crisp and I'm looking with awe at the donkeys and native people who easily make their way up the mountain. Every morning our helpers come to our tent with hot tea from the coca plant to give us an energy boost and to help prevent altitude sickness. When I drink my tea, my breath creates smoke in the cold air. During the day it gets warmer. It's beautiful. With the stunning deep canyons and the snow on the peaks, the scenery helps to pull me forward, to stop and see the beauty as it is, to put sore feet into a stream and feel how it cleans and brings clarity. I get even more convinced. Nature gives us our answers.

The next step on my search for a deeper connection from the inside out became an energy-healing training in the tradition of the native Indians in Peru. By coincidence, I walked into a lecture in Stockholm with Alberto Villoldo from the Four Winds. This was in June 2005. There and then I decided to sign up for a week of training in England. It happened to be a six-week shamanic training that lasted for more than a year. I was not aware of this but felt I was onto something important that could take me further than the therapy. I had the same feeling as when I joined the psychosynthesis training, I just had to do it. I needed to continue to clear out patterns that prevented me from happiness with an approach that was beyond my mind, surrendering to a deeper intuitive knowing.

Death Valley Vision Quest

Nature continued to call me, and in 2008 I decided to go for a nine-day vision quest in Death Valley led by a man named Sparrow Heart. Vision quests are part of a Native American tradition. The quest is vision time spent in nature in solitude.

Part of my vision is bringing leaders into nature for a deeper connection to themselves and all that is. Everything is connected. With more collective wisdom we will have a better world. In order to bring vision quest elements into the corporate world, I knew I had to do the real thing myself. I needed to go first and learn from that experience.

In March 2008, we are a group of eight people who meet up with Sparrow Heart in the desert of Death Valley outside Las Vegas. We are starting a three-day pre-quest where we prepare ourselves mentally and emotionally.

The first night, I'm lying in my tent listening to the sound of the wind and the blowing sand. The canvas is fluttering, making me afraid of it breaking apart. I turn on my flashlight and scribble my intentions in my notebook. On one page I write with big letters "GRACE – less struggle." Underneath I write, "To step into my female power and wisdom becoming who I already am at the deepest level of my being, staying in the awareness of my essential nature." Maybe a bit pretentious but this vision resonates with me.

Three days later, all eight of us step over a line of stones, a threshold ritual, pronouncing our intention and what we want to leave behind. Through the hike, we find our individual power places far away from each other in the wilderness. I'm excited, determined and a bit afraid of the unknown. What if I meet a mountain lion, a rattlesnake, or even worse, inner shadows I don't want to deal with at all.

I'm alone in a canyon in Death Valley listening to the silence with no other gear but my sleeping bag and a too-small sleeping pad. It is the fourth and last night of my solo vision quest. The body is weak from fasting, drinking only water. I'm sitting in a circle of stones that the native American Indians call a "purpose circle." I have put out stones representing all my relations, my allies, who can possibly support me in connecting to my purpose. I'm going to stay here all night. Awake. The sun is setting over the sand dunes and coloring the sky red. In a few minutes, it will be pitch dark. I wonder how I'm going to manage to stay awake. At this moment, I see a scorpion crawl under one of the stones one meter away from me. I feel how fear gets a grip on me. I breathe and imagine the support coming from the stones. I´m not going to give up my intention. If I act from fear, I will call it in. All is connected. My purpose is related to love and wisdom. Agneta be it. Be your purpose. I breathe from my heart and choose to trust. The darkness of the night settles.

We are all earth keepers. We all have a responsibility and we all have a purpose that can serve the greater good. Each one of us adds value in our own context. The vision quest confirmed my path and helped me to connect to my inner wisdom, accepting it as a gift that I can bring forward. I also started making friends with loneliness.

At our innermost center, we are both alone and whole. A few years later I talked to a Buddhist monk who put words to my thoughts about loneliness and belonging when he said, "The way out of loneliness is to love yourself deeply. Let go of the concept that there is something out there. Once you love yourself deeply, you will be happy and also love others more deeply inside".

There are two key elements from these experiences that I hold onto as I move forward in life: to be gentle with myself by practicing loving myself deeply and to connect to nature. When I feel lost, nature is always there for me and can help me to connect to my true self. I can ask for help while walking in the woods. I give myself space and wait for the answer, connecting to the feeling of gratitude and love.

Help will come but we need to ask for it.

My purpose

My purpose is to spread light and love and be a catalyst for people connecting to their inner wisdom and freedom which is ever-present. I want to inspire the steady flow of life force that flows from the depth of our souls. I wish to open doors where people can see more dimensions and thus inspire transformation enabling acts from love and compassion instead of from fear.

I do not give up when something doesn´t feel true to me. I tried new things and learned what works and what doesn´t. It is important to be open to new experiences and not to get stuck in anything as being the one way or the one truth. Different experiences give me different perspectives. I always learn something. Even if some things have not appealed to me, there is a gem in these experiences. I know I don´t need to search for a guru. I need other wise people around me who can inspire me. I feel in my body when something is not working for me, even if my rational mind tells me something different, I have learned to listen to these signals.

I still find myself in stressful situations where I lose my center. I become quicker at regaining my inner alignment. It takes yet practice. Meditation and mindfulness make a difference. Our struggles and failures are gifts. They can bring us closer to the love of ourselves and others since they remind us that we are human.

Difficulties in life can help us to understand that love is more than something that comes from the outside. Love is who we are.

Our mission in life is to connect to that love and from that place. We can spread our wings and walk in purpose. We feel free when we are in touch with what we want to give and serve the world. It is not so much about doing. It is being. When I am authentic, others become authentic. When I am in my power, I empower others to be in their power. When I connect to my purpose it is a form of being. I feel the energy of contribution and from there it is natural to serve, bringing the talents that are truly mine to the greater good of this world.

What is the next step? I´m in touch with my purpose and it is not the end destination for my expression. My purpose continues to evolve as I get to the next level of awareness and the next. Awareness is about knowing myself, listening to myself and making decisions that enable me to be true to myself. I might not be doing the same thing in five years. It can be in a different context. The essence of my purpose will be the same.

Agneta Dieden

Authentic Leadership I Leadership development I Executive Coaching

Agneta Dieden has an MSc in Industrial and Management Engineering from Linköping Technical University. She has studied psychology at Stockholm University and holds a diploma as a Psychosynthesis therapist. She is an ICF certified coach (PCC).

Agneta has worked within marketing and sales at IBM, she has been a partner of Ray & Berndtson, a global executive search firm, and since 2001 she has been working with leadership development and executive coaching. She joined Oxford Leadership in 2011.

agneta.dieden@oxfordleadership.com
www.linkedin.com/in/agneta-dieden-33a939/

Author Of Your Own Life Story

by Abby Barton

I was an anxious child. I can't really explain why, but my default way of being was being worried. As Einstein said: "One of the most important decisions one makes is whether we choose to live in a friendly or hostile world." I unconsciously chose the latter. My mother was a worrier before me, and I remember vividly her telling me, "If we don't have something to worry about, then we'll then worry about that." I think that was meant to be reassuring but it never quite hit the mark.

This default made me strive to make sure things didn't turn out how I feared, which meant I tried to be in control, work hard and always be as good as I could, or better than others. As long as I tried hard to make things right, then surely things wouldn't go wrong – the naivety of youth.

It wasn't always easy growing up, even though I was very fortunate in so many ways. I had a loving family and an idyllic countryside environment to grow up in. I got a free private school education, thanks to my father's job as a teacher, which I know makes me extremely privileged. On one hand, it gave me the best starting place possible and the rest of my academic and career life would flourish because of it. But on the other hand, it severely damaged any self-confidence or self-esteem I might have had. I was different from the girls at school; most notable was not the difference in money and lifestyle (which was also very clear to me) but the fact that I was a day pupil and they were all borders. This difference excluded me from being "one of them," from fitting in, from belonging. In turn, this only served to fuel my habits of worry and anxiety. I struggled to make friends and was always on the periphery of groups, desperate to be part of them. Subtle but long-term exclusion and rejection made its imprint on me here, and it would take over twenty years for me to unlearn the defenses I built up to protect myself from this pain.

At the time, I didn't know anything different so I wouldn't have classed myself as unhappy for these five years at the girls' school, but when I was forced to move schools at 16 to my father's school (where we also lived), the difference became stark.

Finally, I felt like I found a place to fit into, and while I was painfully shy to start with, I started to find the world a little less hostile. I made friends more easily and started to grow in confidence. This was from a very low base, but as a result of this and a more nurturing environment, my academic results rose to the top and my sporting abilities flourished. It was a happy couple of years, not worry-free, but it felt like I'd moved from surviving to thriving and I realized then what happy school life was meant to be like and how absent it had been until then.

This was also a time that I started to realize that I was different in one important way from most people around me. I think all teenagers struggle with emotions and hormones and general growing-up challenges, but my feelings were extreme. They could totally engulf and overwhelm me, both positively and negatively, and it often felt totally out of my control, and even a curse. I could rollercoaster from extreme happiness to extreme sadness, or worry, from one day to the next. My mother and I were very much alike in this, and it was quite apparent if you observed our relationship that it fluctuated precariously between loving playfulness and World War III.

Unfortunately, the coupling of the exclusion in my early school years with this emotional sensitivity drove me to develop strong defence mechanisms to protect myself from further perceived hurt. In addition, there were frequent triggered outbursts of behaviour that would cause pain to those around me and myself. Of course, at the time I couldn't understand the cause of this behaviour, this would come decades later.

The following few years at university, while again not worry-free, was a period of exploration in the world. I lived away from home, made great friends, fell in love for the first time and continued to do well academically and in sport. The worry always made me study hard. I was not a natural intellect but I put in the hours and was adept at recalling information in exams.

Towards the end of university, I'd like to say that I pondered my calling in life and searched endlessly for the career path that would fulfill it. I had finished a degree in Geography and Anthropology but was disillusioned and overwhelmed with the challenges in the world that I had studied. I wasn't inspired by jobs in town planning or going to live half-naked with some indigenous tribe in the middle of nowhere, which seemed to be the only options directly available. So instead I looked at those around me and joined the masses that were attracted by the sparkling promises of bright futures in accounting, law, banking, and marketing. I followed the migration into London and signed up for three more years studying while working and living hard. I fitted in and felt a sense of belonging and friendship inside and outside of work, which is what I had been yearning for since those early school years. The accountancy training with one of the big four firms is still one of the best business training grounds and certainly wasn't a bad stopgap. I just have one regret: I forgot it was a stopgap. I forgot to revisit this decision, and then it became a career path I just slipped into and, true to form, tried to be the best at it I could.

This career path was a successful one for me when measured in the traditional way. I passed all the grueling exams the first time and qualified within three years. The desire for change and exploration motivated me to follow a group of work friends out to the Sydney office for a two-year working holiday. At 25, the years in Australia were a couple of the best; a relatively worry-free and sunny ex-pat life where there is an immediate sense of belonging and kin.

After two years I was forced to face the reality of staying more permanently or returning home, and the draw of the family from the other side of the world made this decision for me. It was hard returning home. It was at this moment that the reality of family life hit home. A fact that didn't seem relevant to tell you until now was that my beautiful vivacious mother was diagnosed with early-onset Parkinson's disease when she was about 30 years old. Of course, it was always in the background of my growing up but not with any seriousness or gravity, though I am sure it was for her. Looking back, she was strong and

courageous and determined not to let it impact her or her family and that is why I think it never really hit me before this point. But she had deteriorated while I'd been away and the starkness of her illness was like a punch in the stomach when I came home.

I settled back into the UK, again moving back to London and reintegrating with my old friends and life in the city. I left accountancy, as I couldn't see myself in the partners I had been working for in the firm, and decided commercial finance in the industry looked like an obvious next step for me. I worked for seven years for one of the UK's largest supermarkets, moving up the ladder every couple of years. I would go home as much I could but often, I was torn between the guilt of not going home and the pain of going home and facing my mother's illness. This came to a head when it was time to buy my first house, and I decided to move back to West Berkshire and be closer to home and family. It was extortionately expensive to buy in London so this also drew me out of the city. It wasn't long after this that I also moved my work out of London and started working for my third employer, one of the UK's largest telecommunications companies. Again, I continued to grow and ascend up the ranks and develop as a leader. I also was in a happy and solid relationship and thinking about the next steps towards the vision of a family life of my own. I thought I could see the path clear in front of me. The path that those around me were also taking and the one that I believed was normal, right, successful, and the route to happiness.

One year later, while waiting for a train in Brighton station, I received the call no one ever wants to receive. "I'm sorry Miss Barton. We tried everything we could to save her, but I'm afraid she died in theatre."

My mother had discovered she had heart damage from all the drugs she had been taking for the last twenty years and had gone in for a complicated heart operation. Despite the odds not being great she had survived the operation. Illness and operations were not foreign to her or us. She had in previous years also had open brain surgery as a test case for radical treatment for Parkinson's and fought off skin cancer. I think this is why I felt she was invincible, that combined with her courage to hide the seriousness of the situation behind humour and light-heartedness. It was during her recovery from the heart operation that she contracted septicaemia (blood poisoning) and suffered multiple cardiac arrests, which this time she couldn't fight through.

The year following was very dark. Grief is heavy, and for some, it is shorter and sharper, but for me, it was long and drawn out. I seemed to sink into it and in some strange way find comfort in the darkness of this place. It was a lonely isolated place, but I retreated further into my cave. I pushed my partner away and decided to suffer the pain alone. I wonder whether I wanted to punish myself, as I felt so guilty for not being able to prevent my mother's death or for the guilt of not being a better daughter to her. Either way, I took the suffering and wore it like a heavy but warm coat. Not long after the anniversary of her death, in the depths of a dark cold winter, I plummeted into depression and deep anxiety that stemmed from the loneliness and guilt. This is when the first pivotal point came in my life.

I was driving home one afternoon, and I remember wondering if I could be brave enough to drive my car off the bridge and take myself out of the struggle of daily life and join my mother. This thought was immediately frightening enough to make me reach out for help as I knew this wasn't right.

The therapy that followed was life-changing. The concept that I was not my feelings was powerful. The idea that I could be in control of my feelings by controlling my thoughts and beliefs. A lot of my negative thoughts and behaviours were the result of programming on my personal hard drive that had happened without me being conscious of it; learning the possibility that I could reprogramme myself was the light I needed to draw me out of the darkness. The journey I started here, to become aware, to understand, to accept, to grow, was my saviour.

As anyone who has made this journey knows, it is long and slow and takes all sorts of twists and turns. I made my way over the next few years to a level of existence that was neither greatly fulfilling nor unfulfilling, neither very happy nor unhappy. Perhaps some people would settle for this lot in life but my subsequent experience is that a lot of people sooner or later decide there must be more to life. I had a successful career and a nice home; I'd worked my way through extreme loneliness and come out the other side embracing freedom and independence. However, I felt that the dark cave entrance was never far away and that I was often just managing to keep my head above the water. It was a life again of surviving rather than one of thriving. This is when the second pivotal point came in my life.

Over one or two glasses of wine with a very good friend we spoke at length about this feeling of being on an escalator without knowing where it is taking us, of feeling like you are on a hamster wheel knowing the next turn will just be a repetition of the one before. The flippant comments about quitting it all and heading off into the sunset with a backpack became less about a dream and more about a necessity. By the end of the evening, we had made a pact to do just this, to jump off the wheel and be on a plane in three months' time with nothing but a small bag and an intention to find some answers.

Six months of backpacking around South America with a rule of no planning in advance was incredible. This was another highlight of my life – the feeling of freedom and space was exhilarating and calming at the same time.

My mantras for the trip were three-fold: "Don't sweat the small stuff (it's all small stuff!);" "What's the worst that can happen?"; and "Shut up and move on."; and my theme tune for the trip was "Let It Be" by The Beatles. These were daily practices to help unlearn the deep patterns of worry, perfectionism, and need for control that were getting in my way of being happy.

I had 200 days just to live and experience each day as it came. I travelled through Colombia, Ecuador, Peru, Bolivia, Chile, Argentina, Uruguay, and Brazil and saw the most incredible landscapes I have ever seen and met the most diverse and interesting people on the way. Life on the move with new experiences around every corner was so exhilarating. I felt I lived more in those 200 days than I had in the last five years in total. This is when I realised what it meant to feel alive again and that life was too short not to feel this way more often.

Each ten-hour bus ride across this vast continent offered opportunities to think. You have so much time to think that you are finally forced to think about the things you are even subconsciously avoiding thinking about. Once you can tackle these thoughts, then you really open up to what is really going on, what the real questions are that you are trying to answer. I can't profess to find anything but bigger and greater questions during this period. No answers appeared as revelations but the realities of what I didn't want were becoming clearer and clearer. The path that I had been travelling, whether the escalator or the wheel, was not one I had consciously chosen or written for myself, but one I had been put on and not strayed from or questioned until this day.

After six glorious months, I returned home; happy, lighter, relaxed, calm and determined. Determined to face my fears and make courageous changes. Determined to find a life that was not about survival but about being fully alive. Determined to find my own path.

Six months later the third pivotal point came in the unlikely form of a leadership programme called "Leading Self."

Under the premise that you can't lead anyone else until you can lead yourself and that the secret to leadership is knowing yourself, I was immersed for four days in a journey of self-exploration like none I had experienced before - or since.

"Who are you? Who is the real true you? Where have you come from? How has this shaped you? What are your light and your shadow sides? What are your gifts? How do you get in your own way?"

And if this wasn't enough, we then launched into...

"Why are you here? What is your contribution? What has life prepared you to give? What are the values that guide you?"

And then the killer questions that floored me:

"What gives your life meaning? What is your purpose?"

Of course, in four days I didn't answer all these questions, especially not the last two. All I could think was why had it taken me 35 years to ask these fundamental questions? But I deeply felt the resonance of these questions and the yearning to explore them. It felt like the answers I had been looking for in South America were going to come from these deeper questions, and I left with more motivation and drive than I had had for as long as I could remember. There was a deep desire for peace, for letting go, for trusting myself, for trusting something greater than me, for finding love, for giving love, and for finding meaning and belonging.

It had been simmering in my mind while I was in South America that I was deeply interested in the diversity of humankind. It had begun in my university studies of human anthropology and geography and now had moved towards psychology and neuroscience. I was passionate about understanding more about how the mind works and the power in being able to manage the mind and behaviour. The cognitive behavioural therapy I experienced a few years earlier, the journaling and self-reflection I started in South America and then the self-enquiry and introduction to the purpose of the programme all kept leading me towards a path of self-exploration, knowledge, and development. This was a path for me but also was emerging as a path for me to serve others and in doing so find a real sense of meaning.

Following the programme, I explored all sorts of study and career options before I finally landed on coaching. It seemed like the perfect combination of my prior corporate business experience and my more recent passion in the human mind and behaviour. My company continued to be nothing but supportive. They enabled my coaching training while allowing me to move out of finance into a number of exciting projects that offered me opportunities to lead and coach in parallel. The more I studied and practiced coaching and saw and felt the benefit it was giving others and also myself, the more I felt the call to pursue it.

The coaching training helped me find many of the answers to the questions I had been asking myself. I began to really notice and listen to my inner voice, the voice of my true self. I began to know myself deeply and to let go of the patterns of thinking that for so many years had held me back. I acknowledged and embraced that part of me that feared rejection and shame. I found greater self-love that fuelled my self-worth and self-compassion which in turn allowed me to gradually let the fears subside. I realised that my high emotion was not a curse but, coupled with intelligence and management, was actually a superpower that enabled me to be at my best – as a coach and as a human being.

I realised that I was good enough as long as I showed up as the best version of myself and did the best I could as often as possible. That is all I or anyone else can ask of me, or themselves.

Finally, after three years of getting ready, I left corporate employment after sixteen years and took the courageous leap into self-employment as an Executive Coach and later as a Leadership Consultant and Facilitator. It was a leap I have never looked back from and has shown to be another pivotal moment in my life.

I learnt that the courage, compassion and caring that I had so greatly admired in my mother was also in me and that this would guide and support me along my path. Four years later, I am still walking this path, feeling alive and living with immense purpose.
I learnt that finding your true best self from the inside out, so you can then self-author your own story, is the most liberating and joyful practice. And finally, I learnt that then writing your story that is full of meaning is the key to a fulfilling happy life for you and those around you.

My primary purpose is to live in the moment and not be caught in the memories of the past or the worries of the future. To be present and intentional as much as I can to experience life as it unfolds and be grateful. My secondary purpose is to help others discover their true best self, self-author their own stories and lead the most fulfilling life they can, in service of what they care most about.

This is my life and I believe passionately that I will not be an actor in a story already pre-determined by society, the expectations of those around me or by any old patterns of thinking that no longer serve me. I will self-author my own unique path and find meaning in being of service to others. I will show up every day in alignment with these beliefs and help others have self-compassion and courage to face their fears, to live their dreams and do the same.

Abby Barton

ICF PCC Executive Coach and Leadership Consultant

Abby is an Executive Coach and Leadership Consultant with a strong commercial and leadership background. She coaches C-suite and senior leaders in global corporations and scaling start-ups. She spent 16 years in the corporate world in the financial services, retail, and telecommunications industries in leadership roles spanning commercial finance, sales, strategy and business development. She also was a leader of Europe's largest corporate start-up accelerator and built a strong understanding of and network in the digital innovation and entrepreneurial ecosystem.

Abby's purpose is to help others to discover the best version of their true selves and live the best lives they can. She helps her clients develop deep self-awareness in order for them to truly know themselves and their potential in the world. She helps them then establish their dreams and aspirations and overcome their fears, limiting habits and beliefs that hold them back from being all they can be. Abby is open for any conversations about her story, finding purpose or her work so please feel free to reach out through

abby.barton@oxfordleadership.com

abby@abbybarton.com
www.linkedin.com/in/abbybarton

Moving From Legal Grounds To Solid Ground

by Andrew Cohn

My story of purpose relates to my career; my moving from a "traditional" job to something more fulfilling for me. It's a story of learning from experience and discovering what has meaning to me. My intention in sharing this is to provide some encouragement to those who might be feeling the inner "pull" toward a new, more satisfying direction, as well as to identify some key self-awareness-producing experiences that helped me along my path and perhaps might support others as well.

When I was in my early 30s, I was a lawyer living in Los Angeles. I had great communities of friends, was making a good living, and had a clear career path and a successful financial path laid out ahead of me. But I wasn't happy. I could not see myself doing this work for the rest of my career.

I always wanted to be a lawyer. My dad was a lawyer, as was my uncle. I grew up very interested in the law, specifically how the law works to keep things structured and fair between people, businesses, and the government. The fact that I wanted to go to law school and practice law was not a surprise to people who knew me. In fact, it was a fairly common career choice for students where I grew up near New York City.

After law school, I joined a litigation firm. I defended companies from lawsuits relating to negligent construction, product liability, and other accidents and breaches of contract. For a while, I really enjoyed the work. I particularly enjoyed helping clients navigate the litigation process. I would receive feedback about how helpful I was in setting their expectations, formulating useful budgets and anticipating the next steps in the often-lengthy litigation process. I was particularly strong in my writing, although I was always much more interested in writing reports to clients, helping them understand what was happening and outlining a strategy than I was in writing argumentative legal briefs. I was focused on resolution, and on learning from experience.

I remember an experience at a deposition. The legal case concerned about property damage resulting from negligent construction. Homeowners were being questioned about the consequences of damage to their home within a condominium development. The seven lawyers around the table questioned them intensively about exactly when the damage occurred and how much they were inconvenienced, focusing in on exactly who may have been responsible for it. I'll never forget a particular discussion among the lawyers during a break from one of these depositions. The lawyers, including me, represented various contractors who worked on the condominium development within which these people lived. Given our role in the proceedings, it's not surprising that the conversation was focused on the economics of repairing the damage in the future and on assigning blame for it. We were also focused on determining when the damage occurred so the proper contractor (typically through its liability insurance carrier) could pay its share of the repair costs and other damages.

What was glaringly missing to me was any attention paid to these homeowners and the harm that they experienced as a result of this problematic construction. Their lives were seriously disrupted because of negligent construction. But this job did not seem to have any place for compassion or caring.

Litigation is about winning. It's about getting the best result possible for your client. It's full of strict rules and procedural deadlines and limitations. It encourages thinking strategically about different tactics that might be taken in order to get the best result, which often means getting the best short-term financial result. In my experience, this system can bring out the worst in people; specifically, it encourages people (particularly lawyers) to be aggressive, super-focused on results, and manipulative in order to win. There were times I felt a strong temptation to take advantage of an adversary's procedural error, for example, conceal important facts, or pay less than an appropriate amount to resolve a dispute because my opponent was uninformed. This would all be "legal," and my client might want me to do it to achieve a "better" result. But it didn't align with my values. I didn't want to contribute to this system.

I learned over time that the integrity of the legal system depends upon the integrity of the players in that system. And some of the players lack integrity. This is not a criticism of the American legal system or any other model, but rather a recognition that different professions can bring out different parts of our personalities. Perhaps those professions attract certain personality types. In any case, over time, I came to realize that these were not the parts of myself that I wanted to nourish and develop to be of service in the world. I was successfully climbing the ladder, but it was not the right ladder for me.

My interests were always focused on people, the interaction of people, the interaction of cultures, and international business. When I was a lawyer, I gravitated toward developing relationships with clients. That's the part of practice I liked the most. My firm appreciated how I helped bring in repeat business with clients and had good relationships with all the support functions in our practice. I partnered well and enjoyed working on teams. I liked the people part of the business, where some of my colleagues would've preferred not to interact with people at all, rather be uniquely focused on issues and on the money.

Being a lawyer provided me with many the opportunity to participate in rich and fulfilling personal experiences. This included assisting and facilitating Insight Transformational Seminars near my home in Los Angeles and in other cities and continents as well. These were public workshops focused on awakening emotional awareness and purpose; they were (and still are) very powerful opportunities to experience deep growth and connection to others. And, in fact, I believe some of what I learned in these seminars helped me be a better lawyer, more able to manage my own emotions, be more focused and listen more effectively.

These learning experiences awakened a deeper spirit of service within me, and helped me recognize some of the ways that I wanted to work in the world, including helping people learn, and apply that learning to the most important circumstances in their lives. I also learned through this experience about the commonality of human beings across the world. Although I had studied international relations at university, it was not until I did this volunteer work in the area of personal development in Russia and Bulgaria that I came to understand that people typically want the same things and suffer the same challenges. I wanted my work to contribute to personal development in the context of business.

There were other important learning experiences that helped me clarify my purpose. After five years of law practice, I took the opportunity to participate in a master's degree program at the University of Santa Monica (USM), near my (then) home in Southern California. This was a two-year program in Spiritual Psychology. People are often curious or confused about this term; it refers to a curriculum of counseling skills with an overlay of universal spiritual principles, including acceptance, peace, forgiveness and loving. The best way to learn about counseling skills is to practice them, so I was able to surface and address some personal issues, including emotional disconnection and mental judgments I had been carrying. And I also focused on what type of work I wanted to do, as it was becoming clear to me that I desired to make a career change. I used the second-year curriculum as a framework for exploring a career in consulting, including research and interviews. At the same time, I continued to use my new counseling skills (and those of my cohort) to clarify my direction and resolve inner blocks related to moving forward. The USM experience was invaluable for me.

I came to realize that I have more choices than I previously thought. I think that's true for most of us. As I started to think about transitioning into another type of work, not surprisingly I became very afraid of giving up the security and certainty of my chosen profession. Why would I want to give up a lucrative profession? Because it was unsatisfying and not aligned with my mission in the world. My chiropractor told me that my nagging neck pain could be the result of a disconnect between my head and my heart.

Being the litigator was good work. But as my self-awareness grew, it became clear this was not the best path for me. There's really nothing wrong with the work itself, but I recognize that there were other parts of me wanting to emerge and be used.

Another important experience that helped me clarify my purpose was the New Warrior Training Adventure, a highly experiential weekend retreat for men. This was a challenging and provocative experience for me. It made me look in the mirror about the extent to which I was living my values and pushed me to step forward toward more of what I am called to do in my life. It also taught me new ways to ask for help and to offer support to other people. It helped me learn how to be a leader in a community.

If my USM experience helped me clarify my purpose, the Warrior weekend helped light the fire in me to pursue it.

One other very personal experience that was pivotal for me in building my self-awareness was my work with a coach, which I did when I transitioned out of my law practice. My coach provided me with valuable tools, including a number of personality and style assessments, some of which I now use with my own coaching clients. One particular assessment she provided to me suggested specific careers for which I would be well suited; at the top of the list was the clergy, which I have never doubted. I provide counseling, support, guidance, and perspective for my clients. I sometimes think of it as a priest or rabbi in a business setting.

In my studies in spiritual psychology, I had an opportunity to do some deep work in which I identified and confronted fears, limiting beliefs, and a number of previously unrecognized blind spots. In addition to identifying some parts of myself that I'm not proud of, I also identified some gold. I began to recognize some of the personal qualities I wanted to make part of my daily work. I began to nurture some abilities and aspirations that could be a part of my next career.

I was introduced to a wonderful little book that provided me with some great directions. It's called "How to Find Your Mission in Life," by Richard Nelson Bolles. Mr. Bolles is best known for his hugely successful book, "What Color is Your Parachute," which is like a job seeker's bible, at least in the USA. But this other book is a little gem, and he's focused on identifying our individual missions at a very deep level. The author has deep spiritual beliefs, and the book is written from that place. It was a terrific resource for me and the "religious "language in it was not alienating for me.

Bolles writes that each one of us has three purposes. The first two purposes are shared with everyone else, although we might manifest these differently. The third is more unique and more about understanding exactly how and where each of us can best serve and find lasting happiness.

He writes that our first mission is to be as fully aware as possible of the conscious presence of God. I believe that each person may do this in his or her own way, at his or her own pace. In my experience and observation, this is what drives people to places of worship, yoga studios, meditation retreats, and the like. I consider the first mission in Bolles' model to be a universal spiritual path. On some level, we all are in the process of recognizing the presence of the divine in whatever ways we might relate to that. Our second mission on Earth, according to Bolles, is to do the best we can every day to make the world a better place, following the guidance of spirit however we may define that. Again, this is something that each person may do differently. Certainly, this is a purpose that most people would agree is worthwhile. I certainly do, and it has become a North Star for me over the years.

The second mission is a criterion we can all use to evaluate our work in the world and, in fact, any action we might consider taking: does this help make the world a better place? If not, then look for another action or another direction. I believe this is foundational for success and living a purpose-driven life, one that helps us feel motivated to move out into the world every day.

Our third mission is to use the talents we believe we came to Earth to use. These are our greatest gifts and those skills and attributes that we are most happy to share. Moreover, our mission is to use these gifts in those places which are most appealing to us, and for those purposes, the world needs most. Of course, this is open to a range of interpretations. But when it comes to purpose, isn't that always the case?

It is the third mission that relates to our individual work in the world. For me, as I reflect on this model and the experiences that I've had which have brought my values and passions into greater clarity, I recognize that the skills I want to bring to my work relate to aligning people and teams; teaching; facilitating solutions to problems, and helping people. The place that appeals to me most to do this work is the business world; I believe that in our current society, the workplace is where people face fears and obstacles, and are challenged to bring their best and make a positive difference to others and to the world. And from my vantage point, the business world needs ambassadors of positive focus and optimism who see the opportunity to use the commercial world for good.

I've talked about these ideas with clients and colleagues who have very limited spiritual inclination. But the principles are transferable to the secular. The first principle refers to gratitude. Can I be grateful for my situations and my gifts? The second principle refers to making the world a better place, the essence of servant leadership and service consciousness. The third principle is about tuning to where good work needs to be done. There need not be a role for God in making that decision if one is not so inclined.

From my experience, I believe that understanding one's purpose is all about self-awareness. Our purpose becomes clearer as we clarify what brings us joy, what we value most and what we want our legacy to be. As these critical personal motivators become clear to us, our purpose comes into view more clearly.

Over the years, I've learned how to choose consulting engagements that are most aligned with my purpose. I've learned that any work I do involves three dimensions: the actual work I will be doing (executive coaching, leadership team alignment, leadership training or workshops, etc.); the people with whom I'm working (my clients and my colleagues); and whatever forms of compensation I might receive for the work. For me, the people with whom I'm working is by far the most important dimension. In filtering work opportunities through that self-awareness, I have a better likelihood of remaining both personally fulfilled and professionally effective.

I have been fortunate to have many learning experiences that illuminated my path forward, moving from a traditional career to much more meaningful and rewarding work. My focus on leadership and team development now supports others in clarifying and walking their own paths. My hope is that my experience can be of service to others, contributing to a world with more purpose-driven and fulfilled people.

Andrew Cohn

President Lighthouse Consulting, Counselor and consultant to leaders and business organizations

Andrew Cohn works globally as a facilitator, consultant, counselor, and coach for businesses and individuals. His work improves his clients' business results and culture and enhances individual performance and satisfaction. Andrew facilitates team meetings globally to optimize achievement, efficiency, engagement and shared learning.
He has coached and trained leaders and their teams on a variety of issues including team leadership, performance management, interpersonal effectiveness, strategic thinking, diversity and women's leadership, conflict resolution, and work/life balance. He works with clients to overcome "right v. wrong" thinking in favor of what works. Andrew practiced law for seven years prior to founding his own consulting firm in 1997.

andrew.cohn@oxfordleadership.com

andrew@lighthouseteams.com
www.lighthouseteams.com

Sunflower

by Ann-Sofie Ellefors

There is a flower that means a lot to me. The sunflower. Read its name. Sunflower. A flower to the sun. "Tournesol" is the French name for sunflower and it literally means "turning to the sun". In reality, sunflowers are always turning their heads to where the sun is. I am not the first one admiring and being taken away by the beauty of sunflowers. The famous impressionist artist Vincent van Gogh made a whole collection of them. The fields of Provence in France are full of sunflower blossoms. For me, the sunflower has grown to become an important symbol in my life. My company symbol is a photo of a sunflower, picked from my garden. My wedding bouquet was made out of three big sunflowers.

However, life does not always give you a bouquet of sunflowers. In our life trajectory, it is more often the painful and difficult phases that give us an opportunity for further development and growth.

Life changing situations

"Mais non, non, non" the words from my French maths teacher hit me hard when I tried making the calculations right. Due to the last maths test where I had only two points out of twenty with red marked notes all over the test, he had now made me come up to the blackboard in front of the class to show everyone how poor I was on these calculations. The class went silent. I was standing there thinking "why does he want me to stand here in front of everyone, knowing that I can't do this"? I can still remember the feeling of being set adrift. Alone. With no other help. A "superior" teacher was using his power in a very negative way. It was now up to me.

Somewhere inside me, I knew that this was a short adventure in my young life, having arrived just a month before to this school in Ferney Voltaire, on the French/Swiss border to Geneva. My family had decided to take a break in life and we moved from the small Swedish city of Östersund to France. Already a tall girl at twelve, I was initially placed in the wrong class, which meant that this class was two years ahead of me in maths. Additionally, I did not speak a word of French. The challenge was evident.

While standing in front of the class at the blackboard, the arrogant maths teacher continued to harass me. I don´t really know from where I summoned my inner feeling of power, but there in the classroom, I decided that his attitude should not hurt my inside. When he continuously asked me to do the calculations on the blackboard and I tried to get them right as he continued to shout "no", I soon understood that this didn't get me anywhere. So eventually, my answer was "I don't know, but I am willing to learn." Despite the pressing situation, I did not feel completely devastated, instead, a feeling of courage and braveness was slipping through. Still today, I wonder where my guts and strength came from because, in this vulnerable situation, I kept fairly calm.

But I was in tears when I went home that afternoon and told my parents about the way I was treated. The teacher's behaviour violated the fundamental values of treating every human with respect.

The next day, my dad followed me to maths class and had a conversation with the teacher, who bragged about his teaching methods. He told my dad that I was a very brave girl. Most girls cried for him in similar situations, he explained. I did not cry, so obviously I was a very brave girl.

The family decision was easy. My parents took me immediately from this maths class. Luckily, I moved to a special maths class in a smaller group with a very nice teacher.

Since the exposure of this challenging experience in a new cultural setting, I have been reflecting upon what this experience meant to me, how it influenced me and how it has been driving my purpose. I strongly believe that we are formed by the challenges life presents us, the choices we make and the changes that occur as a result. These challenges, choices, and changes can be self-driven or forced upon you. My parents decided to move to France, and as a consequence, I received a challenging experience.

The exploration of our life's trajectory, high and low sections in life, is important to consider and reflect upon. My first low point was this school experience in France. Today, I am very grateful for the fact that I had this experience. It created clarity to what is important in life and was an opportunity for inner growth at a young age. It helped drive my purpose with some important life lessons. It taught me courage, the importance of standing up for the deep values of humanity, and the rightness of treating people fairly. Meeting pupils from all over the world and being exposed to different cultures in a new country taught me that we are not so different. We are all human beings born free and equal in dignity and rights. How we behave forms our true leadership.

Ugliness at work leads to strength

After two years on my first job, I was helplessly staring at the office wall with tears in my eyes. I felt drained with no capacity of moving forward. How did this happen?

Upon graduating from Uppsala University with a master's degree in business, I was eager to work in export sales. The reason for this was that I had written my final thesis on export trade between Sweden and Japan. After a trip to Japan to discover the country, I landed my first job, being in charge of the export sales for an entrepreneurial construction company in Stockholm. It was recession time in Sweden in 1994, so I was glad that my dream to find an export-industry job with broad duties and responsibilities had come true.

I was 25 and reported directly to the CEO. He was a good boss. I was in charge of selling construction products with the software on diverse markets. I made several business trips to Germany but also overseas to Hong Kong and Las Vegas. The only pain was that everyone else apart from the office staff and myself were engineers. I was a young woman, in charge of sales to dealers such as Caterpillar and Ingersoll-Rand. The customer side went well, but I felt I had to fight for recognition within the company, showing that I could do the work despite being a young woman and not a male engineer. The culture was not a perfect match but giving up was not an option. With resilience, I wanted to continue to grow and learn.

When the owner stepped down as CEO, they recruited a new CEO. A very negative down-spiraling environment followed. The new CEO did not like me and did not think I could sell. Fortunately, he did not speak German, so I still successfully nurtured relationships with our German-speaking clients. But he saw me as a threat and used every situation to undermine me in subtle and narcissistic ways.

This was devastating. Despite solid hard work, my strengths of perseverance and stubbornness could not help me here. Bit by bit, the belittling atmosphere and psychological terror broke me down. I tried hard to communicate with the new boss as well as with the other engineers, but I had to change my personality so much it made me insecure and unsure. I felt that I had to adapt my communication and my behaviour a lot, leading to not being myself. To be in a stressful, detrimental environment surrounded by people who do not want your best is very painful. The feeling of constantly fighting the dinosaurs almost crushed me.

Bouncing back

How on earth could this happen to a strong young woman with solid values? This scares me still today. But this is what happened. I wanted to leave, tried to apply for other jobs but found myself far too weak, disconnected from my core values and my true self. I felt totally stuck. Who had I become? Being a strong person in a situation without energy and power is self-detrimental. I told myself, you are on your first job, just continue doing it as great as you can. I could not see the damage it was causing to my health, to my self-worth and self-confidence. I just believed in trying harder and harder, not giving up. How wrong I was. With the knowledge I have today, I would have quit when I saw the first signs. But how much easier that phrase is said than done!

I stopped doing many things that brought me joy and withdrew from social connections. It was my body that reacted first. I got the flu, I had back pain and I developed sinusitis. My mother suggested we go for a weekend course in medical Qi Gong. It was a turning point. With roots in Chinese medicine, philosophy, and martial arts, Qi Gong means life energy cultivation and is a holistic system of coordinated body posture and movement with breathing and meditation. I adopted this self-healing process into daily practice and it taught me the importance of always taking good care of my body, mind, and spirit. It also spurred a deeper interest in alternative medicine.

Looking back, I am now grateful for having those tough-and-challenging experiences so early in life. Though painful, I moved on with support and help from my loved ones. I took a break and travelled through India, Nepal and the Philippines for three months, wiping my mental slate clean. When I moved to another job at IT company Oracle, I brought with me the importance of being in a supportive environment with shared values and vision. I knew to trust my feelings, and to quit, if necessary. Being in an unhealthy, unproductive rut for too long eventually led me to great clarity and sense of purpose in life. I was asking myself the questions: "What gives me meaning? What is driving me?".

A sunflower seeking the sun

I knew early in life that I wanted a big family. By thirty I was getting nervous and even ready to adopt a child from China as a single mother. Then I met my husband at Oracle. We shared the vision of a big family, and we are fortunate to have four wonderful children, three girls, and a boy. Having four diverse personalities born within five and a half years is, of course, challenging but mainly an immense sense of joy and purpose. For me, a life without children was never an option. Best teachers ever! They keep me grounded, as firmly as the sunflower is rooted in the soil.

Besides the children, when reflecting on the bigger picture and what gives me meaning, my purpose is very simple. It is to contribute with joy, growth, and happiness to the world. Like a sunflower always seeking the sun. With time, the sunflower has emerged to become my purpose symbol. When doing self-reflection purpose work, the sunflower has followed me on my path in many aspects; as a wedding bouquet, company symbol, own crafted sunflower painting in the office as well as planting sunflowers every year in my garden.

When losing direction on the inner compass, I often turn to the sunflower. Where is the sun? How can I look at a situation differently?

The two mentioned low points on my life's trajectory are experiences that formed and shaped my purpose. My core values of love, curiosity, continuous learning, deep relationships, and connectivity also were molded in my childhood and through my life experiences. They are there as prerequisite for my purpose. Feeding it. Freedom is a quality that is important to me. Freedom of choice, freedom of speech and choosing the life I would like to lead.

True role models guiding me

A true role model in my life has been my grandfather Stig, who passed away at ninety-seven. When the question is posed: Who have been your heroes? he pops up as number one. He had this mindset of curiosity and started art courses at the age of eighty. His passion for life has influenced me a lot. When he passed away, I brought my five-year-old daughter to his death bed. Some people might have opinions about bringing a child to a death bed, but for me, death has never been scary or evil. We are all going to die. I would like to live a long and fruitful life and be dancing at ninety, that's the vision. I can only live in the moment and cherish every opportunity. What then comes along the next bend, I do not know about. I believe that it is important to dare to see and speak about death because it helps us stay true to ourselves and to what is important in life.

For me, it helps to have the end in mind. Sometimes I ask myself "What would I do if I only had one year left to live"? This is a really important question. I believe, we would live more courageously and form authentic relationships if we had that perspective. Not to forget the joy in every moment. I recall when my small son was totally mesmerized by a straw of grass. How it bowed for the wind and back it went. The rich palette of greenness. Gratefulness and amazement of our living planet's wonders.

In 2013, I encountered Oxford Leadership, another important "role model", and did the Self-Managing Leadership program. In the purpose section of the program during a reflective inquiry, my answer to the following question stood out. "What is it that you always wanted to do, but never had the chance… or never taken the chance to do?" The top answer that emerged was to become a professional teacher, working with young adults.

When facilitating this deep self-reflection program with clients it is very important to do it on yourself and also live by its principles. Every time, I applied the Self-Managing Leadership program on myself, the longing for studying to become a professional teacher emerged. I just had to realize this search for more meaningfulness. I truly loved my work as a leadership consultant and executive coach, and still do, but I longed for being part of something bigger and being part of the process of learning and creating lasting relationships for a longer time. When I deliver shorter trainings or workshops for executives, I am only partially on their journey of change and development.

Therefore, I made a conscious choice to go back to university, studying pedagogy full-time for a teaching diploma. It was a lot of pressure steering around daily life with three jobs as a student and mother as well as running my leadership business. When your purpose is clear though, perseverance and lightness follow.

The wheel of life

With my previous experience of not taking care of myself in pressing moments, I did survive with support from my immediate family as well as thorough care of my well-being.

A useful clarifying tool for me has been "The wheel of life". I have also used it frequently with my coaching clients. The eight areas of career, friends/family, physical environment (work or at home), health, money, personal growth, fun/recreation, and partner/relationship represent a balanced wheel. Firstly, I encourage clients to take a look at the eight areas and write down what is working well in each area. We often forget what is working well, so this perspective is important. Then it is time to do your rankings. The center of the hub of the wheel is viewed as 0 (totally dissatisfied) and the outer edge as 10 (totally satisfied). Rank your level of satisfaction in each area by putting a mark on each area. Draw lines to join your markings. The less balanced your wheel is, the more wobbly or rocky your ride through life will run.

When I use this tool to assess myself and my wheel is too "rocky" and not moving smoothly at all, something is needed to be taken care of. I view each area and set a goal or direction in the "rockier" areas as well as appreciating what is working well in the "smoother" areas. This simple exercise of the wheel of life makes a visual illustration of how you perceive your life at a given point in time. For me, it is a resource for a happier and more satisfying life. When we are at ease with ourselves and feeling happy, we are so much more open to giving to others. For example; if I put a 5 out of 10 for health, maybe I would like to make sure that I find time each day for those precious 15 minutes of meditation or find some new group training activities at the gym that I enjoy. Maybe I need reflection time to view how my sleep/eating and exercise habits are doing and then make changes accordingly to get closer to a 10 on the wheel of life.

The path of meaningfulness

Since receiving my teaching degree, I have worked part-time with young adults in upper secondary school. I teach mainly courses in leadership, business, and entrepreneurship. As a teacher, you are on the giving end all the time. Like the harmonic triangle, when you know what the right thing to do is and you connect to your truth and purpose, you also give, give and give back to others without the need of receiving back. Being a teacher is the most complex, demanding, and most rewarding job I have ever had. Working with young adults who have their whole life in front of them with all their ideas, frustrations and commitments give me a lot of meaning.

My job is coaxing the best from my students and nurturing them along the way. But I am not able to motivate someone who doesn't want to be motivated. I inspire. I plant seeds, and I listen. Students will learn when they are ready. My approach is: Be patient. Be authentic. Be generous with our time. Be there.

The combination of working as a leadership consultant with teaching is smashing. I can still contribute to management teams and executives in exciting companies and bring inspiration and experience back to the school environment and vice versa. I keep on living my purpose, spreading joy and growth like the sunflowers. I am confident my life will continue to be good.

Reflections and life learnings

Am I wiser now at age fifty than I was at twelve? Maybe, maybe not. What is wisdom? The more we know, the more we realize we don't know. What I do know is that I have a better understanding of my core values and my purpose. By exploring and pinpointing my most important values to love, curiosity, continuous learning, deep relationships and connectivity, I have gained deeper awareness.

The values I learnt from my parents and through my experiences in childhood have stayed with me throughout my life and I have tried to pass them along to my children. As a parent, my uttermost dream is that my children will find their inner compass and know their sense of direction in demanding circumstances.

Having a purpose statement as well as a purpose symbol as the sunflower is important to lean on when my energy is low. As result of exploring my values and purpose in-depth, it helps me to understand my feelings and consequently take action.

I treasure listening to my children and my students, and I am in awe of their wisdom. At twelve, I learnt how I wanted to treat people, and the first seeds of my moral compass and my purpose took shape. When concluding what my most important life learnings have been, it circles around the wheel of life and well-being. I could never be an authentic leader and parent unless I focus on my own well-being and self-care. There is no universal recipe, but I would like to share some of my learnings.

Most importantly, the focus has to be on sleep, exercise, food, and deep relationships. In my life practice, I include exercises like playing tennis, skiing and going to the gym. Spiritual training such as yoga, Qi Gong and meditation are also important. A good night's sleep where the brain can have its necessary recovery is key. Eating healthy food and cooking fantastic meals creates magic. It is essential to watch my intake of alcohol and keeping a healthy weight. Nurturing deep relationships with the people that I love and care for. We all know that it is not always easy to be the best version of ourselves with our loved ones. But when we let our family and close friends see - and love – our positive and negative sides, it is both comforting and beautiful. Being generous to others with your love and time is also rewarding.

Setting boundaries is another life learning. To say no. As your purpose becomes clearer, this is easier. With the story of my first job, I learned the lesson the hard way. Who do you want to welcome into your life? I am an open person and truly love people. I believe we should socialize with people who give us energy and help us grow, not the opposite. Setting boundaries is very difficult but necessary, especially when you have deep values regarding relationships.

Today I keep a "Feel Good" list. What makes me feel good? What makes me laugh? I pull that list out, especially in turbulent and stressful times. I wish I had had such a list at my first job to draw inspiration from. When I include many feel-good activities such as hiking, cross-country skiing on a wintry day with blue skies, going to my favorite Japanese spa, Yasuragi, floating in their warm spa pools after a well-deserved visit to the sauna, or enjoying the simplicity of daily card-playing with my children, I know I will be a better version of myself. Self-reflection and taking time out are needed. Being in silence and reflecting on my feelings and reactions are key to discovering myself in more depth. Happiness, lightness, and love will be more present. I will be able to contribute so much more to the world when actively seeking moments of reflection and silence. The result is being a leader for good, to myself, to my children, to my husband, to my loved ones, to my students, to my business clients, and the world.

Spreading joy and growth.

Like the sunflower.

Ann-Sofie Ellefors

Owner Ellefors Leadership / Business Teacher

Ann-Sofie Ellefors, based in Sweden and Luxemburg, with former executive sales background from Oracle and EF Education, is currently „Transforming Leaders for Good with purpose and joy". Her leadership work compounds working as a senior leadership consultant, executive coach and business teacher. Her global customer base includes Microsoft, Ericsson, SEB and Sandvik.

One of her most rewarding and demanding leadership experiences is being a mother of four children. Her core values compose deep relationships, continuous learning, curiosity, and sunflower happiness. She believes authentic leadership stems from working on your inner leadership and setting the inner compass for contributing to making a difference in the world.

Ann-Sofie is an avid outdoor lover and globetrotter and this interest has taken her hiking the Inca-Trail as well as hiking expeditions to Nepal and to Laponia. She volunteers as a leader for young children desiring to explore the local nature. Ann-Sofie recently moved to Luxembourg with her family, pursuing a vision to give her children an opportunity for international exposure and getting a taste of becoming global citizens.

Her motto is; Good things happen to good people.

ann-sofie.ellefors@oxfordleadership.com
www.linkedin.com/in/ann-sofie-ellefors-859123/

Evolution Of Me

by Artur Chernikau

Chapter 1: Love

One day when I was five years old, my brother was swimming, and my father took me to the swimming pool, too. From time to time, he took me to the little kids' pool, and I showed him how well I could swim. I noticed how adults swam, moving their arms like a windmill, so I walked with my feet on the bottom of the pool and moved just like I saw the adults do, pretending I was a swimmer. My father laughed.

I swam and danced classical dances before entering school. My mother was happy seeing me dancing. Father enjoyed my swimming. A few months before I started first grade, my parents realized that I could not continue doing both. They were trying to decide which I should keep doing, but eventually they asked me, „What would you like to continue, dancing or swimming?" In fact, I liked both. But dancing was considered more for the girls, so I chose swimming. I was very afraid to hurt my mom with my choice, but she loved me.

Some years later, my brother had dropped swimming, but I continued dreaming that one day I would become an Olympic champion. I wanted my parents to be proud of me. This hope drove me. I worked hard hard, and my results were very good.

When I was ten years old, we started a new training schedule. The first training started at 6:30 in the morning. The day that I woke up at 5:30 am for the first time in my life, I said to myself, "No way! Why am I doing this?" But an hour later, I was in the water. I got used to the early morning routine quickly.

Despite my hope to become an Olympic champion, at fourteen I decided to quit swimming. I wondered: "A swimming career might last up until the age of twenty-five and what would I do afterwards?" I considered making a choice from my own perspective. It was a very difficult decision; I was afraid to disappoint my father, but he loved me.

Chapter 2: Decision

I grew up as a relatively calm boy, but I had strong opinions on a number of serious topics, among them politics, social policies, philosophy, the essence of life, religions. I defended my opinion on every possible occasion.

The topics I was curious about were not interesting to my friends, so the only person I could discuss them with was my father. Sometimes we had different thoughts, my father and I, or he pretended to have a different opinion in order to give me a chance to express and to defend my thoughts.

I grew up in Minsk, Belarus, after the Soviet Union dissolved. It was not an easy time for my family or for the country. Apart from being an engineer, my father produced chairs in our 52-square-meter apartment to survive. Besides that, he always dedicated his time to debate with me on what was important for me. On a big scale, my thoughts were occupied by a single topic: How can I make the lives of others better?

I didn't know the word "purpose" yet. But now I believe that my thinking was the first iteration of a purpose statement in my life. Of course, in my youth, the world for me was confined by the borders of Belarus, so I focused on making the lives of Belarusians better.

I loved my country very much, but apart from believing that politicians should make life better, I had no clue what I alone could do. Even when I realized that I should start with small, single steps, I couldn't find the courage to act. I might notice an old woman on the street carrying a heavy bag, but even then I felt absolutely powerless to help. I couldn't manage to say and do anything. It was a horrible feeling. I blamed myself with negative self-talk: "How can you make the lives of others better if you cannot even help a single woman?" Eventually, I quietly decided on a plan: one day, I would become president of the Republic of Belarus and solve all the issues.

My father is Russian by nationality, and my mother and her family are Polish. By default, my brother and I were considered Polish, since we were surrounded by Polish culture since we were born. In 1999, there was a population census in Belarus. My parents were filling in the questionnaires, and in the field "Nationality of the children," they automatically wrote "Polish." I stood up and said, "No! I am

Belarusian. My motherland is Belarus!" I surprised everyone, but most of all myself. It was the first time I defended not only my thoughts but my own decision. I was surprised by how easy it was to do this! But even more, surprised by the feeling of power and energy this action gave me afterward.

I was seriously considering dedicating my entire life to my "purpose," not focusing on building my own family and what is called a "happy life." However, I realized I could not manage that. Having a happy life and family was so attractive that I decided, "Why should I escape? Let's first enjoy life and then return to the purpose."

Fifteen years later, I found myself living in Latvia, enjoying a happy life with a wonderful family, my wife Aljona, two daughters, Polina and Emilija, and a dog. I was a different kind of me, confident and courageous, and my career was developing well. People would consider someone like that successful, and I would agree with them. But still, something was missing.

Once I was invited by a Latvian university to be a guest lecturer. As a foreign citizen living in Latvia, I was asked to inspire their foreign students to consider staying in Latvia after graduation. I had never done anything like this before. How would I inspire the students? But I accepted the offer because I always embraced challenges and adventures.

I had already graduated as a coach; therefore, I was cautious about any kind of "inspiration." I felt there was always some manipulation involved in that concept, and I couldn't allow it. Day after day, I thought about how I could truly inspire those students, asking myself how could I convince them to consider the opportunity to stay in Latvia? Eventually, I reflected on my past fifteen years, looking for what had inspired me to come and stay in Latvia. I called this story: "Allow life to deviate from your master plan."

Chapter 3: Journey

I finished school in Minsk when I was sixteen. I was an excellent pupil and even earned a graduation medal. I decided to enter the university right away. To enter the university as a medalist, I only had to pass the English exam with grade of 4.5 out of 5. It happened that I passed English with grade 4.4. I decided to turn to another university instead of sitting for the rest of the exams. I was that confident in myself. However, I had much less confidence entering the third university after I did not get the necessary grade in the second. And then, in the third university, I failed again.

I am not ready to recall the magnitude of my disappointment. Millions of thoughts and emotions overwhelmed me. In one moment, the entire world had turned upside down for perfectionist me. "What have I done? And what shall I do next?" These two thoughts trilled inside me. I learned very well what concern, worry, and anxiety are. The only alternative to my self-blaming was to go to work as the loader in a grocery store near our house.

After a short while, I recalled that my uncle who lived in Riga, Latvia, was always telling me, "Come study in Latvia." He brought me a lot of handouts about the possibilities for study in Latvia, encouraging me to consider the move, but I was convinced I was wanted by Belarus. I was blind to this alternative until I had no other options. I was lucky it was possible to start studying after September 1. This is how, in November 2000, I ended up in Latvia.

Only after many years, I realized that Latvia would become my home for the next nineteen years.

Chapter 4: Family

At the end of my studies, six years after the previous story, I was finishing my master's degree. It was the last semester, and I was writing my thesis. At the same time, I met a girl and fell in love. Two weeks before my thesis defense, I received a call from my scientific director who said, "Artur, I won't let you defend the thesis. It is too weak." His judgment was crucial.

I was going to meet my girlfriend's parents for the first time when I got this call. I sarcastically thought I would tell them: "Hi, I am your daughter's fiancé, and I am a loser." I wouldn't say that the director's message killed me. Actually, I just didn't care much because I was in love!

A few months after that, I realized the following fact: my residentship permit in Latvia was based on my studies, and once I successfully defended the thesis, I would have to leave for my motherland – Belarus -- and God knows what would happen with my love. But the director's judgment created the possibility of extending my permit for another six months. It was enough for us to realize that we wanted to be together.

From time to time, when we pass through the Latvia-Belarus border to visit my parents, my wife asked me a question: "So where is your motherland?" It used to be a difficult question for me, but I eventually found the answer: "My motherland is here in the car; it is my family."

Chapter 5: Career

I started my career at the bank in 2006. It was the time when in Latvia a nonqualified worker earned five-to-six times more than an educated banking professional. I had the simplest job in one of the most dynamic parts of the bank, the Trading and Capital Markets Division. We jokingly called our job "F3-F5" because of these two computer buttons we had to press every day (of course, I overexaggerate). I was extremely happy. It was my first qualified job in an international company. However, after half a year of work, seeing no opportunities in the bank, I was ready to move on. One sunny summer day, my Swedish manager came to me and said, "We have just introduced a new position in our division, and I would like you to take this position." I gladly agreed. It was a new and very interesting scope of work for me, along with a salary increase -- everything you need when you are twenty-three. This was the start of my career in the bank.

In this story, I have noticed something interesting for the first time: every time I am standing on the edge of uncertainty, every time I think „that's it, the end," the edge transforms into the next turn of the road, which I had not seen before. I grew within the Trading and Capital Markets operations for the next four years and again reached the ceiling for our Latvian branch. Then, Voila! Restructuring.

Chapter 6: Purpose 2.0

We became a Global Shared Service Center with two locations in Latvia and Lithuania. I became responsible for something very important, but no one could properly explain what. I loved it. At that time I already was a good friend of uncertainty. These few years were interesting; we were building up the Global Shared Service Center, but first, we had to realize what that meant. We all knew the bank had hired an American consultancy to draft the strategy, and we were waiting for the magic suitcase with "Strategy." We got 154 PowerPoint slides instead, stored them properly, and started working on our own. Somewhere in the middle of the process, I noticed a strange, new feeling rising within me. Regardless of any achievements and successes, I was not feeling entirely happy.

I was sent to one leadership course, "Self-Managing Leadership," together with four colleagues. This course was based on the assumption that you have to be yourself in order to be a good leader. It was quite a revealing message in the success-driven environment, where I thought that you had to compete for a lot to be on the top; you had to play the role both at work and at home to comply with the expectations of the boss, colleagues, and family. I thought that for many people in my life, openness would trigger a Pandora's box effect, that it might be dangerous. I thought that the environment we were living in was too tough for the vulnerable truth of the inner self.

After the first day, I texted to our boss. "Isn't it too big of a risk to send five managers from the same division? I suspect people will either be divorcing or leaving their jobs after this type of training?" She answered, "I passed it myself, and I am still a happy wife and enjoy the work."

I remember only two things from that training:

1. It was something very unusual.
2. I rediscovered my purpose. Twelve years later, that has slightly shifted to "Make the life of others a little bit better. Add value."

I worked for six more years in the bank after this training and was still a happy husband. I had proven for myself that your own deeper-knowing is much stronger than any environment, despite how tough it is. This deeper-knowing works as the best navigation system in decision-making, both at work and on a personal level.

Chapter 7: Coaching

A few years later, the-never-entirely-happy tendency reached its peak. It was a crisis on the border of depression. I decided that I had to learn something new. For around six months I was mapping all of my interests, then prioritizing, making short lists, reconsidering again and again. In the end, I came up with a list of two positions:

- CFA certification (trendy banking certificate)
- Coaching

I couldn't explain why I should learn to coach, so I chose CFA. I couldn't say I loved finances, but it would be a great add-on to my curriculum vitae. I applied for studies just before Christmas. The course had to start on January 3rd, and the school promised to call and notify me if I would be taken to the group. Being in the holiday spirit, I only recalled about CFA on January 10th. I called the school, asking what was up with the studies. They replied that the group had started already. I asked about my application, and after ten minutes looking for my file, they said that they did not have my application.

My anger and anxiety lasted for less than a minute this time. I decided to treat it as a sign and to study coaching.

On March 6th, 2014, I was seated on the first day of the first module of coaching studies and was questioning myself: "What am I doing here? What else don't you know about coaching? You have already passed a number of coaching trainings for leaders."

Then the course started, and if you know the feeling when every cell of your body is shouting to you, "YOU ARE IN THE RIGHT PLACE!" you know what I felt that day. I was sitting there absorbing every second.

After two hours, when I already felt that I had received everything I needed, I joyfully said to myself, "It is just the first day of a six- month journey."

My message to foreign students on a guest lecturer at university had been very simple:

1. Define your ambition
2. Create a vision
3. Do the maximum to reach your ambition
4. But allow life to deviate from your master plan

Now I would add the fifth point: Do it again and again until you ensure there is no ambition left, only pure purpose.

Chapter 8: When purpose drives you

After coaching graduation, I faced a few more dangerous turns on my path. I was attempting to build a partnership business in parallel with work in the bank, to ensure a smooth transition from the bank. I was so excited by the vision I had created with my partner that we forgot to pay enough attention to the legal side of the partnership. To cut the very painful relationship story short, we hadn't managed to build a strong partnership, and we failed to fulfill our business dreams. At the same time, I almost lost my family, focusing on two jobs instead of them.

But I learned a powerful lesson about access to my own unlimited resources and ability to define my own boundaries and to stand up for them. I learned that my family is my power and that I shouldn't sacrifice my family's happiness in a given moment for the sake of a better future.

Apart from everything else, this situation also indirectly triggered my leave from the bank.

I do not work anymore since I cannot call what I do work.

I enjoy interacting with people and teams. My own company is called TeamLead; I knew the name long before the company, and I was sure I would mainly work with companies, leaders, and teams, since I know corporate context and challenges well, and it would be the most natural application of my skills. But my first clients were individuals who were experiencing a similar-to-mine, not-entirely-satisfied challenge. Most of them were leaders or business owners; this did not seem to fit my initial concept of focusing on teams and companies. However, I soon realized that my work with individuals is fully described by the TeamLead name. Since each individual is in the lead of the team -- your own inner-team.

I thought I wouldn't become a leader of any kind before I fully realized what it means to give life to your purpose. But life decided differently. Recently, I was elected as a president, not of the Republic of Belarus, yet, but of the Latvia chapter of ICF (International Coach Federation).

When I ask myself now, "Where is your motherland?" I think it is inside myself when I am connected with the self. When it comes to my purpose, it continues evolving. The latest wide version of my purpose is "supporting people in listening to themselves." It gives me a sense of meaning in every action I choose to do.

The current narrowed version is: "I help adults to learn to listen to themselves, to let their children stay connected with their purpose and to make planet Earth a little better place to live for their children." If there is someone looking for the secret ingredient, despite the fact that only you know your own secret, I will share mine: Calm. Love. Concentrate. Enjoy. Repeat.

I am only thirty-five now, and perhaps there are many more tipping points waiting for me ahead. Don't wait until the end of your life to write your memoirs, to realize something important. Do it often enough to understand where you are coming from, what in reality drives you, what your purpose is. And enjoy life.

Artur Chernikau

Leadership Coach

Artur brings more than twelve years of leadership experience from the banking field. His passion is defining strategy, leading change, and cultural and organizational development. After finishing his banking career, Artur dedicated himself fully to the field of people and team development, as an Executive Coach (PCC ICF), Leadership Trainer and Team Facilitator. Artur is based in Latvia and works in English and Russian. Artur has lived and worked in Belarus, the Baltic States, Sweden, the United States, and Singapore, and he has broad experience engaging with culturally and geographically diverse teams. He enjoyed the work both in times of rapid growth as well as in the crisis management environment of 2008.

Artur believes that "everything is personal," and he assists his clients on their change journey toward developing the authentic self. He helps leaders to find their inner compass, purpose, and source of vital energy, to be able to respond properly to the challenges of ever-changing environments.

„'People Profit Planet' is not only popular buzz speak, we all live a very short life on this planet, and I find it meaningful to strive to leave the planet in a little better condition for my children than when I was born," Artur says.

artur.chernikau@oxfordleadership.com

www.teamleadacademy.com
www.linkedin.com/in/chernikau

A Call To Adventure

by Carl Lindeborg

Without knowing it, my quest for purpose started one sunny afternoon in the back garden of a small house in Aix-en-Provence in southern France. It was spring, and I was 20 years old. I had finished military service and then spent an exciting and fun winter skiing in the north of Sweden.

Now I was studying French and staying in the house of a wonderful older woman, Madame Rey. Every evening she made us a delicious three-course meal with wine, and we spoke about life, or at least I tried to, struggling with my French.

I felt free and inspired, spending months away from family and friends, with the future open and full of possibilities. This particular afternoon, I sat down in the shade to write a vision for my life. I can't remember where I got the idea, but it felt like an important moment.

I wrote down a list of things I wanted to achieve in my life. I wanted an exciting, well-paid job and a career that led to a CEO position at some point in the future. I wanted to be very knowledgeable of basically everything, ranging from fine wines and fashion to Greek philosophers. I wanted to be in great shape, to have a cool apartment, to have a good looking and smart girlfriend, to know many languages, and the list went on and on. When I had finished, I looked at the list. I realized it would mean a lot of work to realize this ambition, and I drew an arrow pointing away from the vision, like a "take away," and at the end of the arrow, I wrote, "sleep less."

And without questioning that conclusion very much, that's what I did.

A few months later I went to business school. Soon I was working for a German chemistry company alongside my studies. I loved it. It was challenging and exciting. Next to studies and work there were parties and travel and a good looking and smart girlfriend. Why all this was so important I didn't think much about. I wanted to be someone. I felt invincible, fueled by my ambitions and the sense of being recognized.

Nothing was impossible. Once I was studying three courses instead of the normal full-time pace of two, in addition to my job. To be able to pass the exams and deliver at work at the same time, I scheduled every hour between 7 a.m. and 10 p.m. for 21 straight days with studies and work. There were signs, of course, that this tempo and the lack of rest and reflection had a price. Once during this 21-day period, I was embarking a flight in Munich after a meeting. I sat down and immediately brought up a book on business law that I needed to read to be prepared for the next exam. I opened the book, read a few lines and then felt blood from my nose starting to drip down on my tie. Not good I thought, but it wasn't enough to change my course.

A call to adventure

About four or five years later, I was spending a miserable winter in Brussels. Following business school, I got the job that was most sought after at my school, and I spent a few years working for an American consulting firm. There were ups and downs and a lot of learning in a short time. In the beginning, I was thrilled and also found many of the assignments stimulating and interesting. But something had started to shift after a couple of years living this life.

This damp and gloomy winter in Brussels, I was building a database with a long list of names of employees, basically trying to help the client organization figure out whom they could be without. While I think that it makes sense to do exercises like this in certain contexts, it's important to consider how you do it and why you do it. During this time, my life felt empty. I started to wonder, "What is the point of all this? What is the point of all this running just to achieve another goal?" I was living the work-hard, play-hard life I had strived for since that sunny afternoon in France. However, I was starting to realize that while this lifestyle gave me great kicks every now and then, the sense of satisfaction never lasted. Sometimes I even caught myself playing a mental game on Sundays, thinking about how much I would be willing to pay to make it Friday afternoon again.

Joseph Campbell, a professor in literature and the author of many books, talks about the Hero's Journey as a metaphor for human development. The Hero's Journey starts with "a call to adventure," some signs encouraging you to move away from your current reality into the unknown.

My call to adventure was emotional but also physical. During almost the whole Brussels experience I had a severe cold, which should have put me in bed but didn't. It went on month after month. I also had an inflamed Achilles tendon that made it difficult to walk normally.

Campbell points out that, initially, the hero often neglects the signs and the call to adventure, being resistant to leave the known world, the status quo, the current view of self. In the end, however, the signs become so strong and clear that they cannot be ignored. So, it was in my case too. After three months of coughing, sniffling and mild limping, the symptoms finally forced me to answer the call, to break the patterns I was repeating and to start a journey that would, over just a few months, have me reassess myself and my life-- and then change everything.

Am I really alive?

I realized that my body was trying to tell me something but I couldn't figure out what exactly, working 70-hour weeks with no space for reflection. So one day, I just had had enough. I decided to take a break for three months and managed to get unpaid leave. I made the last push to finish my consultancy project, took a day to pack a backpack with some clothes and a couple of books, and then jumped onto a flight to Asia, leaving my mobile phone and computer at home. I felt I had a debt to resolve when it came to introspection and self-inquiry, so I made a choice to make this journey on my own, with as little distraction as possible. I felt that something really needed to shift in my life and in order for that to happen, I needed to create the space for it to unfold. So, quite exhausted but hopeful, I set off on an around-the-world trip with one question in mind: "What's next?" Leaving Sweden and my familiar hectic life, I could never have imagined how I might respond to this question, how the call to adventure was about me discovering my sense of purpose and then reorganizing my life accordingly.

Three days into the journey, I flew into Laos, one of the most beautiful and tranquil countries in the world. In the small airplane, I was sitting next to a big guy with a bald head. There was something impressive in his appearance. He was the CEO of a Dutch company. Once a year he went to a monastery in Laos to reflect, reboot and then go back into action with more clarity and intention. He asked if I wanted to join him and go visit the monastery, and I thought, "Why not?"

I vividly remember how we walked down a dirt road and saw the golden monastic building where the edge of town met the edge of the jungle. When we arrived, the monks were gathering in the temple. I sat down at the back of the room. There were rows of monks, both young and old, all dressed in orange, sitting in half-lotus position. Suddenly, they started to sing. Absolutely still, they sang hymn after hymn. They sang in a beautiful, harmonic and deep way. The sound touched something deep in me as my brain struggled to understand the abrupt shift from hectic work mode just a few days earlier to now being absorbed into a blissful state by a mesmerizing choir of deep and perfectly synchronized voices.

The thought of whether I was in heaven entered my mind. "Was I still alive?" Then the next thought came: "Maybe this is what it's like to be alive for real. Full presence here and now; no distractions, awakened senses, connection."

Following the gathering, the young monk novices invited me to their room for a cookie and a cup of water. I sat with them on the earth floor. They didn't know anything about careers, businesses or hip clubs. We spoke about life. There was no need for me to keep up a polished and professional façade. I could just be me. I always thought I had been me, so this was the start of an unexpected liberation, that there was something more in me, a deeper sense of authenticity.

That afternoon, I realized that while striving so intensively towards my vision and what I thought would be a fulfilled and successful life, I had lost two important things. I had lost my sense of playfulness, letting everything become so serious. And I had lost my sense of purpose, which could give me a strong sense of meaning from the inside.

Walking home to my hostel feeling happy, free and intrigued, I noticed that the pain in my heel was gone. It never came back. The record-long cold left me a couple of days later. I realized that I had a job to do, finding that which could give me joy and meaning. But I didn't know how to go about it.

An alternative way

Following the monastery experience, I took a riverboat up north into the real wilderness of Laos. After a few hours on the river, we came to a small village with no electricity. I found a bungalow that cost one dollar per night, and I thought, "Wow I can stay here for the rest of my life if I sell everything I own."

The village was located on the riverbank at the edge of the jungle. On the opposite side of the river where green hills. Nature really absorbed me and I felt very far away from the rest of the world. In the afternoons, I lay in my hammock watching lightning play over the hills before the sky opened and I had to flee inside. In the mornings, I was awakened by an energetic crowing rooster, sitting under my bungalow, which was built on poles.

But it was the evenings that were transformative for me. We were only about 10 tourists in the village, and at dusk, we gathered for a beer and something to eat. The people that had made it into this end-of-the-world place fascinated me and we spoke about life, wonder and the meaning of everything.

I especially enjoyed the conversations with two surfers from Hawaii. The kind of surfers who would go out into the waves when there is a real thunderstorm roaring, getting kicks from the electric charges traveling through the water. Maybe they were crazy-- but I think they were crazy in a very intense and alive way. I longed for the freedom I saw in them. I longed to live with more presence, passion, and adventure. I started to see that there is an alternative way of approaching life where material things and prestige are far less important than the actual experience of the current moment. These connections in the Laos jungle made me consciously think, for the first time in my life, that maybe it is the richness of experience that should matter most; the quality of the emotion, the presence with which the senses actually perceive.

I shared the big questions I was pondering with the people whom I had randomly met. "What's the meaning of life? How do we live more fully? What's next?" The last evening on the riverbank, this group of life adventurers put together a reading list for me, a list of 10 books on life and personal development they absolutely thought were essential for me.

I brought the list to Singapore and surprisingly found half of them in a bookstore. I decided to go someplace calm and beautiful to digest them and found an isolated beach on a remote Malaysian island. For several weeks I read, reflected and journaled, and I met more people that shared my longing for freedom and meaning.

The book that affected me the most was Way of the Peaceful Warrior by Dan Millman, a book about self-discovery and self-transformation. I recognized myself in the main character, a young man who is successful in the outer world but unfulfilled in the inner world (Dan himself). In the book, Dan describes how he meets this mysterious character called Socrates who becomes his mentor. Socrates works at a gas station but possesses great life wisdom. He guides Dan to question many of his beliefs, to explore new ways of relating to life and to search for the core of fulfillment not on the outside but on the inside. All this resonated strongly with me, and I became even more disenchanted with my "work-hard, play-hard" life. I was beginning to recognize there was another way of living life, with more meaning and more fulfillment. But what would that life look life for me? What would I need to shift and change?

Facing demons and the rise of purpose

Up until now, my journey had been a great adventure. I expected to see amazing landscapes in these Southeast Asian countries, which I did. But I hadn't been prepared for seeing new and unexplored landscapes in myself. Being far away from my everyday reality, I had been exploring with a sense of lightness and fascination. As the weeks passed and my return back home came closer, fears started to arise. I realized that I had created my life from the outside in. I had been so eager to succeed based on what I had perceived success to be in other people's eyes that I had forgotten about who I really was. Now the consequences of that realization started to scare me; I knew how to be successful in my current life context, but what would happen if I changed course and created life from the inside out? What would

I do? What would people think?

I lay awake long into the nights with these thoughts racing and no one to talk to. My worrying brain, which had checked out in Laos, came back into action to challenge me. Wouldn't it be better to just stay where I was and make a few adjustments?

During this period I moved between meetings with my inner demons presenting the case of how things would go very wrong if I followed this new longing for meaning and freedom, and periods of conviction and strength coming from the emerging new thoughts about what was possible. After many rounds of this dance, I realized that I had opened a door in me that I could not close again, no matter the voices of the demons. To close this door of inspiration and take the old path would have been to violate myself.

More and more strongly, I felt energy and joy when I saw myself making a difference in the world not only in the financial dimension but also in the human dimension. Continuing exploring my book list, I learned more about the inner potential inherent in all human beings, and I also learned about the immense global challenges arising for humanity. It seemed to me that the outer crises, was a manifestation of an inner crisis in people. Inspired by my own journey, I thought that the more we learn about ourselves at a deeper level-- about our beliefs, our values, our sense meaning in life-- the better equipped we will be to make better decisions for the whole. As I started to realize this in myself, it released a wave of energy in me. I was not here just to be an instrument to help companies make more money, I was here to support human beings to make better decisions for the whole; for themselves, their organizations or the world.

The return

Coming back to Joseph Campbell's description of "The Hero's Journey", once the hero answers the call to adventure and passes the first threshold, there is the road of trials where he faces his demons. The hero finally finds what he went out looking for. But it doesn't end there. The hero must return, leave the adventure and come back to everyday life (think of Frodo in the "Lord of the Rings," for instance). Typically, the hero is resistant to return to the former life he didn't want to leave in the first place.

My adventure was about connecting with my sense of purpose in life, and along the journey, I found something important that I knew would change my life. But now I was returning to my home in Stockholm, where everything was the same as when I had left, except that I wasn't. I was ready to return to my friends and my colleagues, where many probably hadn't even noticed that I had been away and where people saw me in a way that would not fully match the person I wanted be going forward. The fears started to arise in me again. "Would I just get sucked back into the old patterns? Would people think I had been smoking something weird in those jungles and get over it eventually? How was I to navigate through all of the changes I wanted to make?" These kinds of questions made my mind race and my stomach tense for many days and nights. And the demons were whispering: "Are you crazy giving up what you have worked so hard for? You just can't do it."

A few days before the return, I was walking by myself on another beautiful beach, this time on the Cook Islands. I still remember this moment. It was a decisive moment, one of those moments in one's life where there a choice is made that puts you on a new trajectory. Suddenly, walking in the lowering sunlight next to the calm ocean, I felt stillness and clarity filling me. The mental rumination stopped, the demons were quiet. And for the first time, I knew with absolute certainty that upon my return I would make the changes needed to align myself and my life with my new sense of purpose, honoring my innate longing for freedom and meaning. No matter the consequences.

I felt at peace with myself when I made that commitment. I felt a power arise within me with a very different quality than the force of performance anxiety, which I often had felt before. This energy filled me with a belief in myself, a sense that I was on the right track and that everything would work out fine. I suddenly felt a rush of positive emotions like excitement, joy and love. Even though the demons and the fear of change would occasionally come back to challenge me, from this moment forward there was an inner foundation anchored in my sense of purpose and my core values. I could allow the fear to be there, but it felt more distant. It was the excitement and joy that would lead the way. The most difficult thing turned out to be making the choice to change, not to actually make the changes.

Changes

After many weeks away I returned to my home. Although I went from the "work-hard, play-hard" life to another kind of life, I still had the drive to be sure to make the change thoroughly, going from one extreme to the next. If I was to live according to my inner compass, I was going to do it fully.

So, during the following weeks, I made many changes. I ended a relationship. I quit my job and career as a management consultant to become a personal trainer, helping people with their health (and lowering my income by 80 percent). I stopped drinking, changed my diet and started practicing yoga and meditation. I also started to read new books and have different kinds of conversations with friends and family.

I wanted to spread my newfound sense of what life is all about and I wanted to help people experience the same shift that I had experienced. When I look back at this period, I can see that the drive to influence the system around me was a way to convince myself that I was making the right choices. A way to calm the inner demons and lingering doubts.

The way I took on my new path, making so many choices that contradicted what I had chosen before. was in a way overcompensating, bringing the steering wheel from maximum left to maximum right. With hindsight, I think it was necessary to do this for a period of time. To be quite rigid in the new helped me break the old patterns, to move from one life trajectory to the next. It was a total disruption and it was probably needed to avoid the risk of gradually returning back to my old way of living.

Following these initial changes, there would be an integration period of several years before I really found inner balance, an inner sense of comfort with myself, a way of relating naturally to purpose and values without having to convince anybody else.

Integration and a whole new education

I felt that my purpose was about inspiring people to open up, to see an even bigger picture and to make better and more sustainable choices for the whole. Reflecting on how I could live this purpose, I had chosen to start with what was most concrete, the physical aspect of wellbeing. I had taken an intense course to become a personal trainer and started my own company called "Energize Stockholm". I was supporting both individuals and organizations and the more work I did, the more I realized how little I knew and how much there was to learn. To be who I wanted to be to my clients, I needed to broaden my approach and return to school, but a very different school than I was used to.

For the next four to five years, I spent two to three months per year in dedicated life education. I went back to university and took classes on topics ranging from religious history to stress management. But for most of these years I traveled with my backpack to new places in the world where I thought I would learn and expand my horizons.

These travels were a manifestation of my longing for freedom and my curiosity about myself and human development. I learned to really enjoy my own company. I always left the phone and computer at home and I brought as few things as possible. I always brought my journal. The journaling helped me process and integrate my experiences, and though I didn't know it at the time, these written reflections would later form the basis of two books.

These adventures influenced me deeply and enriched my own experience of purpose. For instance, I once went to Dharamsala in north India to spend a week listening to the Dalai Lama speak not to Westerners but to fellow Tibetan monks. I bought a small radio through which I could hear simultaneous translation from Tibetan to English. Although I took many notes, I cannot remember any real specifics from what he said. But I do remember two things. One was the numbness and pain in my limbs from sitting cross-legged on a cushion for a week. The other, vastly more significant, was the appearance of the Dalai Lama. During the whole week, he naturally radiated warmth, compassion, presence, wisdom and a wonderfully playful sense of humor. He was such a great inspiration to me. As I write this more than 10 years later, I once again feel inner warmth and a smile on my lips.

Other influential moments from these travels happened in the lush jungle and the high mountains of Peru where I spent time with local shamans, going through deep trainings in psychology in California, climbing a holy mountain with a Buddhist monk in Japan and spending time in a monastery in France.

All these experiences and the reflection in solitude the accompanied them helped me integrate the changes I had made. I could understand myself and relate to myself with more self-compassion. I no longer felt the need to convince anyone in order to validate myself, but I did feel I had a story to tell – a story of self-discovery that could inspire. So, in 2007, I released my first book, "Your Brilliant Self – Creating Life from Inside Out." In 2009, I followed this with "Courageous," which I co-wrote with a friend and colleague. These creative processes were a great way of clarifying and sharing my understanding of myself and personal leadership at that time.

I was 29 years old when "Your Brilliant Self" was published, and looking back at that afternoon in Madame Reys' garden nine years earlier, I saw that there was no need to continue on my initial path. That vision had been so ambitious and I had driven myself so hard to reach it without finding what I really was looking for. Back then I thought that if I only can get that better job or get that thing that is just a little bit more prestigious life would be great. But now I saw that I could question my assumptions and my choices. I was opened up for a whole new adventure, which was about sensing and aligning with my own purpose and values – to peel layers of the onion and get closer to the core.

Moving with purpose

When you strive to live in line with purpose, and when you develop your inner sensitivity to what's next, you never really know where life will take you.

A few years after the episode described above, I saw Al Gore's film "An Inconvenient Truth". Although I had been quite aware of the environmental challenges that humanity faces, this movie created an alarming sense of urgency in me. I remember sitting still in the cinema while the closing credits appeared on the screen and people were leaving. Soon the room was empty and quiet. I remained for some time feeling my fear and worry transform into an inner conviction to do something. My sense of purpose was calling me to act in a new way. It was a new call to adventure.

At that time, I had met my wonderful wife, Julia, we had our first child, Leopold, and we had built our dream house on an island in the archipelago outside Stockholm, just at the banks of the Baltic Sea.

Over the next year, I had the opportunity to lead a leadership development program for the global sustainability group of one of Sweden's largest companies. Throughout the program, we dove into the greatest challenges that humans face and we interacted with some of the leading scientists and thinkers on climate change and global ecological challenges. An important moment for me during the program was when Johan Rockström, Professor in Environmental Science and leader of Stockholm Resilience Center, said, "Climate change is the easy question to solve; then there are difficult questions." I thought, "Humanity is not doing too well on the easy question, what will happen when we come to the difficult ones?"

Julia and I started to talk a lot about the global challenges we faced. We read more, we watched more. How would life be for our son when he was our age? All the signs pointed in the wrong direction and the positive changes seemed to be too few and too slow. Gradually a vision surfaced in us, anchored in a common sense of purpose. We saw the possibility to create a place for learning, reflection, and exploration. A place of inspiration where people could experience real solutions to problems we collectively face and a place that could be a meeting point for people who feel the longing to grow and develop to build an even greater capacity to make better choices for the whole.

So, after all the effort and the love we had put into building our new house, we decided to sell it and move to a place where we could realize our vision. It was a difficult decision since we really loved the place we had created, but the pull of the vision was stronger. We had opened a new door we couldn't close.

We knew that the countryside would be the place for our "sustainable retreat," so we moved to a small town about 100 km from Stockholm and squeezed into a small apartment while looking for the right place. We lived in this apartment when we had our second child, Cornelia. We knew we had to learn more about farming and sustainable ways of working with nature, so in between my consultancy assignments, and while Julia was pregnant with Cornelia, we worked at an organic farm.

A year later, we sold our house and we found our new place by the end of the road, with a lake, forest, and fields surrounding an old farm center. This was a farm that had been neglected for 50 years, and literally everything needed care. It took us seven years to transform the old farm into the sustainable retreat it is today, with new eco-friendly buildings, diverse and edible gardens, and produca harvest of organic grains. We are happy to have built one of the first buildings in the world that is heated in a carbon dioxide-negative way; that is, the more heat we produce, the less CO^2 in the atmosphere. We are also able to demonstrate many other sustainability ideas in practice. But we are most happy to continuously create a space where people and groups can come to step out of the intensity of daily life, to connect with the ecosystems, to slow down, to regain perspective, and to have authentic conversations about that which matters most, whether it is in themselves, their organization, or the world we all share.

This transformation hasn't been an easy journey for us. Tbe stories of ups and downs and learnings could probably fill a whole book in itself. Many times, we have wondered, "What are we doing? Why are we making it so difficult for ourselves?"

For myself and my wife, coming back to our sense of purpose—our intention to make a positive difference in the world—restores our energy and provides clear perspective. I can then see the beauty in the process of continuously taking two steps forward and one step back and then another two steps forward, trusting that by consistently following purpose even in the face of difficulty, I learn what I am here to learn, I do what I am here to do, and I create the ripple effects that hopefully make the whole system more healthy. And that is satisfying, from the inside out.

Carl Lindeborg

Founder of Leader Evolve - Catalyst for Future Proof Leadership

Carl Lindeborg supports the growth and evolvement of leaders and organizations. He is sought after as a catalyst for meaningful change in the roles of advisor, facilitator, trainer and speaker, both to top management teams and to broader audiences.

With more than 5,000 hours of experience from speaking, training and facilitating, Carl has a rich experience from working with a broad range of client organizations and from many speaking engagements including a guest appearance at Harvard Business School.

Carl is the founder of Leader Evolve and Lindeborgs Eco Retreat. He has been a fellow with Oxford Leadership since 2010 and is also an associate program director at Stockholm School of Economics Executive Education. He has a background from McKinsey & Co.

Carl is based in Sweden, where he, together with his wife, runs a sustainable retreat and meeting place. He is also a writer on leadership with two books published and the next one planned for 2020.

carl.lindeborg@oxfordleadership.com

www.leaderevolve.org
www.lindeborgs.com

Discovering My Gifts; The Precious Lessons I've Learned Along The Way

by Dr. Erika Maria Kleestorfer

My experiences have taught me many lessons about living more authentically and bringing my gifts into the world. Both personally and professionally, I have learned what brings me joy and creates more success for me and my clients. My hope is that sharing my story will prompt you to take action to reach your own goals and dreams.

A small child dealing with grief

When I was 6 years old, my father committed suicide. He was 44 and diagnosed as bipolar. His only relief was to leave this planet. And then life changed for me overnight.

The evening my mom informed my 2-year-older sister and me about his sudden death, a new chapter opened in my life - not only on the outside but mainly on the inside. I suddenly felt I needed to be an adult. As a sensitive child, I didn't want to be a burden for my mother. I felt she already had a lot to carry. She was 31, had two kids, a company to run and a few family members who blamed her for my father's death.

My mom never openly shared her pain with us, but I felt it deeply. She wanted to protect us by hiding it. So, I started to function as she needed me to. I behaved accordingly and started to be the funny/entertaining girl in the family to release stress and lighten the grief. When people asked me about my dad, I told them he died of cancer, as I was ashamed to tell the truth. At that time, he was the only person I knew who had committed suicide. I felt stigmatized and thought everyone was talking about us behind our backs.

She told me years later that she thought that if we had questions, we would ask her. But she rarely spoke about it Of course, I had many questions but I didn't ask them. I feared that if I asked, I would hurt her, and that was the last thing I wanted to do. I wanted to protect her from more pain. (Shortly after my father died, we also lost a dear friend of my mom and her younger brother. Both, like my dad, were gone within seconds). So, somehow, I started taking responsibility for her. Something a young girl can't actually do, but as I couldn't save my father, I didn't want to also lose my mother. That unconscious decision was probably the birthplace of my "helper" and "being strong" attitude. Looking back, I realize now that I took over a role that was definitely too big for a 6-year-old girl; however, I learned this only years later in therapy.

10 hours and everything will be fixed

When I was 30, I was in a happy relationship, and we wanted to have a child. For that reason, I wanted to "clean up" inside myself. I had no experience whatsoever with psychotherapy, and thought it would take 10 hours and everything would be fixed/clear. Ha ha! Good joke. The 10 hours turned out to be a two-year journey.

I thought mainly about the early death of my father and other friends and family members who died before my 20th birthday. They all were gone in a second through suicide, car or motorcycle accidents, or a plane crash. No chance to say goodbye.

Everyone who has ever done therapy knows that this is not an easy journey. I was confronted with old, often unconscious topics, very painful at the time and hard to believe, swallow and integrate. There were numerous moments where I thought it would have been so much easier not to start. Before that, life was so much easier – just black and white and easy to navigate. Many times along the journey I felt very fragile, like a newborn baby, and insecure about who I truly was. I realized that I never really allowed my inner child to be a child. I took over responsibilities that were way too much for a young girl. I had, in fact, buried myself emotionally next to my father. I put myself in an invisible inner cage, not allowing myself to be fully alive, happy, light, naughty, and - at times - even demanding. I learned to be the well-behaved girl to be accepted and loved. I didn't want any other person to leave me ever again.

Looking back now, I see that the painful therapy was definitely one of my most important experiences. It was like looking into the mirror and realizing who I really was, what is missing and how to heal open wounds. I struggled and worked hard to heal myself from the inside out. It felt like starting an intimate relationship with myself. And it still deepens more and more every single day.

Vienna, credibility and sports

When I was 14, I moved to Vienna. My hometown was just an hour away, but I had to move in order to attend the arts and crafts high school there. I loved it. I lived at a dorm with nuns in the city. Living with nuns had its good and bad aspects. The good part was that I met lovely colleagues and we played sports almost every day. I felt protected and cared for. What I didn't like were the double standards of the nuns. What they preached and how they lived were often totally contradictory. For example, they talked about love and how important community was, but their behavior showed something totally different. I was quite often confused about what to believe. I sensed something more than what I was being told. I felt a desire to know the truth, because the contrast between the verbal messages and reality was confusing. I wanted to know: What is true? What should I believe? Is what they say true, or what they do? Shall I trust my gut feeling or their words? This experience with the nuns was probably the origin of my excellent intuition and sensing skills. Painfully learned, it is now one of my biggest strengths and gifts in my life and business.

A similar situation happened at home. I understand my mom wanted to protect us, but although she always told us she was fine, I often sensed her suffering and struggle. So, as a child, I started doubting my feelings. Is what I'm sensing accurate? Am I making up a story or can I trust my gut feeling? This is something I struggled with for many years. I truly had to learn this skill – step by step - always connecting to my inside first. I asked myself: what do I really want, feel or sense in this situation? Once that was clear (and, to be honest, it took me a while), I checked my perception with others to get feedback. By doing so I became more and more confident in my ability to trust my gut feeling and sense what's happening around and inside me.

What was fantastic in my childhood was sports! I was encouraged to do many different things – from skiing, vaulting, dodgeball, tennis and my beloved ballet. I guess this was the space where I learned to train and work really hard, to develop my performance-oriented, competitive mindset. To this day, I just love to win, and if I don't win, I want the game to be at least fun and joyous. As with everything, there are always two sides of the coin. What I definitely learned at home, at school and with sports was to perform well, be competitive (healthy!) and goal-oriented. The downside was that I felt that just being was not enough. I felt I had to earn love, appreciation and interest.

I went to ballet from age six to 12 and it filled me up with joy and pride. And when I first stood there and people applauded and my mom gave flowers to me on stage, something magical happened. I realized how much I loved being on stage, being seen and appreciated.

I guess the appreciation coming from the outside helped me to become ambitious and goal-oriented. What I didn't know then was that I can give myself everything I was looking for others to give to me. And I can do this by turning inward, connecting to my needs and fulfilling them either alone or by reaching out to friends or family members.

A retreat and discovering how to love myself

I have also learned that by building up my inside world, I enjoyed being alone more and more. In 2016, I attended a 10-day silent retreat with the spiritual leader Mooji in Portugal. What a wonderful experience. Before going there, I was a bit scared. What would happen? Ten days spent mostly in silence, no eye contact with 400 other participants, no reading, writing, or anything else. Just two satsangs (big group teaching sessions) with Mooji. In these morning and evening gatherings, we could ask Mooji questions. But I never asked a question in plenary. I just enjoyed listening to the questions of others and hearing Mooji's replies. What I loved the most was not talking afterwards with anyone else. I just enjoyed digesting the thoughts and insights with myself in my own, inner world. In my own pace. My own beauty and calmness.

Almost every day, I sat under the same, beautiful olive tree and loved connecting to my inner source. It was a hot August, and I could smell the heat, nature and the warm air. I felt the inner connection to myself become deeper and deeper every day, and by the end of the retreat I had experienced a profound new awareness. I felt such a strong, unconditional love for myself inside. It felt like a white, open space that held nothing and everything at the same time.

After the silent retreat, it was hard for me to go back to my "normal life". I wanted to stay in that lovely inner space. I felt whole, protected, and loved. When I arrived back home, I realized a change. I was much calmer inside, centered and grounded. And I realized that this profound space was always with me. In fact, I am that space. I am everything and nothing, wherever I go. And I could see changes in my work. I was even more calm when meeting clients. I didn't need to prove myself anymore. My presence alone was enough. And my work became more enjoyable and effective, just by me being present without seeming to do a lot (or showing how smart I am) and just sensing when an intervention is needed. It's like working out of the here and now. It is holding the most powerful and transformative energy possible to support clients in turning their visions and ideas into concrete results, whether the work is individual coaching, strategy workshops or organization culture change processes.

I felt also a difference in my private life. I had no need to prove myself anymore. I realized I am absolutely enough – actually overflowing with love and richness. And that I could only be in a relationship again with a man who is also full and willing to share his overflow with me.

I am always whole

When my father died and there was not much communication going on, my child's mind started building up stories. I don't know why, but somehow, I strongly believed that now that my father is gone that half of me was missing. So, only if there is a man in my life will I be whole again. It was this concept of two souls. I needed a male partner to be and to feel complete. And as this was my strong belief, I had to find the other part to feel whole again. And I found them. Over and over again. The first at 16. I was constantly in relationships until the age of 37 when I realized I still didn't feel whole and complete with all the men, their love and appreciation. Something was still missing. All the external appreciation and compliments didn't really land inside. I heard what they said but didn't believe it. I didn't feel it inside. Looking back, I feel a bit sorry. They gave me a lot, but nothing was enough for me, as my inner foundation was still missing. There was still this empty hole, I was searching for something. My own love and appreciation were missing. The love, respect, gratefulness and nourishment from the inside out.

During my therapy, I learned about the "inner child", the parts inside that didn't get enough love, space, appreciation, or attention in our early childhood and thus, drive us to seek those things from people on the outside. It can happen in relationships when we attract-- over and over– partners who are similar to our parents. We want them to feed something inside that our parents couldn't. Not that they didn't want to, but they just couldn't. And as long as we attract similar people, we can't get the gifts we are looking for. I experienced that a few times. I wanted a man to tell me how wonderful I am. I wanted him to cure the loneliness I often felt as a child; however, they couldn't give that to me. This is something I have to do for myself. I learned that I can connect to my inner child and give her everything she needs to feel unconditionally loved. This is a lifelong journey and relationship with myself. It's like growing older together, staying in touch with my inner child; loving, protecting and caring for her. Showing empathy and compassion. It's about inner abundance, joy, love, boundaries, achievements and fulfillment. This means love from the inside out.

Awakening. Who I am is the gift!

It was in my early 30s and I still remember the exact spot in Vienna. I was waiting for the streetcar to get to my office at IBM. I think I forgot something at home, and my inner critic started shouting at me...nasty words, yelling and telling me over and over again how stupid I am. And then- BANG - it was like a light bulb lit up inside. I suddenly realized how I was talking to myself!! How unkind, disrespectful and rude I spoke to myself. I realized that I treated myself in a way I would never allow others to treat me. I was my worst enemy!

At that time, I had a spiritual coach and we went for a one-week retreat to the Austrian mountains. Our first task was to be alone in silence for two hours and to spend one hour for writing down every single thought. Hallelujah! What a simple, yet very powerful exercise. I was amazed about the amount of trash (we have up to 65,000 thoughts a day) I unconsciously thought every single minute about myself and others. How judgmental I was about myself and others. What the heck? At that same retreat, I was also introduced to the "law of attraction," Simply put, this means that we attract what we think, feel and are (the energy we radiate). Similar thoughts, ideas, people, situations and circumstances are drawn together. Wow! I was fascinated. I love knowing that my mindset and attitude matter and make a huge difference on my outer reality. This was something I felt since I was a child but now, I learned about a "law" that supported what I believed.

With this idea in mind, I started being much more conscious about my thoughts toward myself and others. Whenever I noticed self-limiting, negative thoughts about myself, I changed them immediately into thoughts like "I am a wonderful woman," "I am very smart," "I am beautiful," "I love myself," etc.

In 2016 I started an experiment. I love to test everything for myself before offering it to my clients, because credibility is very important to me. It's called "50 days to be your lover." It's all about mindset/attitude and the effect thoughts have in my life-- a bit like self-fulfilling prophecy and law of attraction combined. Every day, I tested a different mindset/strong belief and its effect on my behavior and results. For example, one day I focused on the belief that everyone loves me. Wherever I go, whatever I do, everyone loves me. I could be sitting in a meeting, saying everything that was on my mind without the fear what others could think – because on that day I strongly believed "everyone loves me." My experiment the next day was quite different, as I focused my thinking to believe "I can't trust a single person. I have to control everything." With that mindset, I approached everyone with a more suspicious, controlling behavior, and I got the result I expected; narrow-minded, shallow ideas and conversations. It was amazing to see the difference in outcome depending on my beliefs and mindsets. Through this experiment I learned how to attract more of what I want by directing myself in a focused manner.

Judgment is separation

One of my toughest lessons in life has been learning not to judge. My rational mind will argue that judging is important, otherwise it's hard to navigate through life, and that it helped me so much in the past (which is true) to have my black and white boxes. However, my inner wisdom knows that judgment is separation. It takes away the colors and possibilities in life. Judgment doesn't accept the full person or situation. It accepts only what seems okay or right for us. The moment I judge (myself or others), I separate good from bad, right from wrong. I actually quite often separated parts of myself I didn't like that much. If I separate parts of myself, I am not fully present, alive and powerful. I might be a well-functioning facade/machine but not a lively and emotional person.

Because I was left alone so many times in my early years by sudden deaths, I started leaving myself unconsciously over and over again. By judging certain parts of myself I was not loving my whole person unconditionally. I left certain parts behind. I wanted to stop that. Just realizing that I judged myself made me sad. Something had to change. However, changing a very strong belief/behavior needs a lot of attention.

I have always had a very strong mind and ego (Taurus!) that was not very happy when I decided to take back the control of my thoughts and well-being. There were many moments where my inner critic judged myself. It was almost a reflex. So, I started to play a different music in my mind. Whenever my mind went into judging and criticizing, I immediately thought about something positive; something strengthening, appreciative and nourishing. It felt like re-training a big muscle, turning the reflexive muscle of judging into a kinder and pleasant muscle. A muscle full of self-love, self-compassion and appreciation.

Breaking free, spreading my wings, and becoming my own source

After participating in different coaching sessions and spiritual retreats, I felt an increasing need to break free. I wanted to break out of my inner limitations and self-criticism. My coaches helped me come home to my true self and accept and fully love the person I am today. They helped me to celebrate the here and now and everything I have achieved so far – inside and outside.

It was time for me to fully show up. To stand behind myself. To say what's on my mind.

One big step in that direction was starting my own company in 2004. Before that, I worked at IBM, holding both European and global roles in the area of management development. I loved it. I loved to lead people and projects and to learn from the best in the field. However, after eight years It was time for me to leave. The students in my "Inspirational Leadership in the 21st Century" class at the Technical university in Vienna sometimes ask me, "Why did you leave such a great company, salary and job?" The reason was that I felt as though I was not fully spreading my wings. I had the feeling of flying with retracted wings and I wanted to know what it would be like to spread my wings 100%. I could not do that with a safety net beneath me, and IBM had been the safety net.

I finally left in 2004 and never regretted it for a second. Before setting out on my own I had thought that starting my own company would mean working a bit less after my 60-to-70-hour weeks at IBM (I traveled to work with leaders all over the world). However, I was too eager and ambitious and wanted to prove that I could make it alone. I didn't take a single client with me or start working as a consultant for IBM as many colleagues did. That was not my way. I wanted to succeed on my own feet. I was very lucky. Shortly after I left, I was introduced to Duke Corporate Education in the U.S. Deutsche Bank was a big global client and they asked me whether I was interested in leading a European project, implementing the first-ever global leadership initiative at Deutsche Bank. What they wanted was very similar to the work I had done at IBM. It was a leading-edge leadership program, combining top content with the latest technologies. I loved it. I adapted the global program and process to European standards and trained all future consultants and trainers to run different programs, as well as delivering many myself. I was back to 50-to-70 hours a week, but it felt different. Now it was my own company. My own money. My decisions. My quality. My standards. My mindset, and an awareness of the difference I was making.

In my new company, I decided what to do and with whom I wanted to work. I began to build a global network of excellent colleagues from around the world. I always wanted to have a small boutique consulting firm that could stay flexible and independent. I am proud that I have never abandoned my high ethical and moral standards. Having said this, I have also withdrawn many times from work with companies whose values didn't match mine. I don't like employees or managers who take everything for granted, who don't see and appreciate the incentives, benefits and goodies companies offer. I don't want to have to convince leaders in workshops to participate, bring the right attitude and mindset. They are all adults and it's up to them to take responsibility for their lives and the impact their behavior has on their employees and results.

Working at IBM was like attending a tough school. In my early days there, we delivered five-day leadership programs for managers from all over the world almost every week. Workshops for 24 participants, sometimes men only, sometimes a few women. Quite often some participants resisted for the first one or two days they were sent and didn't want to be there. And my colleague Sys Boe from Denmark and I tried everything to convince them about the benefits, what was in it for them and what they would gain by the end of the week. I gave everything! All my energy. And I was exhausted by the end of the week. Usually, 97% of them loved it. They were happy, fulfilled and stronger than before. But I felt exhausted, tired and drained. I unconsciously took over their responsibility! I thought it was my role to convince them. However, looking back now, I know this was not my responsibility. But this insight came only years later, with much more experience and confidence.

Nowadays, I don't accept program participants who don't want to be here. I don't want to waste my time and energy with people who are not serious or committed. I want to spend my lifetime with people who want to make a difference in this world, in their own lives and the lives of their employees. For them, I give everything, and I still have more than enough energy.

I really love my company. We have achieved so much during the last 15 years, and I can't wait to explore even more. I will expand offerings and add more online coaching and consulting work. I love to combine technology and leading-edge content and methods.

Business and spirituality

The freedom of having my own company has made me stronger every single day and help me merge my spirituality and business side. In the past, I often felt like living two lives. There was my business life on one side and my spiritual life on the other side. I even had two separate groups of friends.

Earlier in my career, I didn't want to share my spiritual side with my clients because I was afraid they might think I was odd or unprofessional. I felt I needed to play the "normal" game so as not be judged. To avoid that, I rarely mentioned words like spirituality, love, kindness or mindfulness in my business context.

My business life brought me many achievements, successes, money and great clients, however my spirituality filled up my soul and provided a sense of belonging and purpose. Within my spiritual circles, I became stronger and stronger from the inside out. The more I loved and respected myself, the less I could deny my truth. And my absolute truth is my spirit, my essence, my core. I can't say that there was one moment where it all changed. It was more an ongoing process, development and growth in that direction.

But over time it did change, as I became more comfortable sharing my spiritual side. I still remember an experience with one group of leaders I have worked with for many years. Most of them are very rational, goal-and- results-oriented. We meet four times a year in a 'Leadership Circle' in my office. The goal is to address day-to-day leadership challenges and leave with a concrete plan or action on how to tackle or solve the issues. One of them is an especially smart and reflective man. And just recently he said at the end of the workshop, "Isn't everything just spirituality?" I had tears in my eyes. It was so deeply touching to me as I realized my inner YES to spirituality (not doubting or denying it for a second anymore) was positively affecting their thinking and behavior.

Who you are is a gift to this world

It took me almost 45 years to truly feel this with every cell in my body: "Who you are is a gift to this world." Who I am IS a gift to this world! My being is enough. My pure presence is enough. If I am not sharing who I really am with the world, then I am robbing people of something they need. By showing only parts of myself, I am not showing my true, rich and abundant self.

There have been many times I've asked: Am I really allowed to be happy? Can I be joyful when so many people around me have died? Was I not good enough for them to stay? What must I do to show the world my worth-- that I am worth being loved? But through my experience and learning, I no longer linger in these doubts and fear.

I couldn't save my father. So I made up my mind, behaved well, was the funny, entertaining, good girl, and I learned to work really hard and function well. And although there was very often resistance inside, I didn't face it because I needed to survive. I needed to adapt to be accepted and loved. That was the old Erika. The Erika that was searching for everything outside.

Today, I try to give myself everything I need. I have a lovely relationship with my family and if I am not happy, I change it. If I don't have enough clarity about a client project, I ask for more clarity. If I feel upset in my relationship, I start a conversation or find a way to cheer myself up. If I feel bored, I try to find something that lightens up my day. It's MY job to make myself happy and look after myself. We are adults and we are responsible for our own happiness, health and well-being. It's not those outside (family, friends, partners) that need to make us happy and fulfilled, it's ourselves.

I have learned to own my own story and to rewrite it in my own voice. Every single moment, one step at a time. I have learned to stop telling the same old stories over and over, which actually were prolonging my suffering. I have stopped waiting for others to save me.

I started looking inside. I started connecting to my inner source. I started loving myself from the inside out. I started saying "YES!" to myself. I strongly believe that we are all here for a special reason. That we all have our very unique place on this earth that only we can fulfill. Our job is to find it and turn it into reality. Our highest self wants to have fun, play and serve others, and each of us has the ability to make this happen.

The greatest gift, freedom and source of peace for myself has been to find everything inside. To become my own source. Owning my own life, love and happiness. To never leave myself alone and be there – especially when times get tough – with a kind, loving and supportive mind and heart. This is inner leadership at its best. And once this becomes second nature, it overflows to the outside and brings even more richness, fulfillment, love and success into our lives.

I am very grateful for my life and for my journey. I believe that our toughest challenges are our greatest gifts for inner and outer liberation and development.

I have arrived. I am here, not waiting anymore.

Dr. Erika Maria Kleestorfer

Entrepreneur, Leadership Expert/Coach

Erika loves to (re-)activate existing resources, mobilize talents, bundle the energy available and turn it into measurable results. In her work, she focuses on leadership consulting, organization development and executive coaching. She is particularly interested in supporting senior executives and entrepreneurs in their decision-making processes, tackling the real issues and supporting individual and organizational growth. She is also a keynote speaker for inner and outer leadership.

The success of Erika's work hinges on her approach; which is systemic, holistic, spiritual, multicultural and networked. Erika has worked alongside a wide range of clients, such as ECB, IBM, Deutsche Bank, Baloise, Sanofi-Aventis, UBS, BASF, Telefonica, etc. Since 2004 Erika is part of the Global Educator Network of Duke CE, US. In addition, Erika is a partner of Oxford Leadership since 2009. Erika is very fond of supporting, encouraging and mentoring young professionals around the world and lecturing at some Universities in Vienna (Uni Wien, TU, WU) as well as teaching Coaching since 2004.

She is also part of the Supervisory Board of the ‚Architects of the Future'. The architects are pioneers of a new economy that connects holistic thinking with successful entrepreneurship, compassion, and solidarity with social activism.

erika.kleestorfer@oxfordleadership.com

Leaders, The Shamans Of A New Paradigm

by Eve Simon

Nanoseconds often define our lives. These short moments steer us in a new direction of change with no return. They are often turning points and guide us to live a life with passion and purpose - without even intentionally knowing it.

Nothing will ever be the same. These breathtaking moments lead us into transformation for an astounding impact.

And that was also for me the case.

After 17 hours of intense labor, I found myself faced with death - for me and my daughter. This little human being was trying to make her way into this world. Drifting away as both of our hearts slowed, hearing the doctors speaking from afar "to act right now with no time left" - my impulse was a cry of prayers. All I was hoping for was to have the chance to hear her first little scream on this Earth.

It all ended in an emergency C-section, so I didn't have the chance to hear this first little scream. But after waking up from anesthesia, it was the most precious moment to hold a healthy baby in my arms.

That moment, when I was holding my little wonder, everything changed instantly. My world view, my focus, my heartbeat for life - even I did not realize this at that time.

Spending many years in my career on change-management projects, as a professional I knew how to move things and even people from A to B, and often also to Z and back to A. I was a master in changing the outer world, studying all that was available, from cutting-edge systems, the newest business models, technologies, leadership theories, human potential topics, even to topics such as cosmology. But much later, I realized that change only gets us so far. True transformation has another twist – it changes from the inside out, and not the other way around.

So where do we start? Do we always need high emotional live-changing moments and catastrophes such as death, sickness, loss, new love, or birth?

My personal moment of transformation was this nanosecond of understanding how close birth and death are and how precious life is. The moment of transformation was not the outer requirement of being responsible as a mother for another human being that would fully rely on my care for many years. It was an innate impulse of course direction. From this moment on, all my decisions came from another perspective than before. My horizon widened based on the well-being of this little human and the next generation she will grow up in.

My new perspective didn't only apply to my role as a mom; it deeply affected my being as a business builder, change consultant, executive coach and leader. A much deeper dedication grew inside of me, aligning all areas of my life. Instead of only the mind, my purpose shifted into an integrated motor of heart, gut, and mind - driving and influencing the outer world with a much larger impact.

Transformation is rooted in a deep yearning for change, which is unfortunately often created by crisis. Nanoseconds lead us to this fundamental change in perspective and priorities.

Even though my birth experience was in many levels traumatizing, I wholeheartedly believe that it was meant to be - for both me and my daughter – and the interrelation we interact in. It gave me another level of consciousness and urged me to deepen my work. Instead of fine-tuning the outer world by new concepts, systems, designs or orders, my inner focus and wisdom shifted, leading to another driver and greater impact.

Are leaders the "shamanic" healers of a new ecology?

We find ourselves in a world that is in the most developed state we've ever reached. We face fewer wars, deaths or catastrophes than ever in history - and still, that is not at all how we perceive it. The United Nations rightfully defined 17 sustainability goals. With our resources, knowledge and human power today we should be able to solve these challenges in a heartbeat. But we don't. We hype the entrepreneurial startup world without looking at the solutions we create. More than 70 percent of our workforce is unhappy and not engaged. Not to mention the increase of depression and obesity. And the devastation in several areas of the world where people are facing political tumult or have no access to basic necessities, such as clean water. Even as we approach Mars, consume lab-created meat and use self-driving cars, the world is not healthy.

Our children are walking the streets to protest for climate change with Fridays for Future. It´s time to wake up as leaders and become wise adults - or to be more exact, become a fearless mothering-kind species, making every decision instinctively based on the well-being of our children and society.

In the moment of becoming a mom, I knew intellectually that an intrinsic motivation took over which from now on was leading all my thoughts and decisions.

The world of the future needs wise Evolutionary Leaders who heal the unhealthy status quo.

We know we can tackle every problem to solve the challenges of today, and yes, we could create Utopia in some form or another. And for that, we need a fully new mindset connected to a purpose higher than ourselves.

Many years ago, I had the pleasure to study with Chip Conley, a conscious-business leader who integrated the wisdom of Maslow's Hierarchy of Needs into his hospitality company to successfully navigate the bubble bursts of Silicon Valley. He proved that when you see beyond the basic expectation of clients, shareholders and your employees and fulfill a peak experience, you create a deeper form of relationship and a new "Mojo" will securely navigate your company through many storms.

In so many ways, Chip is for me an amazing example of an evolutionary leader, a new form of shaman of the emerging business world, transforming the many lives and businesses he touched.

It's time to look beyond the known

Back to my own experience of enlightenment. I learned fast. Only when we face our inner landscape, our shadows, our inner cosmology and quantum fields, will we be able to embrace transformation and lead a life with impact. In so many situations we see it's time to design new solutions from the inside out – just as Chip did with his approach of embedding Maslow in his operating system. I believe we can draw on our intellect and Artificial Intelligence, but even more, we need to lead with our higher instinct and a holistic, more integrated wisdom. We must bring together the whole available intelligence of body, mind, and spirit, with the relevant knowledge we have today from bioengineering and neuroscience. Learn from history and our ancestry. And embrace a larger quantum field we can't even imagine today. It's time to find better solutions for the greater good and make decisions based on the interconnection of the triple bottom line – People, Planet and Profit.

In my career, I am and was in charge of many initiatives, strategized and designed workplaces, events, departments, products, and services. In this nanosecond of being faced with death, followed by the moment of holding my precious gift in my arms, I realized, "I can't hold back any longer." I became more of a peaceful warrior who spreads the message of conscious change and holds the space to shift from an outer design into an evolutionary creation. Instead of playing small and nice, it was time to find this voice of inspiration and activism to inspire leaders to shift their perspectives and take action to collectively create a healthy business environment in which everyone can thrive and where solutions are created to lift society to a healthier paradigm.

Well, I do have to confess that it is more than scary. Stepping forward, swimming against the stream, is uncomfortable and sometimes even dangerous. I am not always the most liked or booked consultant in the field. For me, it would be so much easier to sell my deep knowledge of leadership, innovation and digitalization and "the Silicon Valley Mindset." But I can't, knowing how dangerous our decisions and resulting consequences are when we focus only on profit and quick results.

No wonder Eric Ries and a group of executives are pushing the long-term stock exchange right now. I am thrilled to see their great results, just as the group of B-Corps, for-profit organizations with a higher purpose for society such as Patagonia.

Another example that fires me up is a group of executives from Silicon Valley who formed, with strong conviction, an alliance to step up against the "free-range" development of addiction-based applications. They founded a non-profit which is now helping digital addiction victims; they have a voice out there to warn about the results within many apps, and they are working on rules for business to follow an ethical code. The same executives who were in charge to create these apps are now stepping up. Why? Because they have children, and they feel firsthand the negative impact of their own action and creation.

Let's not wait until it's too late

My purpose of being a change agent for the business world by inspiring others to look beyond, face the shadows and paint new horizons, isn't a walk in the park, but it is the only way to bring humanity back into the center of a healthy society. When our intentions and decision-making are driven by a purpose beyond ourselves, it's a process of healing.

Is your purpose is based on love, with a twist of heroic action, evolving and aligned, inspiring others and a natural thing to do? Then you are on the right track.

The purpose discussion shouldn't be lip service for marketing and profit, but show action in role modeling, leading with a bigger impact than just your personal or business benefit.

We human beings have a gift within us - to create beyond what we know. Robots and AI are not a curse; they are our chance to focus on what is truly needed - a human connection, love, and care for each other and the planetary family. Would you rather work in an environment of fear and pressure, mistrust and unhappy colleagues, or in a workplace that cherishes your talents and dedication, one where you can laugh with colleagues and co-create wider global ecosystems?

No wonder the Conscious Business and Mindfulness movement is so popular right now. Salesforce.com just hired its first Chief Ethical Officer. Companies such as Haniel as a 200+ year old company remember again what they're standing for – an entity for society, with offerings which are 'enkelfähig' (for grandchildren). Society is ready for change. Are we as leaders ready to go the extra mile and create impact for the greater good?

My message: We have to shift from profit to impact, from success to significance, from performance to aliveness.

We, as leaders, have a responsibility, just as mothers, to care, create and hold the space for others to flourish in a safe environment.

Business can be sexy instead of evil. We are able to transform business into a force of positive evolution for our people. Instead of seeing the corporate world as a prison and an enemy, we can start seeing capitalism and the economy as a source of energy for evolution. My question is – which are the KPIs that drive us?

I am thrilled to see role-model nations like Bhutan and New Zealand that defines their political success by the health and happiness of their society.

When one starts dancing, it's potentially just a sign of craziness, but when one more join in it is the start of a powerful movement.

In 2005, I started a women's network in the U.S. based on circles of sharing and support. Everyone thought I was crazy to put so much of my effort and money into this initiative instead of spending my little time with leisure. Well, in the bigger picture it paid off, as the movement took off. For me, it was never driven by the monetary payoff but by a deeper innate purpose to spread inspiration and courage. But even then, I didn't feel the urgency of change as I do today. So purpose can build up in its intensity.

Circles became big – whether it's "Lean In" by Sheryl Sandberg, Women in Digital or the Working out Loud movement. People finding their power through intimate circles of peer support, even when it's a stranger (who quickly becomes a friend). They help you become the best version of who you are, with no personal agenda, selflessly, collectively and for the greater good – not just for women, but for everyone. This experience led me to start the Future of Leadership Salon in 2018 which holds the space for inspiration beyond technology and controversial dialogue for leaders.

We are not separated from each other

Every interaction has a wider impact than we can even imagine. Every thought creates a ripple effect of dimensions much larger than our own being.

I strongly believe it's time to define a new business matrix. The status quo is proving this. Every company is an organism with a soul and a DNA. Every company, every service and product is part of a larger ecosystem. Every person in this equation is as important and relevant for survival as the other. Instead of increasing our mechanical ability of functioning, it's time to become alive again.

In early 2000, I became very sick. For months I was fighting a virus that was shutting down my ability to function - the worst thing that could happen to me. Through the course of my life, I had mastered the ability to function as society had required of me. I was the good girl, the caring daughter, the dedicated wife, the committed, responsible and focused leader. I was all of that, but not alive. My system needed to shut down, to make me realize that I had to shift from functioning to aliveness to stay alive. And we see the same in businesses. We have plenty of examples in the economy where businesses drove their way of functioning too far, forgetting why they existed in the first place and who the driving force was: the human source. They became strictly machines ... and died.

Transformation is painful, it´s scary and it´s needed

One crucial thing differentiates us from all other species on this planet - our conscious choice. This conscious choice we can direct to things that matter most.

More than 80 percent of the day we run on autopilot, which means we are driven by automation of experiences and conditioning. If these are old patterns and survival mechanisms from our early days of existence, we are driven by our reptile brain. Decisions based on this conditioning will not birth anything new and for sure nothing better. It might be different, but not substantial. And substantial change is what we need, so our children can grow up in a healthy world.

Consciousness is the key to transformation. Transformation is the only catalyst to create a new paradigm.

You heard the quote by Einstein a million times: "No problem can be solved from the same level of consciousness that created it."

This quote alone is not as powerful as his additional statement: "A human being is a part of the whole called by us universe, a part limited in time and space. He experiences himself, his thoughts and feelings as something separated from the rest, a kind of optical delusion of his consciousness. This delusion is a kind of prison for us, restricting us to our personal desires and to affection for a few persons nearest to us. Our task must be to free ourselves from this prison by widening our circle of compassion to embrace all living creatures and the whole of nature in its beauty."

In 2007, I started offering Innovation Learning Journeys to Silicon Valley, showing executives cutting-edge new business solutions. Today my heart starts racing when after a transformation journey to Silicon Valley, Stockholm, Austin, and other places of impact, I see what change the participants personally went through. Then I know I lived my purpose. My offer is not a safari where you look from the outside at innovations and models. We go into much deeper conversations of the core of leadership – with ourselves and other great leaders in these hubs of innovation. And we also look at the shadow sides of these places and products - and ourselves. The impact is a deep reflection on how our actions can have a positive influence and impact. It's not an easy journey. At times, it might be challenging for everyone involved, including me, to stretch out of our comfort zone and examine the ugly, relating it to us and changing to an unknown perspective.

Through many years of studying great evolutionary leaders as role models, I saw that Leadership of the Future is built on these six characteristics:

- Conscious
- Collective
- Creative
- Compassionate
- Continuous
- Courageous

To live on purpose is brave, not always easy and requires alignment in every step you take. In my mind, I often hear this voice: "Do you really have to take this job and fly around the globe? What about my carbon footprint?" or "Salami is so delicious, but to stop global warming, it's time to let go of meat. Do I really need it?" Or, "Again you are away for days for work, is that really good for the little one?" For every decision I make, I also have to ask myself hard questions about consequences that might not fulfill my pleasure, luxury or personal need but pay into a healthy future for my daughter and my mission. And surely, as a human being, I am not always on track.

The good thing is that through years of practicing mindfulness, the inner critical voice which keeps me on track shows up faster to allow me to make a conscious choice.

When you read this book, are you eager and ready to drive change? For you and the people you lead?

In my experience, the best way to do this is to first look at your inner landscape to be successful in transforming the outer world with tremendous impact.

Are you ready to start more meaningful and crucial conversations with others but especially with yourself? Instead of monkey mind chatter, create focus and clarity? And are you ready to understand when your values are at stake to stay alive and not just perform?

Become your inner engineer

Being a mom and business leader isn't a walk in the park. Many times stress takes over. When that happens, my best mechanism is to STOP and breathe. I put in the effort to understand the full context (from the insights available to me right now) to decide from a space of care'ship beyond the obvious, free from ego, driven by the urge to create a world with less misery based on my purpose. When I get into this state flow happens, and existence makes sense. People join my dance. It's so thrilling to see when leaders are open up and explore a different path. At the annual Future of Leadership Salon, we hold a space to explore deeper inspiration, crucial conversations and an evolutionary co-creation. And even though every year we plan to officially finish at 6 pm, participants are still in deep exchange of thoughts and laughter at 9 p.m. It's alive, full of energy - a circle beyond, in full flow.

Our ego and desires too often lead as the drivers of our actions. How consciously are we directing our actions toward influence and impact? The end is clear for all of us; the road we take is up to us. Let's all be more aware on this journey. Life is a precious gift, and leadership is a privilege to be in service not for one but many.

Being aligned with your purpose gives life a direction and meaning. But don't ask yourself only what the world needs; start with what you can give - unconditionally and intrinsically - just as the love of a mother. What brings you meaning or where can you spread meaning? It's not necessarily the big things. It's the little actions when we touch people, create a smile on their faces, encourage them to follow a new path, give hope or lift the burden of their pain and pressure just a little bit.

The UN sustainability goals, many unsettling statistics about satisfaction at work, social conflicts ... which challenge are you most passionate about and eager to address? Listen to this inner voice and do THE work.

I encourage you to explore your inner landscape, be a detective of your unspoken world, and you will find a path with meaning of no return to create true transformation. The purpose calling is usually close to your heart and doesn't leave any space for reasoning – just like a parent's intrinsic motivation to keep a child safe.

I am deeply grateful for my nanosecond of painful transformation. When you almost lose life you know how precious it is. I don't want my daughter to have to walk the streets and dare adults to face their responsibility just as young Swedish climate activist Greta Thunberg does. It's my job; it's our job as leaders. Will you start dancing with me? I know together we can create 'Utopia', a healthy place with a happy society – and this is not on Mars, but here on Mother Earth.

Thank you for being you, being on this journey with me – for the children of today and tomorrow and our beautiful planet.

Eve Simon

Expert in Leadership Transformation, Igniter for Innovation and Inclusion, Executive Coach, TEDx-Speaker, and Serial Entrepreneur

German by nature, Californian by heart - that promises an unusual approachg in all Eve does. Eve works as a creative and systemic business builder with corporations, executives and start-ups all over the world to empower radical self-awareness and agile leadership for a more sustainable business approach.

Prior to starting her own company InspirationsWithoutBorders in 2005, Eve managed national marketing, communications and change at E-Plus, as they transitioned from start-up, through rapid growth, and into the maturity phase.

Since 2005 she is a driving member of the Conscious Capitalism movement, bridging the gap from success to significance. As a futurist, Eve founded the initiative LadiesLead Change and the Future of Leadership Salon; both movements that foster co-creation and inspiration in a powerful network.

Eve holds a master's degree in Marketing and Economics from the University of Basel, Switzerland. As a constant learner, she is further qualified in Executive Coaching (NLP), Mindfulness, Scrum, Design Thinking and Open Space and various human potential methods.

Eve lives currently with her daughter on two continents – Silicon Valley, CA and Düsseldorf, Germany.

eve.simon@oxfordleadership.com
www.futureofleadership.salon
www.ladies-lead.com

The Road Home

by Fredrik Lyhagen

I'd lost count of how often that nagging question ambushed me. As I did every workday, I charged down the narrow road to the highway to work, my brain on fire. Not with ideas and energy, but with a morbid calculation that had become routine. So routine that I'd even gone through my old college physics books to refresh my memory on kinetic energy.

As I eyed the thick, ancient trees lining the road, that question, which had gripped my mind so often, came up yet again. "What's the optimal speed to hit one of those trees, so I don't kill myself but hurt myself enough to get a three-month break from work?"

I'd "made it" but my heart was crying

I was 32, had a six-figure salary running a $100 million sales department for the coolest IT company at the time, and 65 people working under me. Most people would say that I'd made it. And yet, here I was, considering self-harm as my only escape. Maybe I needed a break from work, not hospitalization.

Except, I was already taking all the breaks the system allowed. That's to say, 25 days of paid holidays, but never more than 2 weeks straight, where you spend the first few days fidgeting nervously while trying not to check your work emails on your phone every couple of minutes, and the last few days with a creeping sense of nausea at the thought of going back to the office. Sandwiched in between are those fleeting, euphoric moments where you tell yourself, "Screw slaving away as a corporate drone, let's sell all our things, move here and open a bed and breakfast." I'm pretty sure I said some version of those words at least once every vacation I took.

To be fair, though, work wasn't all bad. The best parts of my job involved collaborating closely with my team members, engaging with them and challenging them to overcome their fears, nudging them in the right direction, and seeing them grow and prosper as individuals. That energized me, making me feel like I was doing something worthwhile. But such moments were very rare. My reporting requirements kept me buried under Excel sheets for days, pushing numbers up the command chain so the top management could further "motivate" my department with targets, metrics, and benchmarks.

The other problem was that I'd chosen to be there. No one was forcing me. And yet, I felt like a hamster on a wheel, always running but going nowhere.

Every workday, I left my heart at home and replaced it with my laptop. From 8 a.m. till 7 p.m., I was busy with tasks, responsibilities, and obligations that meant little to me. Days, weeks and months disappeared in a hazy blur of repetitive motion. It was making me sick to my stomach. But I'd no idea how to get myself off the wheel without throwing myself off and crashing into a tree. And the wheel was just spinning faster and faster.

I needed something to happen. To dig deep, close my eyes, and jump off that wheel.

So, I did. I jumped. And I didn't crash into a tree or anything else. In fact, I landed on my feet. But nothing turned out as I expected or planned.

An interlude with lasting impact

This journey had started many years before, back in my last year of business school in my native Sweden.

As both my parents were teachers, an academic path was always a given. Not even discussed, never questioned. From the start, I'd bought into society's prevailing narrative of success: study hard, get good grades, land a good job, get a mortgage, and save for retirement. The whole enchilada. My strongest motivation to do anything different was simply to leave Sweden and see the world. I don't know where it came from, but I've always had this urge to see more, experience more. Anything that allowed me to do that while checking all the boxes in my life plan suited me just fine. If I had any sense of purpose, it was merely to get out – and fast.

But then, in the year of completing my bachelor's degree, I struggled with some exams. It felt like I'd failed myself, and for the first time, I began questioning whose dreams I was trying to fulfill. Was it really me who wanted to do this, or just what I thought society expected of me? What my upbringing caused me to expect of myself?

These questions and the sense of failure led me to take a sabbatical and go to guitar school for a year.

Yep, you heard right. Guitar school.

I moved to London and started at the Guitar Institute of Technology. To say I was the odd man out and that I didn't fit the guitar school mold would be an understatement. For one, I was probably one of a few students who'd complete basic school. I was also probably the only one not to spend every waking moment in my room practicing scales. The other thing I didn't share with my classmates was talent. They had it in spades, whereas I … well, I enjoyed playing guitar. So, I accepted that I'd never be a rock star and moved on.

But it did me good to be in an environment so unlike the one in which I'd spent my entire life, and to encounter backgrounds and dreams that were so different from my own. And it may have planted some seeds that wouldn't blossom for another two decades. But, at the time, it didn't really change anything. I finished my sabbatical at guitar school and then had a free semester until my last year of business school. With nothing else to do and thinking it might be fun, I accepted an offer from my parents to substitute teach international trade and accounting for one of their colleagues at a high school.

The two-week stint turned into a month, which turned into the entire semester.

It was my first taste of teaching – the first time I felt the excitement of seeing a student get something and grasp things from a new perspective – and I liked it. Indeed, were it not for the lack of career progression and the fear of getting stuck in Sweden, I'd have liked to be a teacher. But my ambitions were bigger and I returned to University to do my master's degree, with no real change in my own perspective. If anything, my year in guitar school and my semester teaching were mere interludes in my planned trajectory, opportunities to take a break, nothing more.

Quitting a guaranteed career

The questions I'd started to ask myself before starting guitar school had drifted away and then disappeared altogether. Rather than following any purpose in my life, I was following a plan. And that stayed the same as before: good school, good job, good retirement. Any sense of inner purpose remained out of sight and out of mind. And so, in 1998, I graduated from business school and landed in the management trainee program at a large, Scandinavian consumer goods conglomerate.

My life plan entailed climbing the career ladder and creating a comfortable spot for myself in the world. But, as I mentioned, one constant factor that didn't fully fit with this plan was my desire to get out and see more of that world. So, when the management trainee program ended, I left that guaranteed career path and took a job in Amsterdam, at the IT firm, where I'd eventually find myself driving to work dreaming of crashing my car into a tree.

But everything started well. I worked in sales. We had a great, young pan-European team, all with similar life ambitions, and everything buzzed with energy. Soon my career took off and within a few years, I was running that $100-million-dollar sales department. I'd even won an award for best account manager in Europe and found myself on stage in the US with the global CEO and other important people. I thought I was having the time of my life.

Except I didn't.

I was working hard, putting in hellishly long hours building and expanding my team while telling myself that all the hard work would pay off in the future – when I'd be a global CEO. When I'd made it to the top. My trajectory was taking me there and then I'd get my reward.

Except, my colleagues at the pan-European level didn't remotely inspire me. The place where they'd worked themselves toward didn't seem a happy one. And the place where they'd reached in their lives – working incessantly and neglecting their families and their dreams – didn't inspire me either. And I felt like I was joining them in the same uninspiring place.

From the outside, of course, I'd made it. I'd left my little hometown. I had a good education. I traveled, I was living abroad, working for a great IT company, earning good money. I was starting to become a bigwig. I had a wife, whom I loved. We had a daughter, whom we adored. Everything should have been perfect. But on the inside, my heart was crying – though I didn't know yet for what.

And once again, those thoughts that had led me to guitar school started to creep up on me.

"Was this it?" I wondered. "Was this all there was to life? Was this what I was working so hard to achieve? Whose dream is this, anyway?"

My workload at this point was crushing me. An iron yoke pulling me along and dragging me down as the invisible hand of my plans whipped me relentlessly forward. Meanwhile, around me, my colleagues were smiling and laughing, giving each other high fives. I thought to myself: "Am I the only one struggling here? Am I not cut out for this? Am I not good enough?"

I couldn't accept that, and so I worked myself harder and harder. It got to the point where, on the last day of my 2005 summer holidays, I was sitting in my parents' garden, talking to my father and lamenting that I had to get back to the office on Monday. I wanted an escape. A way out. At the very least a break. But the birth of my daughter and having a new family to support didn't allow me the luxury of another sabbatical. That autumn I started contemplating those trees on the road to work, thinking about ending up in the hospital and finally throwing off the yoke of work, at least for a while.

Escape, lawsuit, and vodka

I mentioned initially that my career path didn't end up as I expected. I'm a thoughtful, careful and sensible man by nature and not given to rash behavior. So, I quit the IT firm, but not with a bang. Instead, after a few more months of grinding away, a friend suggested that we both jump off at the same time and set up an IT management consultancy, which we did once we'd secured our first client.

Initially, being an entrepreneur thrilled me, and in the first 18 months, we secured a couple of big-name accounts and hired six consultants. But my heart wasn't in it. My business partner was, and is, a highly driven and successful entrepreneur and passionate about building businesses regardless of the sector. But for me, the project was more of a means of escaping corporate employment than a way into something inspiring.

On top of all this, my relationship had become strained and I was beating myself up for putting us in this situation. Leaving corporate to set out on my own I had pulled my wife away from an exciting career and an environment with lots of friends and put her in an apartment in a new country, with a language she didn't know, without friends or family around, taking care of our baby daughter while I was away all day "entrepreneuring" without bringing home much money the first 12 months.

Then 18 months into my adventure as an entrepreneur, the thing I treasured the most, my marriage, was falling apart, a major client refused to pay us, and we ended up in a legal battle facing all of our work leaving us with empty hands.

After three sleepless months, the client finally owned up to what was right. But my wife and I decided we needed a fresh start to heal ourselves and our marriage, we decided to move to Prague, my wife's home town. I exited the business I had helped to build.

To cut to the chase, I got a consulting contract back at, of all places, the IT company in Amsterdam. That carried us through the relocation and starting anew in Prague. Then the financial crisis hit in 2008, and only a few months after I'd started, my contract was canceled. So, after six months of unemployment, I took a job at a telecom company in Prague. Not long after, I felt the familiar stress building up in me again. Soon, I found myself stopping by the corner shop on the way home to down an airplane bottle of vodka as a way to decompress, and then going through a pack of chewing gum so my wife wouldn't notice.

Unfortunately, the vodka was followed by a bottle of wine at home. Things, as I said, weren't turning out as I'd expected, and I found myself back on the same hamster wheel, the same worn path I'd been on for most of my life, this time with the added weight of too much alcohol and some extra years pushing me down. It was then that I promised myself that I'd quit the corporate world for good by 40, only four years out. But how to do that? As I said, I'm a sensible, rational person.

My escape route first emerged while doing consultancy for the IT firm I had worked for in Amsterdam, to which I owe a huge debt for teaching me a lot, for building my resume and for helping me finally leave the corporate world. One of my assignments there had been to coach and mentor junior sales managers, and I'd quickly discovered a deep pleasure from helping people. It reminded me of my semester of teaching at the high school. Now, some years later and once again finding myself utterly worn out, it seemed like coaching could be a way for me to heal, and maybe even a way of jumping off the corporate treadmill. I'd finally find some meaning beyond working for the idea of a more fulfilling future.

The first steps to explore purpose

My lucky break came, once again, from the very corporate world from which I was trying to escape when a global networking company offered me a position. The job was actually a breath of fresh air – this was a smaller, younger, more vibrant company without all the stifling bureaucracy – but the bitter taste of my time at the telecom company remained. I hadn't forgotten my promise to quit the corporate world by the time I hit 40. Yet, as the sensible man I am, I realized this might be financially challenging, so I decided to seriously explore coaching and get my professional coaching accreditation. It would thus be something to keep me sane should I be too afraid to honor my promise and quit.

So, for the next year, twice a week, I'd get up to have a training session between 5:30 and 7:30 in the morning, then wake my family and start my workday. And what an amazing experience it proved to be. As much as I was learning about how to coach others, my mentor took me on a journey to explore who I was, digging deep into my motivations and fears. Helping me hold conversations with that little devil perched on my shoulder, who kept whispering in my ear: "You can't do this. You're not good enough. People will laugh at you," and more.

I found the tools to work with all the indications I'd had of something being not quite right. The questions about whose dreams I was pursuing, the feeling of failing at the IT firm, and the conflict that had raged inside me for so long – and was still raging.

These factors, combined with an interest in Buddhist philosophy and meditation, which had been growing inside me, prompted me to join a small Buddhist community for regular meditations. Conversations with a Buddhist priest helped me by grounding myself in who I am, and I started to think in terms of my purpose, for the first time in my life. Simultaneously, from the conversations I was having with friends and colleagues, I realized that I had quite a lot to offer other people. And so, what had for so long been a fog of poorly defined and fleeting ideas scrambling my mind became a clear vision of wanting to use my experience to help people overcome the challenges that I'd had, to reconnect them with who they truly are and create a path towards living it.

Except, I had no idea how to make that happen.

Walking in the light of purpose

That answer came in the form of my coaching accreditation, which finally gave me the confidence to start working with clients. Eventually, this led to partnering with Oxford Leadership, and in turn, opportunities to go into large companies and work with leadership development until, a few years past my 40th birthday, I left corporate employment behind to dedicate myself full-time to explore my passion and purpose. And it was such a relief: the dissonance between the life I had been living and the life I wanted to live had become so strong that the consequent pain had become unbearable.

In doing so, I finally feel that I am, if not yet fully expressing my purpose, at least walking in the light of it. And on my path to here, the corporate years served me well; I wouldn't be able to do what I do now without them. I'm also grateful for all the role models of the life I don't want to live that I've met over the years. They have unknowingly pushed me to explore my path to avoid my biggest fear in life – ending up as a grumpy old man, bitter for never really having lived. And please don't get me wrong: walking in purpose doesn't make life easier, but I find that it does make it simpler. I see my way forward, and even if the exact path is unknown to me, my heart is in discovering and exploring it.

Reflecting on my inner journey, I now have a sense of coming home to who I am. I can now show up 100% as me, no longer feeling that I must assume roles to fit in I am helping to create a sustainable and inclusive world, one conversation at a time.

This could mean inviting a single person to explore their shadow sides or to be more conscious of what they support with their spending. Or it could mean working with a room full of corporate leaders on how they can have a sustainable and inclusive impact on the people their businesses touch.

Whether with one or many, it's one conversation at a time. A conversation that's taken me half my life to finally have – first with myself and now and with others.

Fredrik Lyhagen

Leadership Consultant, Facilitator, and Executive Coach

Fredrik draws on 20 years of experience from consultative sales, sales management, talent management, alliance management and consulting, mainly from international IT and telecom companies. He is an experienced executive coach, passionate about conversations that explore intrinsic motivations and push the boundaries of the comfort zone.

As a leadership consultant, his work is centered on raising self-awareness for the integration of the self and leadership from the inside-out to transform organizations. Fredrik's clients highly value the combination of his strategic approach with grounded presence. His entire career has been in multicultural organizations and he has lived abroad close to 20 years.

Originally from southern Sweden with an education and a career throughout Northern Europe, he has been settled in Prague with his wife and daughter since 2008. To reenergize he enjoys woodwork, traditional archery and spending time in nature.

fredrik.lyhagen@oxfordleadership.com
www.fredriklyhagen.com

My Path To Purpose –
A Series Of Dots

by Graham Bird

Apple co-founder Steve Jobs once said in a Stanford University graduation speech, "You can't connect the dots looking forward; you can only connect them looking backwards. So, you have to trust that the dots will somehow connect in your future."

My story is evidence of that and I am keen to share the story of my journey to finding my purpose. This journey has taken me down many different religious and spiritual roads, most of which were dead ends but a few, just a few, took me that one step further to answer the questions I'd asked myself for many years. I feel clearer now, after a long and eventful journey, I feel that I can now take some satisfaction that I am far closer to knowing myself, and therefore my reason for being, than ever before. The irony is that it was there all of the time. Discovering my purpose has not been easy; it has taken time, deep reflection, commitment, and much self-reflection.

Dot No. 1 - From humble beginnings

My story begins in childhood, which by all standards was pretty normal. I was born into a working-class family living in a small two-bedroom apartment in an industrial town in middle England. Although I have an older brother, he left home when I was 6 years old, and I have very few memories of his presence. This rendered me in some ways an only child. Without going into the reasons why, my mother kept me very much by her side during pre-school years which meant that when I first attended school, I had very little experience of being with other children. Therefore, I did not know how to behave. This meant that for the first few years of schooling, I was pretty much a loner and extremely shy; in fact, there was only one other kid whom I called a friend. This made me different from most of the other children at school, and we all know what happens to children who are seen as different; they can become the focus of intimidation and bullying, and that was certainly the case for me.

I was quite a sickly child and this kept me away from school a lot during the early years of schooling. This meant that I fell behind with my schoolwork. The result of this was I did not earn a place at the grammar school. Instead, I went to the local comprehensive school, an institution where, by definition, "pupils with all aptitudes and abilities are taught together". The comprehensive I attended from the age of 11 to 15 was a particularly unpleasant place. My experience during those years was dominated by fear. There was a very powerful negative energy in that place, an energy of intimidation and threat. The teaching staff, or at least some of them, behaved in an autocratic and quite intimidating fashion, which of course just fueled an energy of retaliation and violence from the unruly element. Bad behaviour was punished with physical punishment. In hindsight, those early experiences of fear and intimidation began to cultivate in me a bullying of violence. This manifested itself in what I felt at the time was my only option, avoidance. I would find any opportunity to skip school whether that was through genuine, or more often than not, contrived sickness. Looking back, I was a frightened and lonely child. I did have a few friends who were much like me, bullied and lonely. Finally, at just 15 years old, I walked away from that school, a place where the primary education had been emotional and physical survival, with a great sense of relief that my days going forward would be free from fear– or would they?

Dot No. 2 – A wake-up call

Just before my 16th birthday, my family moved to a seaside town on the south coast of England. Having just left school and moving to a different part of the country meant that once again, I found myself without friends, and the feeling of loneliness reappeared. My father had bought a small restaurant business, so I worked in the business during the daytime and spent the evenings alone until the restaurant closed around midnight. I didn't see much of my dad during those days as he was still living and working in our home town so I guess this didn't help the isolation I was feeling. It was during this time that something began to happen, something that would be a wake-up call. I became ill. More specifically I began to lose blood due to internal bleeding. At first, my mother took me to doctors and the prognosis ranged from 'growing pains' to poor diet. I knew instinctively that none of these explanations were true. I also knew that even at just 16 years old, I was beginning to get into bad habits, habits of smoking cigarettes, drinking alcohol and experimenting with recreational drugs. The bleeding continued and I became physically weaker and more and more anaemic day by day. More doctors and more medication failed to stop the bleeding until eventually, my parents took me to an old family doctor back at our home town. He examined me and immediately admitted me to the hospital. I was suffering from a burst duodenal ulcer which, it was believed, was the result of the years I'd spent in fear. The acid my stomach had been producing was literally eating away the lower intestine. By the time I got into the hospital, I'd lost approximately half of the blood in my body, a life-threatening situation that was luckily caught before it was too late. Once in hospital, I received a blood transfusion and over the course of two weeks, I slowly began to regain my health and the colour in my cheeks! However, what was to happen while in the hospital really shocked me. In the bed next to me was a Portuguese man, probably around the age of 40. I don't recall his name but I do recall that he did all that he could to make me laugh, I guess to relax me. He would tell me jokes, he would make funny faces, he really was a funny man. Then, in the middle of one long night, I awoke to a ward full of doctors and nurses, surrounding the bed of my new best friend who had fallen out of bed onto the hard ward floor during his sleep. He wasn't in his bed in the morning when I woke. I asked where he was, and I was told that he would not be returning. I learned later that day that he had passed away during the night. I was shocked, and I was deeply sad. This, in hindsight, was my first experience of the fragility of life – here one moment and gone the next, an experience that shifted something inside of me.

Dot No. 3 - The search inside begins

Leaving the hospital, I no longer wanted to work in my father's business; I wanted to go my own way. However, searching for work at 16 years old with no academic qualifications or work experience, meant only one thing, little choice but manual work. However, despite holding some pretty menial jobs during the first few years of full- time work, I always felt that I had more to give, I just didn't know what that could be or even what that meant. As a result, I drifted from meaningless work to more meaningless work. I saw work only as a means to a pay packet, no more and no less. However, regardless of the type of work I did, whether it was in a factory or pumping fuel, I was always aware of something inside of me that yearned for more meaning. I sensed deep down inside that I had more to give but I had no idea of what, let alone how. Alcohol and drugs were everyday pursuits for many and being vulnerable as I still was, I found myself slipping into that dark, yet in many ways, exciting world. It was around my early 20s that I began to realise that the fear that I'd experienced in my early life had not left me, it was still present. I also became aware that I was now angry – angry with myself and angry with life. I would feel angry if I saw other others being abused, or if anyone tried to abuse me. Although I was living a pretty unfulfilling life, looking back, I realise that this was a major turning point in my life.

Dot No. 4 - From self to others

Religion played no part in my life as a child. In fact, my parents never spoke of the subject and the only visits to churches were for weddings and funerals. I was an unintentional atheist. Yet, deep down inside, I felt as if there were more to my existence and life than I believed there was. I began to read about different religions. I began to visit religious buildings, all in the hope of finding answers, answers to questions that were beginning to occupy my mind. I also began to read self-help books which, along with my introduction to spirituality, began to open up my mind to another reality – one far removed from the life I had lived up to that point. Eventually, in my mid-20s, now married and with a large mortgage to pay, I applied and was successful in securing, a role with a large global organisation as a sales executive. The company at the time was the 8th largest privately-owned company in the world, so heaven knows how I got through the interviews. My brother had introduced me, so that no doubt played a part. Thankfully I was successful, and this was to provide me the opportunity to make a fundamental change in the direction of my life. For the first time, I was challenged, challenged intellectually as well as emotionally, and for the first time since leaving school, I began to realise a deep lack of self-belief and confidence in myself which was to keep reappearing for many years to come.

Being in a professional environment, my lack of academic education and writing skills would be put to the test, so I had to work evenings and weekends in an attempt to educate myself. However, despite the feeling of low self-worth I carried around with myself, I became aware that others saw something different in me, some saw what I could not: my potential. True to form, I dismissed these well-intentioned compliments as people simply being nice or that they really did not know the real me. Nonetheless, I grew in that company. At last, I found something that I enjoyed and was good at. This new role allowed me to attend many training courses, and I absolutely loved them. I became fascinated by learning about and experiencing a world that up until then, I had no idea existed. What was most significant, however, was that I was attracted to what I saw training do – it encouraged people to grow emotionally as well as intellectually. Not only did I learn valuable life skills, but I also learned to see myself differently. This world of helping others appealed to me. Maybe part of the appeal of wanting to help others was a cry from myself for help, too. Inspired by my new discoveries about myself and the support that I was receiving, I set my career sights on becoming a trainer. I spent the following couple of years in that training role enjoying pretty much every moment of it and learning so much about life, others and, ultimately, myself. I also began to read, something even through my school years, I'd done little of. I read anything and everything I could find on psychology, religion, spirituality, and self-help. I started to attend many courses, some to develop my professional skills and some more personal skills, eventually, gaining qualifications to fill the educational gap left from earlier years. I became obsessed with self-discovery and I knew that at last, I was beginning to find some meaning in the work I was doing and ultimately life itself.

Dot No. 5 - The road less travelled

Now in my early 30s, things were going well, and I was gaining a solid reputation as a dedicated and loyal member of the organisation when one day, out of the blue, I was invited to the Managing Director's office. That day once again shifted the trajectory of my life. I was offered the opportunity to take over the role of head of training. I had just 2 days to decide if I wanted to accept this new role and although it was an exciting opportunity, accepting meant moving my wife and two very young children to a different part of the country, leaving our friends and families behind. Of course, career-wise, the opportunity was far too good to miss. So, unanimously, the decision was made. We put our house up for sale and while waiting to sell it, I began to make the 200-mile-per-day round trip to my new place of work, the UK HQ in Henley upon Thames, England. The timing was not in our favour as it was to take almost two years to sell our home and find a new one. Learning my new role, and having direct reports for the first time challenged me. To make matters worse, I was living out of a suitcase driving many miles each week, and this took its toll on me personally and on our marriage. Being in this new environment and having much responsibility to prove my worth, the old pattern of self-doubt began to re-emerge. I began to be highly critical of myself, again, blaming myself for every mistake that I made, even for those my team made. I realise now that during this time of self-centeredness, I took my eye off the ball as far as my relationship with my family was concerned. I was so focused upon my new job, that I was unaware of the pressures my wife was experiencing back home. She was left to look after our home and two very young children while I was away. Slowly our relationship deteriorated and the fabric of our marriage sadly began to come apart. To add to the pressure at home, the earlier promises of excellent career opportunities, the promotion and subsequent personal and family sacrifice we'd made, my future with the company came to an abrupt end one February day in 1994, three years after our move. That eventful day, the whole of the training and marketing departments were closed due to the recession hitting the world at the time. I found myself amongst 92 others on a list of the largest redundancy programme the UK company had ever seen. This was to be a very eventful and emotional time as within the very same week that I had lost my job, our home was burgled and our third beautiful daughter was born. When I called my wife with the news that I'd lost my job, and therefore the much-needed income to pay for our large mortgage and general living costs, she naturally became very upset. Yet I sensed, deep inside, that all would be well and that this was meant to be. Now, in my late 30s, I was about to take the road less travelled.

Dot No. 6 - A call to purpose

The company was very supportive to me during this time, offering to help find me another position. Although I did apply for management roles, nothing materialised. Then one day, out of the blue, my wife suggested that I follow my passion for the career that appealed to me so much, freelance training. Considering that this idea had slowly cultivated in my mind over the previous few years, I failed to understand why I had not pursued this route before. I guess that my immediate concern was in securing an income, a goal that at the time made perfect sense, but, in hindsight, was a path that would have kept me secure on the road to mediocrity. She was right, navigating my path was what I'd always wanted because I wanted to make a difference to a wider audience than my previous corporate role. The fact that I had no clients, no network, no understanding of what it would take to set up and run my own company, to take 100% responsibility for the large financial obligations we had did not deter me. Despite the big risk I was about to take, I felt driven by my dream. It took about six months and many sleepless nights before I finally landed my first contract working with a UK-based 500-store retailer. The next three years were a rollercoaster ride of travel, nights away from home and 70-to-80-hour workweeks. But I now felt that I was doing what I was meant to do.

Dot No. 7 - My dark night of the soul

I hit hard times in 1999 when my mum passed away. I had been very close to my mum and spending the final months of her life, watching her health slowly deteriorate was a very difficult time for me. The following year, the relationship with my wife deteriorated further, so much so that we decided to divorce. I had spent a lot of time focussing on building my business and travelling and I guess that I had taken my eye off of the ball and neglected her and time with my three beautiful young children. This behaviour, although well-intentioned, was to cause me many years of guilt. We didn't fall out, we simply accepted that even though at some level the love we had experienced together still flickered below the surface, we had grown apart. Maybe it was depression that brought on a feeling of having lost my passion for the work that had driven me for the previous six years. I was living alone, my debts had doubled, and I began to seriously question my life, the life I had strived so hard to achieve. It wasn't the separation from my wife so much that caused me the pain, it was living apart from my children. The house that was once full of children's laughter now felt cold and soulless. Even though my wife and I had decided to part, I felt guilt, guilt that in some way I had abandoned my children, something that violated my values as a father. The truth of that matter was, I probably saw more of my kids after the separation because I made sure that I did – it was a perceived loss of identity that I now know was causing me the pain. This period in my life was my 'dark night of the soul'. Still working for myself, and feeling pretty low, I took any training work that I could get but now I was not driven by any sense of purpose anymore but of a sense of meeting the obligations I needed to meet.

Dot No. 8 – Light at the end of the tunnel

Maybe it was denial, but I eventually turned my thoughts outward trying desperately to shut out the hurt I felt. To do this, I became a volunteer charity worker, mentoring disadvantaged children. I met and worked with young people who were suffering mentally and emotionally and somehow, this experience helped me to put my own life back into some perspective. I felt the real pain these young people were feeling, and I began to cultivate a desire to do more to bring about a better and fairer world, a world where emotional and material poverty could be addressed. It must have been Christmas 2002 when I was invited to a party by the charity I was working with. At the party, I sat next to a woman I'd never met before and we began to talk. I mentioned my growing interest in spirituality, and my desire to learn more when she told me of a meditation course which was to commence the very next morning in a nearby town. I attended that morning and the subsequent six-week programme that followed and was sufficiently intrigued by it to sign up for an advanced course at a meditation centre in Oxford. During the many weeks, I attended the programme, I became aware of another programme the centre offered. This was a two-day leadership training course which was titled "Self-Managing Leadership". I was intrigued, so I attended this leadership programme and it shifted the trajectory of my life yet again. I don't recall how, but I somehow got to meet the founder of the Oxford Leadership Academy, an Australian named Brian Bacon, one Sunday morning in Oxford who invited me to join his company.

The forming of dot No. 9 and beyond - Finally, on purpose

For the last 15 years, I have worked with Oxford Leadership, travelling all over the world delivering transformational leadership programmes and working as an executive coach. "Transforming leaders for good" is at the heart of the work we do and certainly at the heart of what I do. However, I now realise that I had not only been pursuing a career purpose, I'd also been pursuing something much more personal. Eckart Tolle in his book, "A New Earth" talks about having an inner and an outer purpose. An inner purpose is that journey of discovering the self, who we really are beyond the ego, whilst outer purpose is our mission in the world, how we live our purpose through our work. Looking back over the years, I realise I tried to be someone else, as I did not like the person, I thought I was, therefore my inner purpose has always been to reconnect with my true, authentic self. On the other hand, my experience of fear and intimidation cultivated in me a deep sense of compassion for others and this has driven my outer purpose. I thank God that I finally found the work that I feel I was meant to do, the work that truly inspires me. As I began, looking back on my life, I can see how the dots line up, how every event in my life, good and bad, positive and negative, has led me to where I am today. Rather than being angry for the hurt and the missed opportunities that my early years produced; I now see that it was all part of a much bigger plan. Rather than despising the years of intimidation I experienced, I now see how those times have helped me to understand myself and my mission in life.

Now in my 60s, I feel privileged to do the work I do with Oxford Leadership, which has provided me with the vehicle to live my purpose. I can genuinely say that my work is helping, even if just in a tiny way, to make this world a better place.

I cannot predict where the future dots will land, but I do know, deep down inside, that my life has been, and continues to be, a path to living my purpose.

Graham Bird

Executive Coach and Leadership Consultant

Graham is a passionate leadership consultant and executive coach based in the UK. Since 2003 he has been inspiring the leaders of some of the world's largest corporations to find their own sense of meaning in the work they do. He is driven by the belief that each of us has the potential to be more than we currently believe ourselves to be, a belief that often limits leadership to mediocrity.

Graham is known for the authenticity he demonstrates in the work that he does. He believes that the very best leaders are those who are aligned to a deep sense of purpose, a purpose beyond self-gratification and self-gain.

Graham has worked with thousands of executives from all over the world during his career and this has led him to nurture a profound belief in the potential purpose-driven leadership

graham.bird@oxfordleadership.com

www.linkedin.com/in/graham-j-bird-ab2b335
www.oxfordleadership.com/authors/graham-bird/

I Did It!

by Hans Veenman

I did it. I resigned. I quit! Tears wet my face even before I called Klara to tell her. I felt so relieved by saying it to her out loud.

It was December 8, 2005, and I was driving home to Badhoevedorp after a meeting in the vicinity of Utrecht. It was dark and raining, the road was glistening. Combined with the tears, I had to concentrate on my driving. We did not speak much, but we stayed in touch through the telephone connection, throughout the drive home.

How did I get here?

Nearly 28 years before, I started working for KPMG, straight from University, 21 years old, as a youngster. First as a software engineer, and before I knew it, I commenced developing my leadership skills in roles such as team lead, manager and senior manager. I loved my work.

Klara and I got married in 1980 and started our family (two wonderful sons). Soon after that, Life showed me the way and was easy. I must say, in hindsight, I lived my life on a not-too-high level of consciousness. It just happened. I was content in my work, Klara took care of the kids and we were happy and wealthy to have what we wanted.

The work environment was wonderful challenging assignments, great colleagues and always people around me who showed me the way.

When I was 26, my father passed away very suddenly. It was a heart attack. I was devastated and did not really know how to handle this event, other than by putting even more energy into my work. Life just continued. No questions asked.

I traveled a lot for business and loved working together with others on the most challenging projects. And while people still saw me as "the technology guy," I was step-by-step realizing it was not so much technology that made me happy, but people. I thrived by making my teams work.

I remember giving a Christmas speech to my team. About a hundred at that time, I told them what I felt. "If we start a shipyard tomorrow, we will be successful in that as well." The funny thing is that only years later, I started to realize what this message actually told me. With a good team of motivated people, anything is possible and fun!

Looking back at those roughly 30 years of working in the consulting business and 50 years of living, I now realize there were people around me regularly, who fed me with advice, questions or behavior that helped me find my way in life. Let me share some.

Who showed me the way?

To me, the best way to learn has always been through guidance from a mentor. Of course, my dad was my first and best ever mentor. He taught me about right and wrong, about the revenue of working hard, and that anything can be done or made if you set your mind to it. The most important value I developed through his guidance, is the importance of togetherness, of connection through the heart with other human beings. He was loved by the people on his team for who he was. He showed me the way.

My great friend Han, with whom I stayed during summer holidays as a youngster and during adolescence, was also a role model. I recall working on his farm and camping in the countryside during the daytime. We discovered new friendships, nightclubs, and alcohol. Han gave me trust in being good at what I was good at. He let me explore and expand my limits and enjoying life next level. He showed me the way.

At work, it was my first boss, Herman, who showed me the way in his particular style. He was a partner at KPMG and always full of energy and new ideas. He loved technology and was regularly judged by his colleagues for spending company money on the newest technologies and pushing his team to test them to the limits and see what was possible.

I was involved in the development of the first-ever commercial chipcard application in the Netherlands, and in professionally hacking the Dutch banking system to prove their weaknesses. It was assigned by the Dutch National Bank, of course. I loved those projects and doing the most challenging things as a team. Herman taught me to act first and ask for forgiveness afterward, instead of asking for approval upfront. He showed me the way.

In the late '80s, I was asked to set up a new consultancy practice in telecommunications. With a lot of help from the people around me, I did one of them was another Herman. In my eyes, he was an old and wise man. He was a technology engineer and business advisor with a vast amount of experience in large-scale infrastructure and telecommunications projects. He was my personal coach for two years, supporting me in setting up this new business. In my view, he was stubborn, sometimes grumpy, and never satisfied with my answers, never a compliment. And with that, he taught me the importance of always looking for opportunities for improvement, not to settle for mediocre solutions. I learned to ask myself the questions I hoped others would not pose to me, to challenge me before others did. He showed me the way.

So, what made me do it?

Around the turn of the century, the world of accountancy and consultancy was in turmoil. The Enron affair – about the segregation of responsibilities of financial auditors and business consultants – triggered a fundamental change in the consultancy industry. As a result, KPMG decided to sell its consultancy business to IT outsourcing giant Atos Origin. Employees and partners went with it. I was one of those partners, and loyal as I was (am), I moved with my team to this new business environment. I felt it as of Day One: a culture of fear, of individual targets, of personal success, in which failure is not an option.

I tried to blend into this different culture and adapted my behavior. As was expected from me, I focused on realizing short-term revenue, on sales and on my weekly reports, on getting my figures right. In hindsight, my attempts to be the tough, result-focused manager must have looked pathetic.

I did it because I had the feeling of being forced to do so, not having a choice. Although I was not good at it at all – which showed in my results - senior management let me continue, probably because they liked me. I was a nice guy. But I never asked.

Soon after August 16, 2002, the day of the takeover, I found an opportunity to use my strengths in team building and recreate some of the old KPMG culture. An internal training program on personal leadership, team development, and customer focus that we ran for years before the takeover could be dusted off and reintroduced to get back to some of the old feeling, to which so many consultants hungered.

Together with some dear KPMG friends, we did it. In a couple of weeks, we redesigned the program (most important criteria: under the radar, no cost involved, no impact on billable hours) and found a low-cost training environment (a refurbished pig stall in the countryside). Just these activities alone generated a buzz of excitement among the consultants.

Is it true, will the Core Skills training really be there again? We managed to run a number of those programs, one every two months, asking participants to take care of their billable hours and to give up their free Saturday. It was a great success. It recreated the feeling of togetherness, of being seen and being part of creating a great culture. As a partner, I was responsible for the program, budget, and, in terms of delivery, logistics and the lot. And I loved it. Energy flowed. When people asked me how I was doing, I started talking about this training program and its impact. I forgot to talk about the rest of my work, my prime responsibility managing revenue, risk, and spreadsheets.

One day, a dear colleague and friend (still working with her today) asked me this same question and mirrored, "Hey Hans, if you're talking about Atos business and your responsibilities as a partner in the firm, I feel a heavy load, but as soon as you start about this training, your eyes start to glisten. Isn't it about time to listen to your heart?" This remark took me by surprise. It made me aware of what was happening. The balance of "must-dos" and "want-to-dos" in my work was not level, far from it.

A few weeks later, on December 7, 2005, I was in Arnhem, a city in the eastern part of our country. A strategy consultant and I delivered a workshop with the board of NOCNSF (the Dutch chapter of the Olympic Committee) and it was awesome. Energy flowed, the board members were thrilled and motivated and we over-achieved what was intended.

Later that morning, we drove back to our Utrecht office, happy with the result, together in my car. In my mind, we were just chitchatting, but suddenly he said to me, "Hey Hans, why don't you quit your job, take some time off, and then find your new challenge with the old KPMG or one of the other consultancies?" This remark really took me off guard. What signals was I giving? What had I said to make him say this?

Back in the office I found myself a work cubicle, called one of my dearest colleagues with whom I was working closely in redesigning and delivering the Core Skills training program. I asked her whether she had time for a coffee and chat. As always, she had time. After two hours talking, she left the room by saying, "Tell your secretary you're out for the rest of the day. Take time to think and think hard."

The next day, I told my manager, the leader of our consultancy practice, "I quit."

With resigning in December 2005, it was me, telling myself what to do.

I learned to listen to myself, to dare and act on what I needed, what I felt was best for me. And that same moment it was so crystal clear to me what I needed: space. I needed room to maneuver, room in my head, and I see it clearly now, room in my heart.

I sent my resignation letter a few days later. It was titled "Space."

Visualizing the next chapter

During the weeks following my resignation, I was asked to keep it a secret until early January, I took time to reflect and think about what I wanted next. I felt my energy level rise and I started to think about what to do. What is important to me? Which values drive me? Should I go and become a partner at one of the other consulting firms or to KPMG?

It did not feel good, not again this same process. I had seen it, done it, got the T-shirt. Or should I do something else?

The answer came to me very clearly. I'm on this planet to help other people. People like to be around me and trust me. Confide in me. I like to have the freedom to do so in my way, on my terms, following my heart. The collateral and approach of the Core Skills training, based on self-organization and experiential learning, would be a great foundation to start. I also knew for sure that I never wanted to work alone. That's not me. I want to work together with others and I know I'm good at it.

I want to work together with others and in direct contact with those asking for my help because I love being around others. I'm good at bringing out the best in people. Curiosity is key to me. I honestly hate it when people make assumptions and judge others or opinionize based on those assumptions. The world would definitely be a totally different place when people, leaders to start with, would think and act based on curiosity instead of opinionizing first and then looking for confirmation. Therefore, it was clear that my way of working should be about letting people discover the power of asking questions, to themselves, and to others.

Chatting with Klara about these results of my brainstorms on the purpose, focus, and name of my new business, she said "Why not use some Latin words since that language is part of your education?" Through that, Rogare was born – my own company! Rogare is the Latin verb for asking questions. No better word than that, describes what is important to me. A week later, I had my logo, business cards, and rudimentary website. With the help of a lot of lovely people, of course.

One of the commercial banks in our country uses the slogan "Follow your heart and use your head." I love it, especially the order. First, listen to your heart, and then subsequently use your head. My purpose is to stimulate people to listen to their heart, or to put it differently: always use the filter of their heart in observing, deciding, reflecting.

When I said goodbye to my colleagues on February 28, I had a short speech and a sweet treat for each of them, which is the typical way to celebrate in the Netherlands. I had it specially made: a piece of pastry ("gevulde koek") in the shape of a heart. It was my message and wish to my colleagues and to the company.

Reactions on my announced departure were all positive and heartwarming. They understood, wanted to stay in touch, and quite a number of them shared that

they thought it was brave to quit my job and become self-employed. Clients were informed about it as well. And a number of the clients I worked with expressed their preference to continue working with me! All this positive feedback gave me a wonderful feeling. My self-esteem lifted.
Impact

About five weeks later, on a Saturday afternoon in mid-January, we were all home, Klara, both our sons and some of their friends. With a pot of tea and cookies on the table, all of us sat around, having fun, uncomplicatedly joking, laughing. Then Bart, our youngest and 20 years of age, rises from his chair, comes to me and hugs me intensely. He says "I'm so glad that I have my father again." That remark goes straight to my heart and will stay there forever.

Was it that bad, in the past months, years? Had I been too occupied with my own issues that I hadn't been there for my family? I will be forever grateful to him for expressing his feelings. If I had ever been in doubt whether I made the right decision, now I was 1,000 percent sure. I learned how important it is to regularly check my connection with the people around me, the people I love, and the people I value.

What also helped me make the decision?

Long before that evening in the rain, I knew that I would not stay and work for Atos for another 25 years. Why? Because I had to do my best to do what others wanted me to do. Focus on short-term turnover, and earn as much money at the lowest possible cost. I felt the pressure to perform, but not the support nor atmosphere to cooperatively work towards results in which we jointly believed, in a way we strongly believed in.

Two years before I left, I was invited to join a personal leadership program. The outcomes were two possible scenarios for my future, prioritized clearly. The first was to move to another country for a couple of years, a slumbering wish I had for some time. The business consulting practice in Spain was small in those days and together with my Spanish colleagues, I developed a business plan to grow that practice.

The business plan included a seat for me in the management team. It got serious. Klara and I went to Madrid, to explore the city, the local living, and housing. One thing we realized during that exploration; when we would move to and work in Madrid, my salary would be roughly half of what I earned in the Netherlands. We both knew that that would be enough as well.

The approval by the Spanish board of the business plan was stalled and stalled. In July 2005 there was still no decision. I decided to ask for a yes or a no. Spanish culture is not so good at answering that question in a straightforward, Dutch way. There was not enough support so it was a no. I stopped the initiative. Sad at one end, on the other, we realized that we could do with a lot less and would still be rich.

This insight helped me a lot to step out of my golden cage a few months later.

Living my purpose

I'm on this planet to help other people, that's what I feel very strongly. It helps me to express that out loud when introducing myself to the people I work with. And how do I do live my purpose? I check the impact my interventions will have on others. I explore the questions that they have, whether personal, organizational or on a team level. Which change do they want to achieve?

I guide them in a process of experiencing their desired situation step by step; letting them reflect and experience it again and learning by doing, individually, and in teams.

I regularly check expectations.

However, living my purpose is far more about how I do it. I have learned in those first 30 years of my working life what I am best at. First of all, I learned that I can best help others if I take good care of myself. So checking what I need, assessing how I feel in interacting with others, I recognize and value my boundaries. By showing myself, opening up and being vulnerable, those around me are invited to open up as well. This way, it is easy for me to connect with others, which makes it easy for others to trust me and feel safe. My impact is best when I feel the connection on a heart-to-heart level. Then I feel free to confront, mirror, listen, to do what's needed. Exemplary behavior is powerful. That's what I want my clients to discover. I'd best show it myself, as well, in my role as coach, trainer or facilitator.

I love working this way. And honestly, it does not feel like work at all. Regularly I'm asked to facilitate teams in their search for better performance and to coach people. The earnings are good and that way I have the freedom to also help people straight from the heart, without financial reimbursement. (Via Rotary and other institutions and networks.) Money or no money, the most beautiful gift I can receive from the people is that they leave with a smile on their face or with a different look in their eyes, a different color on their faces. That's my humble way of contributing to a better world.

Now, over 13 years later, I still find it difficult sometimes to decide without thinking, "What will others think of it?" By now, I have learned not to take myself too seriously and freeze, not to stall, not to be afraid about what others will think. Instead I make sure that I dare to be honest and sincerely answer the questions, "What do you think of this? Is this what is really necessary? Is this the right thing, or the easy thing?"

Wealth is not about money at all, it is about happiness and making a difference, to have an impact and to feel seen. If people approach me to be coached or otherwise ask me to accompany them in their development for a while, I feel seen and I'm grateful for that. What I also learned is the closer people are to me, the stronger the heart-to-heart connection, the stronger the gratitude.

Winter of 2010 I was in my car driving the A2 heading for home. My son David called. Dad, will you please help me? He finalized his Ph.D. and had scheduled his promotion ceremony, sent out invitations nationally and abroad. All set, he thought. And then, out of the blue, one of his promotors called and proposed to promote him "cum laude." He was a bit too late in commencing this procedure and therefore asked David whether he would like to postpone his ceremony.

I felt his struggle strongly. How unfair to ask this! What should he do? And what could I do to help him? I asked him what the options were and what was most important to him. We explored the pros, cons, and options. Some 10 kilometers down the road he found his answer. The "cum laude" label was less important to him than finishing this ceremony. David decided to tell his promotor that he would stick to the original date and took the risk. He thanked me for listening, and I shared my gratitude with him that he reached out. Wow.

My purpose is to help others. I´m grateful to experience that people ask me to do exactly that. (Help them in finding their path, help their team to find a better way to collaborate, help their son or daughter to explore what their future would look like.) I´m most grateful for being able (and allowed) to be there for our sons and their partners and children. to meet them where they are, walk along their sides, and ask the odd question, from the heart.

Hans Veenman

Facilitator and Coach

Hans Veenman (1956) coaches individuals and teams through performance improvement processes by focusing on attitude and behavior, leadership, governance and organization and on activating the individual's personal motivation. His affinity and strengths lie in working with people in their business context.

With his understanding of culture and operational management, he supports a variety of organizations and teams in their growth by leading workshops and training sessions. After a career at KPMG Consulting, Hans launched his own business in 2006. His defining outlook in life is to remain curious and open to surprises, to learn continuously and to offer others the opportunity to experience this outlook.

hans.veenman@oxfordleadership.com
www.rogare.nl

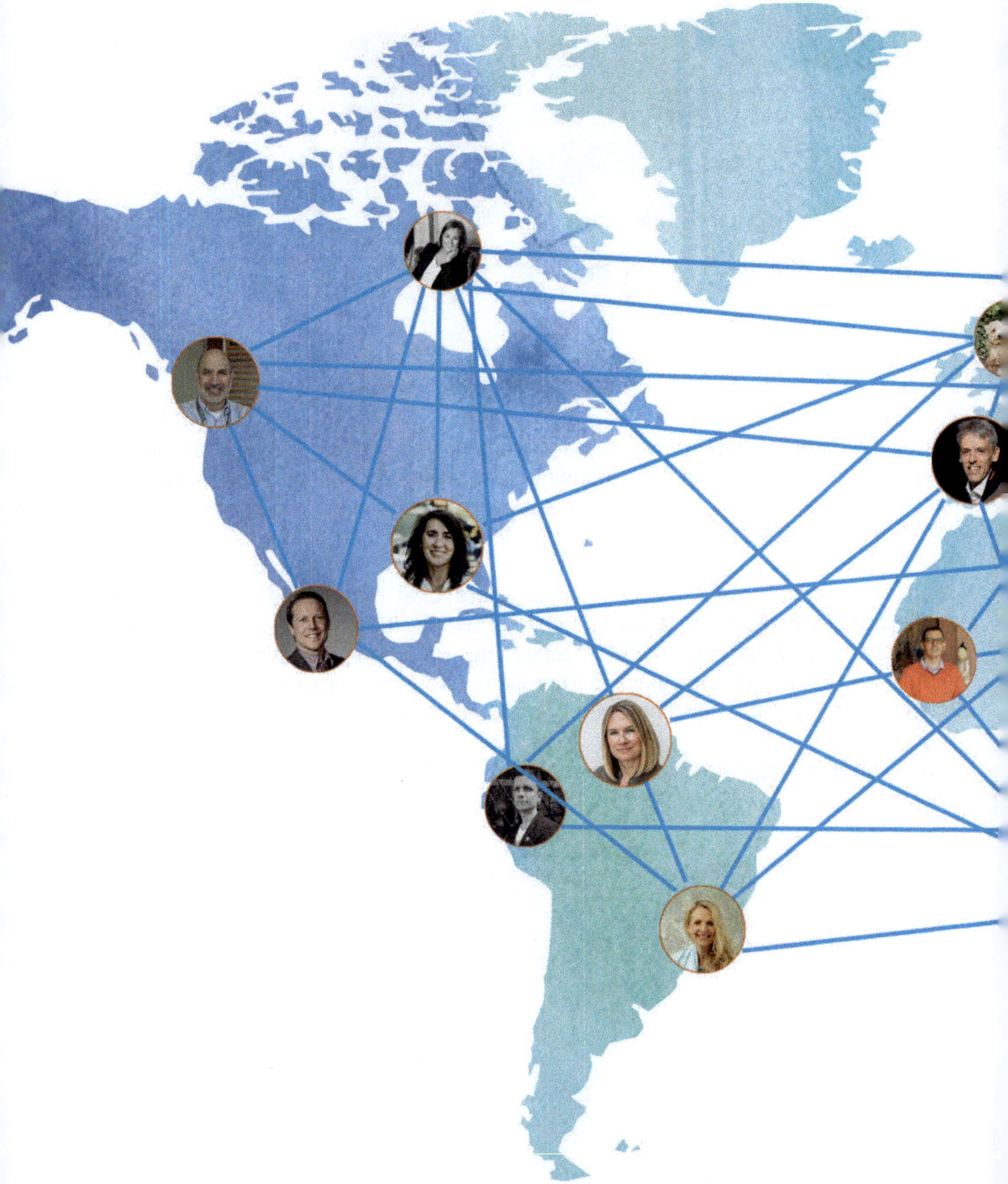

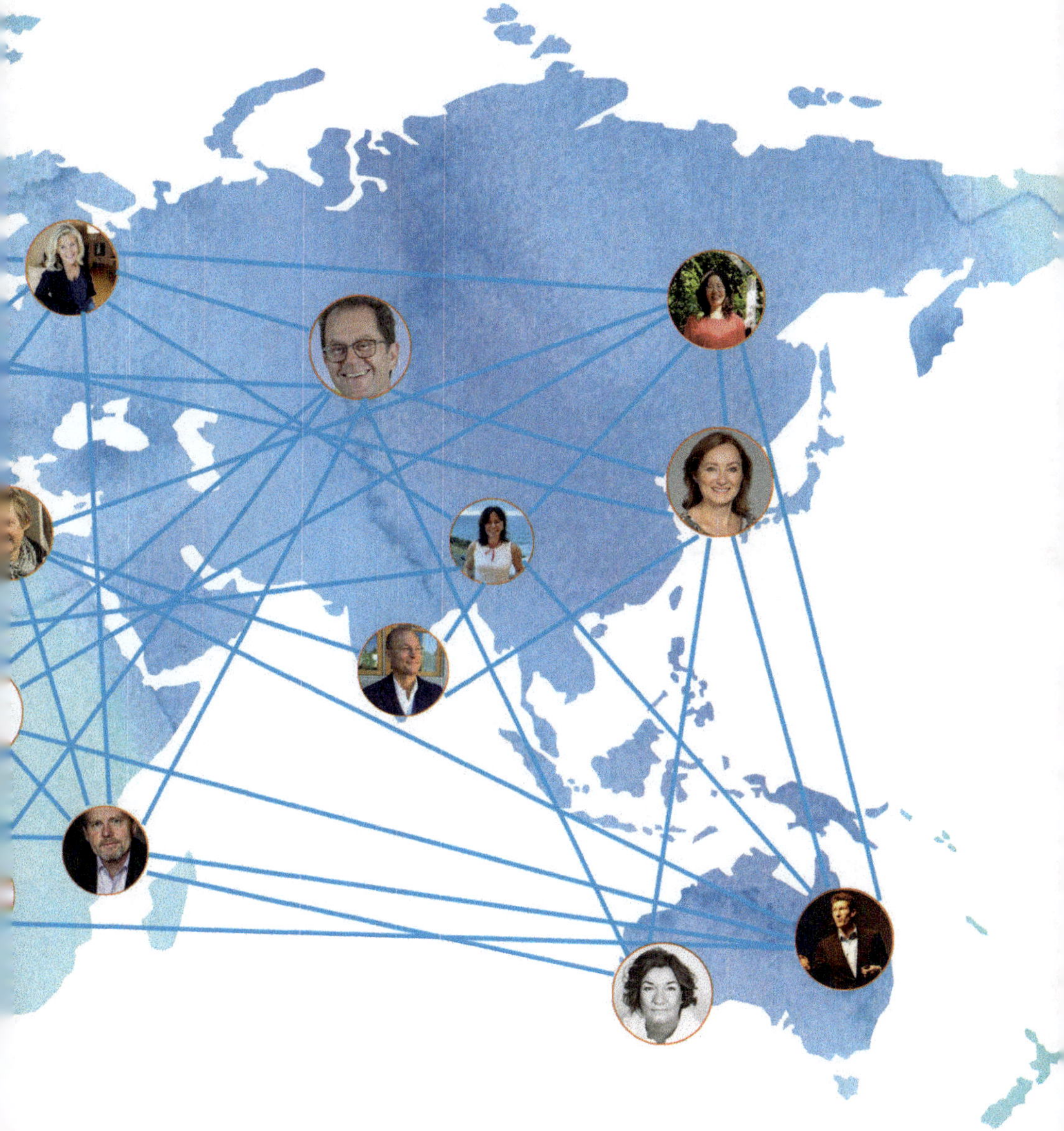

Dare To Be Happy

by Jean-Christophe Normand

I saw it coming again like a rippling wave of frustration and anger in my heart. We had been on the road for less than 30 minutes and already I was having problems with Mignonne. I had carefully said my morning prayers and set an intention for a day of peace and happiness side by side. Furthermore, the day was crisp and clear and echoed well of my commitments to get a good start. Yet once again, I was experiencing the weakness of my communication skills. It was even more than that: it was a blunt revelation of our inability to understand one another. I was starkly reminded of past times with my children when they were still little ones. Of anger erupting, because they were not cooperating to finish up their plate, tidy their room or simply hurry along to get going to school. In essence, I was stripped bare and left to ponder on how much work I still had to do to just be mindful of what was going on and what was needed from me, attitude-wise.

So, I had set out two weeks ago from Paris with a 5-year-old donkey to walk toward Le Puy en Velay, a small provincial town some 750 -kilometers (500 miles) south. I had decided to take a long walk as a token for the change in my professional life that was occurring. I was leaving a very well-paid job in corporate finance to move into the- unknown for me דדד- world of coaching, facilitation and leadership training. I felt the need to fully adjust myself to this major change. And I had imagined something extravagant and daring. A project where I would confront myself physically and mentally to the unknown. I was going to do a serious walk through France, my native country.

And since I did not believe I could walk with (20-30 pounds) on my back, I had chosen to take a donkey along, Mignonne, to carry my equipment.

Donkeys are funny creatures. They are curious, sensitive and challenging. In the prior three years, we had gone on family walks with friends and experienced what it was to have the company of donkeys. It had proved great fun. But this time it was a different story. I was going for a month-long hike on my own, and this was quite different compared to a few days with friends and the reassuring presence of the not-far-away owner. For this trip, Mignonne had been driven up north some 800 kilometers (about 500 miles), and I was left alone to take her all the way down again. I had learned that donkeys are gregarious animals. On their own, they feel lonely and anxious. Mignonne was upset about leaving home. And she made her point on the first day we set off. She charged off with haste, and I had a hard time following at first. She was also a real beauty, stunning in appearance: she was tall, Andalusian with a very handsome grey-white robe. I quickly understood that she had intelligence of situations and clearly a mind of her own about how long she was going to walk or which way she was going to go. And we argued over and over again on such issues. I remember to this day, the glares we would exchange on the odd occasion when we were misaligned and confused.

There were, however, also times when we cooperated nicely, generally at the end of the day when we were both tired and anxious to find a place for the night. We would open our eyes and ears and seek a bearing toward a safe haven. Funnily, she was then my best ambassador. People are less afraid of a man with a donkey than a stranger walking by. And I witnessed some amazing examples of kindness and generosity along the way. As a man of Christian faith, I saw this as an expression of God's love for humankind, which theology defines as the expression of divine Providence. In the 30 days I walked, I was overwhelmed by a feeling of love and gratitude for all the care and attention I received along the way.

When we look back, it's always interesting to try and pinpoint events or encounters that were decisive for the future choices made. As I turned 40, something snapped inside me. It started with an urge to be outside and see the world for what it was and not for what I had been told it was. But it wasn't just about being outside to discover landscapes and take a deep plunge into nature. There was also an urgent cry to be me and to make choices of my own. This issue of being self or of independence in the way I was leading my life, was the outcome of a rising awareness that I was not happy and satisfied by what I was doing. As a financial controller working for a large group, I had the feeling that after 15 years of professional experience, I just hadn't really lived my life. This feeling is described magnificently by American author Matthew Crawford in his book: "Shop Class as Soulcraft: An Inquiry into the Value of Work". Matthew reinvested time, money and stamina to start a business as a motorcycle mechanic, leaving behind a handsomely paid job as executive director at the George C. Marshall Institute. He defines this clear-cut decision as the appropriate answer to his need for both alignments to his purpose and values and his need for a profound sense of accomplishment in his work. I read his book many years after the walk but fully resonate with this idea of emptiness or lacking sense of accomplishment one may feel in his life.

The paradox was that I had always received consideration from my senior management. But my work context at the time was filled with insecurity and absence of vision: the cable industry I was working for in 2000-2002, was taking the full blow of the price drop due to competition from emerging countries (Turkey and China in my case). We repeatedly ran strategic planning exercises, which generally all proved unsuccessfully and sterile in terms of business acumen. This transcribed into considerable frustrations and heated discussions with senior management, who were confronted with situations they were not in a position to manage. I felt depressed and unable to make some sense of the situation. To some extent, I was going through a similar phase I had experienced at the age of 12 when I had reintegrated into the French education system after five years of school in Australia. At the time, I experienced the shock of losing space, friends, and a very open education system. I had to adapt quickly and demonstrate resilience to adjust to an altogether different environment.

The second major event, three years before engaging on my catharsis trip, was a personal and family traumatic shock: my parents had a car accident that left my mother paralyzed from the shoulders down. The pain and the grief in the weeks that followed whenever I would visit my mother were acute, and they reinforced the feeling of emptiness and desolation I was experiencing in my work life. Nothing seemed right, and I was craving change without being able to define how to start the quest. This was extremely frustrating and induced a form of constant restlessness. I started finding myself interested in all sorts of experiences without being able to follow one down the road. But I had my "search mode" on, and my decision to start thinking of an alternative career, to accomplish things on my own and thus "find myself" had been taken.

But, having been employed over 18 years in the cocoon of a large organization, habits had grown. I was used to have everything taken care of for me: office logistics, IT tools, travel arrangements, health, and insurance programs. And above all, I enjoyed a nice monthly paycheck which had enabled my family to make a nice living, including mortgage, a school for the children, great vacations. Therefore, the frill of engaging a 180° change was quickly cooled down by the chilling effect of the prospect of losing all of this (false) sense of security. I had to take it step by step.

The salary issue was, in the beginning, the first major hurdle. I had here another great opportunity for sleepless nights. Although my wife had started working again, her salary would not cover the expenses of a family of four with a mortgage. I needed time to think things out clearly. My first discussions had gone the wrong way: my senior management did not show any sympathy for a personal project outside the group. This implied that I was free to go, but I would have to resign from my position without any form of compensation. A risky situation to start again from scratch.

The resignation option goes against all uses and habits in France where the social insurance system is highly protective compared to many other countries. Some will argue, overly protective. My company was highly interested in my resignation, versus a redundancy plan, because it would not have to commit to severance pay, which can reach up to 18 or 20 months of salary. Also, the person made redundant can then claim pay to cover the time it will take him to find a new job. For senior employees in their mid-50s, finding a new position can be a major challenge, and unemployment benefits can potentially breach the gap of their last years before claiming their pension fund.

But, at the bottom of my heart, I just could not bring myself to negotiate a severance contract. Nobody was asking me to leave the company. I had not breached any professional code of ethics or engaged the group's responsibility wrongly in any form or matter. I just wanted to change the course of my career and that decision was purely personal. This meant, in my view, that I had to assume the full responsibility of the decision I was taking. Consequently, I chose to be authentic in the discussions with my senior management and human resources department. And I also decided that I was going to trust my partners. People may argue that I was naïve or simply lucky; that, in the real world, it's a question of striking the best deal, regardless of any feelings or values. I like to think that I was able, at the time, to engage in real conversations with intelligent people. The deal that was put on the table was to have training funded by the group over the three years before my resignation and a solemn promise between partners that in the immediate months following my leaving the company, I would be given some work on a consultancy basis. This is exactly what happened, and I was given sufficient work to build initial funds to get started in the first three years following the resignation. The success behind this story had to do with trust and openness between persons. I had taken a risk, it proved a sound bet, and I'm proud that it worked out.

The second source of my anxiety was ambiguity. On one side, there was the yearning to be the master of my destiny and to go my way. But on the other, there was also the sharp awareness that I was going to be alone out there. There would be no one to fall back upon in terms of work and responsibilities. A void suddenly would emerge in the daily rhythm of things. Being your own boss can be appealing, but it also leaves you with a sense of sudden loneliness. I can still remember in the first few months after leaving my company, feeling sometimes a sort of envy for those that had a fixed job; they knew what they had to do, and it was simply a question of getting on with it. In that change period, I could very well be sitting at home and wondering what I was up to: had I made a mistake? I had to learn to define my personal strategies based on a vision of who I wanted to be, rather than what I wanted to do. I discovered how finding a purpose for oneself is often mistakenly taken for defining what you are going to do. Simon Sinek is famous for explaining: before stating your what, you need to find your why.

Walking alongside Mignonne in that glorious summer of 2005, I had ample time to figure out which of the whys I wanted to live. Sometimes, I would imagine myself in the figure of Strider, Tolkien's human hero of the "Lord of the Rings." I was leading a path with smoothness and care, sharing kindness and responsibility with whomever I crossed. Translated into work, this could mean helping others find their own paths through, coaching, training, facilitation. The only problem with that is when you are less than 50, there are a lot of people who have twice your experience and more to say or teach to others than you do. Other times, I would see myself as a new emerging Gandhi or Lanza del Vasto, building the bases of an alternative form of community living that could offer at last real answers to the strains and burdens our civilization is putting on Earth's natural resources. Was I not experienced now in handling a donkey and living simply off Mother Earth? These utopian thoughts would fall through the roof when I was reminded of the family that I had and the financial needs that had to be met if our children were to enjoy the same level of education, from which I had benefited. Generally, I was left with a feeling of uncertainty. If I was happy with the choices I had made, I was certainly still very vague about how I was going to lead my life onward. So, my purpose at the time could be summarized by simply learning to accept the uncertainty of having to earn a living on my own. And this adventure was a real practical case: I had planned my trip by choosing the paths appropriate for a traveler with a donkey, but there were no nice and cozy hotel rooms booked in advance. On these pathways, crossing rural villages, there were seldom any restaurants or convenient take-aways for lunch or cheerful breakfasts. Shopping along the way was hazardous. You don't just park a donkey in a convenient parking lot. If ever, I got out of her sight, Mignonne would pretty quickly start fretting and call for me. So, going for groceries needed careful planning, and the strain was to keep the pace to reach a monastery or abbey before the next Saturday. That was the deal between Mignonne and me: if we got to the next monastery by the following Saturday evening, we had the Sunday off to rest.

This adventure turned out to be one of the most profound personal experiences of my life. My family joined me for a week, and the last few days were also shared with friends. When I returned Mignonne to her owner, I felt a feeling of pride and inner accomplishment. No doubt was Mignonne even happier to join back with her fellow companions. This experience provided me the self-esteem I was looking for. I still didn't know clearly how I was going to lead my work-life onward, but I had the feeling I was finally going to find a sense of purpose for myself - even if there was still a long road in front of me to settle into my new life.

Back home after my trek with Mignonne, I was left with open questions: How was I going to give a new vision to my life now that I was the master of my own destiny? Aside from assuming my marriage and my responsibilities as father and husband, I couldn't go much further at the time. What could I do to find the resources to transform myself into the entrepreneur I wanted to become? Where would I find them? There were so many options and possibilities in terms of training courses or learning experiences. One of Brueghel the Elder's paintings (16th century) illustrating a parable from the New Testament, depicts a column of blind men falling one after another into a ditch. Unaware of where they are being led, they are following one another by holding the shoulder of the companion immediately ahead, and as they stumble forward, they realize only when it is too late, that they are heading into a trap. That was precisely the image I had of my life at the time. Being led forward in a clumsy way, without a view of what was to come, always hoping for something better than yesterday. Like these blind men, I was afraid of taking the wrong path, of wasting time, money and energy in pointless investments. I felt as if I had had everything so far, the easy way.

And I indeed belong to a generation that has neither experienced war, nor famine nor any form of poverty outside of moral perspectives, perhaps. We may argue that this is fine: Who wants a life filled with fears, disease, and hunger? Yet does not human nature need some form of adversity to build itself upon? As a father and married man, I have experienced, like many, family issues. Discovering that I was suffering from an incurable autoimmune disease at the age of 30 was one blow. Adopting and raising children born overseas has been another major challenge to face.

So, by the time I reached 40, it suddenly became clear that I had to come to terms with this issue of defining who I really was and what I wanted to do with my life. And nobody was going to do this for me. I had to do this on my own.

I would start working on this at the beginning by simply stating that I was going to stop doing what I was doing. This got unsurprisingly a very fresh welcome from my parents, friends, and relatives. To their understanding, I can now say their concerns were also the reflection of my being rather vague about the form my future job would take. You cannot transform yourself overnight, and setting oneself into a new job requires stamina and time. In the first couple of years, I needed to learn by reading, meeting others and looking as closely as possible into how things were done in the field of human relationships. I desperately needed time at an age when it seems unsuitable to be planning a new career. And I had to believe in myself. I have to give credit, at this point to my wife, who showed undisputable faith in my project, however shaky it may have appeared at times.

Yet, if I had ambition for myself, I was unable to give it shape or form because I just didn't know clearly where or how to start. For example, it took eight years before I was ready to believe I could start a business of my own and stop working for others - simply because it was not clear in my mind what I had to offer specifically that others didn't have. I had not invented a new management technique, nor could I say I was more expert than others in leadership skills or employee retention. I couldn't argue about a specific skill that would have market value. In contemporary wording, I would summarize the situation by saying my pitch was weak and my vision too conceptual. You don't convince people with great ideas that could change the world. You can catch their interest, on the other hand, by offering them something that can make a difference or can effectively solve one of their problems.

I like to think of the shaping of my purpose by using the metaphor of listening. In the first five years as a coach and facilitator, I listened more than anything else. I started by listening out of habit. It is like being slowly conscious that something in your daily life is out of scope, or that things are just not fitting in anymore. "I should be doing this rather than that," or "I'm never going to succeed in doing this or that." At this stage, I was indulging in judgments and beliefs. Initially, when I first started to think of a new purpose for my life, I decided I needed help to assess my personality. I worked with a retired psychologist who gave me a broad rundown on my values and main personality characteristics. The feedback, however, lacked empathy and vision. And I remember sitting at home with a sense of deep gloom after being told I had not chosen the adequate path career-wise. Judgments on myself and others would cascade down on me, leaving me with further anxiety for the future. I got out of this state of mind by getting to work with a professional coach. This introduced me to a newer form of listening: listening from outside to another voice which was much more factual and open, providing me with new lenses to see things differently. Having set aside past judgments, I could see differences with an open mind. What seemed yesterday a failure, was now an option or an opportunity. There was excitement in this process. I was discovering the power of coaching work, and I marveled at what could be done. I wanted to be doing the same thing.

The third step was another shift in my listening: a subtle move from the outside to the inside. What does this mean? I believe there is nothing that we do or think that does not come from somewhere or someone. I have received life as a result of a loving relationship between my father and mother. I surely cannot say that I am the only architect of my life. Some choices and acts reflect weaknesses in my character. By adapting myself to the trials and errors however, I found I had resilience I could build upon. I also modeled myself on those I grew up with: not just parents and family, but also teachers, mentors, and friends. And there came the point when I was ready to trust the world enough to move into the space of empathetic listening. This meant that I could start giving in return. As I opened my heart to my true self, my listening became deeper, more challenging. I engaged myself in a progressive process of deconstruction of the self, or ego. After leaving my C-suite executive position, my first job was to manage a Catholic chaplaincy for teenagers where I experienced deeply enriching relationships with others through religious education. I fully engaged myself in activities and events I had missed out on years before when I had their age. My ambition was to experience authentic relationships and enjoy a new form of recognition. This meant working with a new pair of glasses or seeing things through a different perspective. When we can go through this process, we are like clay in the hands of the potter. We are remodeled internally; values and beliefs are set upon what we can do for others instead of being constantly focused on what you can get out of others.

My fourth step was built upon this firm foundation of an open heart. The path of an emerging future came up naturally. This new form of listening qualified as generative in the sense that it produced something new and authentic. Instead of desperately trying to seek the attention of others, I focused on doing what I had been asked to do in the best possible manner. No more complaining, no more explaining: I was intent on following the guidelines and opportunities provided by others through an open-will attitude. There is something incredibly human about this transformation of our identity and self. I believe we are all born with charisma, energy, and faith to build something or to leave behind a form of legacy. Sadly, not everyone can go to the full extent of this transformation because fear, pain or grief holds them back. Or, because they never get to meet the right people. Or, because circumstances are unfavorable. However, we do get the opportunity of responding. This is what I understood about free will and self-determination. In my new position as facilitator and coach, I have often felt I did not have the experience or the resources to meet a specific client request. I have instead always shown the will to learn and the eagerness to do a good job. And that reflected in my attitudes or behaviors with others. I think that people are happy to work with me because they feel I am enjoying my assignment. Who wants to deal with people who are always grumpy or unhappy about everything? I have learned to see such character in the people I mingle with daily: the smiling baker, the happy bartender, the good lawyer, the curious physician. Happiness is the best thing that can be offered around. It is also a good omen. It means that he or she who is reflecting such inner radiance has found his or her purpose in life; he/she is living at this very moment. And if it is happening to this person, it can very well happen to you.

As the Roman statesman and philosopher Seneca quite rightly expressed it: It isn't because things are difficult that we do not dare to change, it's because we do not dare that they are. I have dared to be happy about my life and I dare to share it with all those I meet and/or live with, regardless of the difficulties and challenges that I, like every human being, am confronted with. Many will argue I belong to the happy few who have got the best out of life because of where they were born. I will take their point and respond that that's precisely the reason why I cannot afford to be unhappy. That would simply be unfair.

Jean-Christophe Normand

*Professor in management and leadership for Church functions,
Founder of RH-INC*

Jean-Christophe Normand is a French coach and facilitator in leadership. He has previous experience in the industry in corporate finance in various countries and moved on to coaching and training of management skills in his mid-40s.

He features a specific interest for Corporate Social Responsibility and has invested himself in extensive research and training work in the Christian Tradition to find inspiration and answers for contemporary practices of leadership. Jean-Christophe is married with children and was elected as a permanent deacon for the Roman Catholic Church for the dioceses of Paris in 2014. He currently lives in Nantes.

jeanchristophe.normand@oxfordleadership.com
www.linkedin.com/in/jeanchristophenormand

Invent Yourself, Then Reinvent Yourself

by Karin Verhaest

Homecoming - Berkeley, California.
As I walked into this beautiful Julia Morgan-designed house south of the University of California campus and saw the beaming faces of my roommates-to-be, I felt that I crossed an important threshold. Nothing would ever be the same again.

It was Halloween evening 1981 and I was 25. Some of my roommates were hopping around naked, trying on outrageous outfits in preparation for a party. They loaded me in their car, included me in their lives, and became my close U.S. family for the next couple of years.

A Jewish acupuncture student from New York, a medic at the Berkeley Free Clinic and his art student wife, both from Montana, a very California aerobics teacher with her two young kids, and another East Coaster who rambled Marxist theories nonstop were my new family.

My home country of Belgium felt very far away among this diverse population of passionate people. It was as if that evening a deep yearning in my soul and my deep craving for "space" in all its connotations had been answered.

My life with its highs and its lows could be read as a journey in which I walk alongside myself. I have a picture of myself at age 4 going for a walk in the countryside with an uncle. Carrying a small cardboard suitcase, the walk felt like an exciting world voyage of discovery and feels today like a metaphor of my lifelong quest for space and meaning. It took me onto a path of over 60 years of learning, re-inventing careers, deep friendships, great losses and living in many different places. During those younger years, I can detect the curiosity, spaciousness, and presence which became my signature in my later calling to host spaces for others. As a facilitator of learning journeys and an executive coach and as the owner of a B&B.

Daydreaming and looking through the window

Born in Gent, Belgium, as the eldest to a medical doctor and a homemaker mom, I was raised in a conservative, middle-class setting. I was an only child until the age of 5 and did not go to school nor did I need any toys to entertain myself. My main activity was daydreaming and creating stories around street scenes and people I saw through the window. I remember spending long summer days at my grandparents' house in the countryside, scouting for a place in which I would not see any signs of humans around me, longing for a place with only nature around and far horizons.

School at age 6 was an enormous shock and an abrupt stop to my happy childhood years. I abhorred the bars behind the windows of the school building, the dark green uniforms, the girls-only environment, the curtsying to the Catholic nuns and the harsh, cold atmosphere.

My physical space felt infringed upon and so was another sense of space. There was an implicit class system. Kids from "good" families had better teachers and birthday parties with girls "of your own kind" only. I loved the Bible teaching to "love your neighbor like you love yourself," which I understood to treat everyone as equal. I was shocked by the discrimination I saw around me.

I would sometimes pinch my skin trying to understand what life on earth was all about. What did it really mean to be human? Why was I here in the first place?

In hindsight, I can discern some more seeds that would determine my journey through life. My love for reflection and sense-making, my need for space and my deep longing for an inclusive community would start to emerge.

Free spirit rebellion

My free spirit took over when I became a teenager and I rebelled. I was a girl, OK, but I no longer wanted to play that game. I would grant myself all the rights that boys were claiming – boozing, partying, free love. I shaped my own identity in terms of who I did not want to be, a "nice girl." Boys loved me because I was like one of them. Many other people turned their backs on me and I felt very misunderstood.

As I approached the end of high school with A+ grades in sciences, it seemed normal that I would become a medical doctor like my father, or a civil engineer. I broke out of this mold and chose a master's in mathematics out of pure love for the subject.

I enjoyed studying. Even more so, I enjoyed student life when I moved to another town and was finally living on my own. In the last year of my studies I realized that my degree could lead only to teaching. Inspired by my father's international career in pharma, I was curious about working in the "real" world and so I completed a second master's in computer science. The world was buzzing with the birth of the computer age in the mid-'70s. I felt thrilled at the perspective to be part of that!

During those years, I discovered other values that would continue to be important to me. My love for learning, my sense of adventure, and my curiosity for everything that is leading edge was my driving force.

So, who am I, then, really?

As I completed my studies, I saw many people around me scurry and getting quite serious about careers and marriage. These were not motivating options on my table, more like doors closing in on my precious space and possibilities. Luckily my computer science degree was my ticket towards broader horizons. My father understood my longing for freedom and a greater sense of living and became my biggest ally in applying for a research grant in the U.S.

So at age 25 there I was, settling down in Berkeley with a one-year paid internship at UC San Francisco. Living in this crazy funny household, working within an international team, continuing my computer science education at UC Berkeley.

My one-year internship shifted into ten years of California residency, and a series of IT software development jobs in a big variety of settings: a big corporation in Silicon Valley (which felt very out of place to me given the blue streaks in my hair), and a series of jobs closer to Berkeley with IT startups. It was wonderful. I felt very much at home in that geeky world with so many eccentric people many of whom are still my friends today.

According to the American Dream, I could be anyone I wanted to be. Exciting perspective at first, giving rise to deeper and more complex questions that were harder to answer. Like, if I stopped defining myself as not this or that, then who was I, really? I hardly knew myself. Luckily, I had all the space around me that I had ever dreamt of, the free spirit of the '60s still being very much alive in Berkeley at that time. I was living in the Mecca of New Age with lots to explore- consciousness-expanding experiments, different forms of relationships, new age ideas and therapy.

Gradually I gave shape and form to the important seeds that had been popping up in my life. I started a regular meditation and yoga practice. I collaged and discovered a love for making art and for artists. I became a homeowner, sharing my duplex house with inspiring friends, while loving the community life. I volunteered on several local projects, especially enjoying being part of a San Francisco collective publishing a free avant-garde art magazine and running a gallery for starting artists.

As software development jobs were abundant, I had the luxury of being able to quit my job whenever I felt like it. Several times I backpacked on my own for a couple of months in Southeast Asia, working here and there, enjoying the discovery of other cultural paradigms, the beautiful landscapes, and many wonderful random encounters.

In my job-hopping, I experienced a wide range of leadership styles and organizational cultures. My curiosity was triggered by new questions. What does it take to create a sense of excitement within organizations? What is the role of leadership? So when my U.S. employer opened an office in Amsterdam and asked me to start working as a liaison with European banking clients, I was eager to get out of my cubicle and work more directly with mapping out new ways of collaboration. During the next five years I worked and lived in Amsterdam, Oslo, Copenhagen, and Stockholm.

In that period, I attended a personal leadership course from the founder of Oxford Leadership that gave me many answers to my question of "Who am I, really," and provided me with a compass for life. I discovered how I wanted to make a difference as a bridge-builder and I wanted to work with leaders to help them get over the gap between their reality and their aspirations. I wished for people to experience the spaciousness I found in my own life, and to see and shape their own dreams from there. As a consequence, I enrolled in one of the first coaching trainings in the U.S. at Coach University. I was going out on a different ramp again!

Who do I choose to be?

After five years of being a nomad living out of a suitcase in furnished apartments, I was becoming tired. While there were beds for me in several places, I did not have a place I could call my home.

My house in California was rented out. U.S. Immigration had me on their radar for being out of the country more than what was allowed with my green card. My job with my U.S. employer did not offer any learning anymore. I had a community of friends dispersed throughout the world and no stable companion. My relationship life was nowhere and everywhere as I put other things first.

It was time again to undertake a big leap and this was the scariest thing I ever did. Having no partner, no family of my own, no home and no more job, I decided to move back to Belgium after having being abroad for 15 years. I felt the pull to live closer to my aging parents and to take up my role as godmother to my brother's children. I was so afraid of the small world closing in on me. My inner voice was whispering to me. "If you can be happy here in Belgium, you can be happy anywhere." My challenge became to really anchor myself in the principles that were so dear to me – space, adventure, learning, meaning and shape-shifting.

It was hard to rebuild my life from scratch and it took time. After a couple of years, I found myself in charge of internal change projects for a fast growing startup in speech technology. It was super exciting and I felt very proud to be there. I became a homeowner of a beautiful modernistic building in my hometown in which I opened a B&B called "Four Corners". It was a way to call on people from all over the globe to come and stay over. And I was in a "living-apart-yet-together" relationship with an artist who became my best buddy. So at 40ish, life looked quite promising.

There is no uphill without downhill. My employer was accused of fraudulent financial transactions and went bankrupt. This was heartbreaking. I lost track of my compass and I ended up accepting the first leadership job that came my way. From the moment I walked in the door on my first working day, I sensed that it was wrong. I stayed on anyway and quit only after two years of barely surviving in a culture driven by fear and aggression.

I reconnected with my love and took a leadership position with a local college. The department was doing action research projects around change and leadership. The job gave me a unique opportunity to be entrepreneurial and to deep-dive into change related subjects. Unfortunately, I kept running into walls when I offered out-of-the-box ideas to my bureaucratic management.

In that period, my partner was diagnosed with incurable cancer. He moved in with me and for six months I was combining a full-time and frustrating job with being his main caregiver. Taking leave from my partner was sad and raw, and yet also, in a strange way, the most beautiful experience of my life.

Maybe for the first time ever, I had the sense that I was no longer standing behind the window looking at myself and life. I was doing something of real value. It was as if all of a sudden, I found myself in the midst of life and of what matters most. The grief and loss, combined with the accumulation of jobs that had turned sour somehow took their toll. I crashed with burnout just before my partner's death.

It was a wake-up call to go back to the drawing board. Which signals had I missed? Which turns had I taken and why? Where had I been untrue to myself? Most importantly, who did I choose to be? I returned to the essence of the personal leadership course I had taken many years before.

I was organizing my work and my life around the purpose of helping people and organizations to bridge the gap between where they were and where they wanted to be, symbolized by my beloved Golden Gate Bridge. I realized that I was using this purpose as a measuring stick of success, cultivating a sense of failure when the other side was not reached.

As part of my recovery, I went walking often in nature and took a mindfulness course to settle the unrest in my head. I discovered several schools of conscious movement that were not only fun and healing, but also helped me develop my own somatic intelligence. And slowly but surely, a variation on my purpose did crystalize. I still saw myself on that Golden Gate Bridge; not as someone who needs to get others across, more as a "compagnon de route" (companion) who walks along, listening, sense-making, nudging, bringing spaciousness and a sense of what is possible.

I reinvented myself again in 2010 and started my own business as a consultant, coach, and trainer. I got involved with the biggest charitable NGO of Belgium as a project member working on leadership development among disadvantaged youth. I reconnected with Oxford Leadership, where I am celebrating my 10th anniversary as a leadership consultant.

I feel very, very fortunate to be surrounded by a global community of talented colleagues who have become dear friends and to do meaningful work that I love.

The loss of my partner brought me closer to a new companion whom I had known for many years. We got married in a small Buddhist ceremony in the Bay Area, overlooking the Golden Gate Bridge, surrounded by my American circle of friends. He is a true "compagnon de route" to me and we continue to shape our lives together around art, family, travel and hosting people.

Eldership

Three years ago I turned 60. I had a bicycle accident. I broke my shoulder. It healed badly, so bye-bye perfect downward-facing dog in yoga class. A confrontation with the frailty of my own body giving rise to sometimes paralyzing questions such as what still needs doing and what truly matters?

I observe others who are anxious and rigid becoming older. Some deal with grace and ease. I'm watching my 88-year-old mom who is slowly losing her cognitive capabilities, yet I see so much delight in her. Which brings me back to the key question - Who do I choose to be now as an elder?

How real is it to see aging only as a diminishing or a restrictive condition? Some friends of mine decided they would start counting backwards at each birthday. They found it a liberating experience, stepping away from identifying with a number.

My world may become smaller, more centered around a specific place. I have the choice to continue to nourish the sense of spaciousness within. There is so much more to be curious about, inside and outside.

Work and retirement are fluid concepts. What matters is what is present to me and how I am present to that.

I have a strong ground under my feet carved out over time by my trajectory, my values, my loved ones, and my meditation practice. I can trust that life does take care of itself and that I can shape-shift into what is needed at the moment. The loop feels closed for now.

I see my life as putting one foot in front of the other. As I have done all of my life, really, only now with more with ease, presence, and intentionality. I savor and love to share the wisdom and the wildness that come with eldership, especially with younger women professionals still exploring who they are to become. Joy and gratitude take a more prominent place in my life. Small and slow have become more and more beautiful. A warm get together with friends or family, watching birds in the garden, an impactful conversation, the spaciousness of a beautiful landscape.

I get up each day and I sit on my pillow, opening up to the surprises the day will bring with the firm intention to be a kind "compagnon de route." That's all that needs doing. Being is more than enough.

Karin Verhaest

Executive Coach, Leadership Consultant

Karin has over 35 years of professional experience as a change driver. She is passionate about being a "compagnon de route" to leaders on their journeys of transformation. She works with global clients as a coach, trainer, and consultant.

Prior to joining Oxford Leadership, Karin had an international career in the IT sector leading large digital change projects. From there she moved on to business process, quality, and operations management. These experiences inspired her to focus on leadership development.

Karin is based in Belgium where she is also a wife, daughter, sister, stepmother, godmother, and friend. She is a world traveler and a mapmaker of life on a journey of discovery. Her passions are learning, art, nature, and yoga.

karin.verhaest@oxfordleadership.com

www.linkedin.com/in/karin-verhaest-2039925
www.oxfordleadership.com/authors/karin-verhaest

Where There Is A Will There's A Way

by Kristina Zumpolle Flodin

When I reflect on where I am today and how I got here, I can see my drive to help others is the product of growing up with dysfunctional family communication and experiencing first-hand the devastation of bankruptcy and a bitterly contested will. And who would have thought that an "expensive hobby" combined with a cheeky monkey and a chance encounter, would lead me here? Let's start at the beginning.

It was 2008, I found myself living in the Netherlands with my husband, Jan Mark and two young children, Diederik, 2, and Oscar, 1. I never imagined I would end up in this country. Destiny had other plans for me. I was living and working in London when I met this tall blond Dutchman at a party after he flew over for the weekend.

When Jan Mark asked me to move to the Netherlands with him, I was excited about experiencing a new country, culture, and language. It was by no means easy. I felt isolated not being able to understand what people around me were saying, even if it was just on the tram or in the supermarket. And although English was the corporate language of the company I was now working for, everyone on my floor was Dutch and hence spoke Dutch. It was a new job, a new role, and a new industry for me, so it was difficult to be proactive. I felt very insecure and my self-confidence was decreasing by the day. Then I started to get physical symptoms. After breaking down in her office, my doctor ordered me to take two weeks off.

At first, I thought it was ridiculous and unnecessary. I was fine. However, with a lot of convincing from my husband and father-in-law, I took the doctor's advice. I went back to Sweden and spent time with people who knew me all my life and helped me realize I was okay. I still wonder how I could have let myself get so negatively affected by work.

Slowly I managed to detach my self-worth from my work. And soon, my confidence in my abilities returned. I left the company and eventually ended up working for Cisco where I could fully contribute and grow personally and professionally.

In the meantime, my husband proposed. We got married in Amsterdam on a crisp and sunny February day with family and friends from near and afar celebrating with us. It's still one of the highlights of my life.

My department at Cisco moved to Copenhagen and, simultaneously, we decided to move to the suburbs.

So, I was 32 years old and had resumed my career after having my second child. I was working three days a week at an executive search firm but I wasn't happy. I loved visiting companies so I could understand what made them tick and help them identify the right candidate for the right job, I had to go through so many resumes.

Finding the perfect candidate was an incredibly long process. It would take months to find the right one. And if just one person out of five decided they didn't like the candidate for some reason, you'd start all over again. It was brutal. I was totally bored, unfulfilled, unmotivated, and consequently, unproductive. One day, it dawned on me that the only reason I was there was so I had a job three days a week. As I stared at a fresh pile of resumes on my desk, I knew something had to change.

My 'aha' moment

I decided to try coaching to see if I could figure out what I wanted to do with my life. I knew I wouldn't get my dream job the next day, yet if I knew what it was, I could start working towards it. At the end of my first session with my coach, Willemien, I realized I wanted her job!

I continued with regular sessions, carefully observing how Willemien worked. As my last session ended, I knew I wanted to coach individuals and teams at international companies. Coming from an international background myself, I knew that's where I could add value. As I thanked Willemien for all her help, she surprised me "I really like your energy and would love to work with you! Let me know when you're certified."

Can I afford to make the change?

I couldn't wait to take the next step and undergo training as a coach. Then I realized

I couldn't afford it. I was still paying off my student loan from my degree at the European Business School in London. Amazingly, my husband offered to pay for it, saying he would support me if it was something I really wanted to do. I wouldn't have been able to do it otherwise.

So there I was, juggling children and coaching and continuing to work at my dead-end job at the executive search firm three days a week. All the time I doubted whether I made the right decision. I remember that time vividly. Two images would constantly play in my head. One was of an ambitious career woman. The other was of a calm, relaxed coach. It was an intense battle. Ultimately, the coach won.

Inspired by what I was learning, I tried to find a way to integrate it into my work at the executive search firm. The opportunity to combine coaching with searching for candidates was staring me in the face. Not only could I place people, I could help onboard them and make sure they would succeed in their new roles.

My bosses, however, couldn't see the connection. When my six-month contract came up for renewal, we agreed it was probably best to part ways. When I look back now, I realize what a blessing in disguise that was.

Not another coach

To get certified as a coach, I discovered I needed to have several paying clients. I might as well start my own company, I thought. And just like magic, my inner saboteurs emerged:

I'm too young.
No one will take me seriously.
I'm not smart enough.
Why start a company when it's bound to fail?

I sought reassurance from others in my social circle. I could almost see them thinking, "Oh no, not another coach!" Then one of them said to me, "Look at how many restaurants there are. Everyone has different tastes and different needs." Exactly, I thought.

A working mom

In the beginning, it was very challenging being a working mom, especially one who was setting up her own business. I think my husband expected to have a stay at home wife. That's why when I decided to go back to work after the birth of my second son, I arranged au pairs for the children and decided to pay for the childcare myself. After all, it was my choice to work I thought. By doing so, I felt I relevant. The feminist within was slowly emerging.

Thankfully, I was entitled to a six-month subsidy from the government when on February 1, 2009, I started my own business, Zumflow. I had no financial support after that. I barely survived. However, I was so happy to be making money for myself that I didn't really care how little it was.

My husband also had his own company and would receive a fixed salary at the end of each month. Sometimes, we'd look at each other and say "We have two weeks until the end of the month and no money left. What can we sell on Marktplaats?"

I remember, having to cancel a holiday with friends that we'd both been looking forward to as we realized we simply couldn't afford it. Our friends offered to lend us the money. We didn't see how we could to pay it back. Those were tough times. Our financial situation was completely at odds with the affluent area in which we lived and the circles we moved in.

I also appreciated that time in our life. My husband and I became very creative as a couple when it came to money-saving ideas which only brought us closer together.

A chance encounter

Then destiny intervened again. One afternoon around five o'clock, I was sitting in the cellar of an Italian restaurant eating pizza with my children. There was only one other family there so we struck up a conversation. At one point, I asked the youthful grandmother if she worked. It turned out she was vice president of human resources for a large American retailer. I asked her if she worked with coaches and trainers. When she replied she did, I told her about the training business I set up and cheekily asked if she might have time for a meeting. "Yes, of course," she smiled.

Afterward, I phoned my former coach Willemien and told her we had our first potential client. Both of us were used to working with results-driven American companies so this would be good practice for us.

Willemien worked in human resources for Nike for 11 years. Before the executive search firm, I worked in sales for Cisco and Gartner. While I saw this meeting as more of a "test run," we actually walked away with a huge deal. My company, Zumflow, had its first proper client. Willemien and I went full speed ahead running workshops and coaching sessions together.

A bitter family feud

Then life threw me some fresh challenges. I became pregnant with my third child, a daughter we named Elsa. I had three miscarriages by the time I was 28 so I didn't take getting pregnant for granted. I was delighted!

As my husband and I celebrated her imminent arrival, my grandmother died. When her will was released, a bitter family feud erupted when my aunt and uncle contested it. The family split further when I didn't take my father's side. I wanted nothing to do with him financially. I inadvertently became embroiled in an ongoing legal battle that would last more than two years.

Then, while all of this was going on, my mother was diagnosed with breast cancer. A friend of mine was diagnosed with tongue cancer. I was soon spreading myself thin, trying to be there for everyone while the stress of the lawsuit was exhausting me. Although I really cared about my mother and friend, this is when I learned the importance of setting boundaries. It was something I had always struggled with. Now I had a family to take care of, my business and myself. It all got to be too much.

Where there's a will, there's a way

I remember sitting on the floor one day playing with my children and noticing I wasn't "there" with them. My mind wandered to the impending court case. I realized I no longer wanted all this negative energy and that I had the power to change things. So I picked up the phone and called my aunt.

I hadn't heard my aunt's voice since my grandmother died two-and-a-half years earlier. It was very nice to hear her again, especially as she, too, was now battling cancer. As we spoke, I could apply everything I learned from my coaching and training sessions which elevated the communication. Of course, she was upset and let off steam.

I could truly listen to her. I understood where she was coming from. I didn't engage in the blaming and defending pattern prevalent in my family. One person would blame the other. The other would defend themselves, and repeat.

In the end, my aunt and I managed to find a win-win situation. It was the eve of the court case and I was just about to board a flight to Stockholm when I got a phone call saying an agreement was reached. That moment was such a massive victory for me. I savored the realization that I had come from such a toxic place to a place of understanding, compassion, and connection. I walked away from that situation in a way that felt good for everyone.

No doubt what helped me most was learning about toxic behaviors – the blaming, the stonewalling, the defense, the contempt. All four were the norm when I grew up. I came to realize that these behaviors got you nowhere and led only to short-term solutions with either a winner or a loser. Reading Leadership and Self-Deception: Getting out of the Box by the Arbinger Institute taught me how to be genuinely open to others' points of view. I discovered it was possible to find long-term, win-win solutions when you understood everyone has different perspectives and usually also the best intentions.

An expensive hobby

The next challenge arrived in 2014. Elsa just started school. I found myself at another crossroads. I realized I needed to get a full-time job so I could earn enough money. The thought of it suffocated me. However, it was always in those moments of utter despair and hopelessness, when I was questioning what I should do, that the phone would ring and it would be a client. Somehow, I always seemed to get a "sign" telling me to keep going with my coaching and leadership development business.

Although my husband was very supportive of me at first, he started referring to my coaching as "an expensive hobby." I was furious. On the other hand, I had to admit he was right. I wasn't giving it my all. Only working half the week meant I was only putting in half the work. I had to give it a hundred percent.

I also needed to work on my relationship with money, something that was complex and rooted in early childhood. My mother had a fear of not having enough money when I was growing up. I would get into the shower and before I barely put soap on my body, she would shout at me to get out because it was too expensive. Then I had a father who would fly first class and was extremely generous and had no clue about money. When he went bankrupt, we lost everything. Strangers came into our house and took away the carpets, the paintings and all we had! The auction was the final nail in the coffin.

For the next six years, I struggled. At one point, I was working 54 hours a week while studying for my international business studies degree. I also had to lend money to my father because, of course, he didn't have any. I got a stomach ulcer from all the stress and from trying to keep up appearances. I didn't want people to judge him. Now I realize I didn't want people to judge me. That's also when I came to understand that it wasn't about what you had but who you were that mattered.

The flower girl

Because I really enjoyed what I did, I would say, "yes" to everyone and everything. I was doing so much work for free that I realized I had become "the flower girl." Clients were constantly giving me flowers to thank me for my help. One day I came to a realization. I don't need fricking flowers. I need money so I can pay my bills.

Later, when I discussed this dilemma with a colleague from Oxford Leadership, he or she told me how they tackled it. "I first make sure I do the work I need to do to pay the bills. Only then, do I give my time to charity." That was great advice.

Then another colleague revealed how much they'd earned the previous year – double what I had. I thought to myself if they can do it, so can I. That mindset brought me to where I am today. I don´t compare myself to others, I´m inspired by them.

As I mulled over the advice my colleagues gave me, I set about making a "vision board." I stuck a number on it that was more than double my revenue from the year before. And that year, I made more than I had envisioned. It was the first time that I used a goal as a strategy and not the last. Since then, my business has gone from strength to strength every year. And yes, my husband is really proud of me.

The cheeky monkey

And as for the cheeky monkey? Well, that was always in me. While earning my coaching degree, I discovered that my purpose in life was to be the authentic, loving, "cheeky monkey" who creates aliveness and connection, a connection of people with themselves and connection of people with others.

I should explain that I grew up with an English stepmother from the age of 4, and I could never keep my mouth shut. In a negative way, she always called me a "cheeky monkey". So I tried my best to suppress it, although I failed at it most of the time.

Similarly, when I first started working in London, my boss took me aside and said, "It's great that you're so direct with me, as I'm also Swedish. It would be very helpful for you if you could learn to be more diplomatic." It was true. I didn't always tone it down. When there was something that no one else would dare voice, I was always the one to speak up.

However, when I started learning about coaching, I discovered that this cheeky monkey I tried to suppress was actually an asset. After all, it was, my job to be a mirror to the client and reflect the truth. Finally, I found the profession I fitted into, instead of always trying to fit in.

The cheeky monkey pops up now and again to remind me of the importance of playfulness in our lives and how we shouldn't take ourselves too seriously.

A future goal

I'm probably not alone when I say one of my biggest role models is Oprah Winfrey. On my journey towards connecting people with themselves and with others, I discovered I secretly wanted to be the European Oprah.

I love how she inspires millions to read and how she opens peoples' minds. She allows people to look at things from different perspectives without being judgmental. She's able to have constructive conversations with anyone and everyone, yet somehow manages to stay true to herself without compromising her values. Millions of viewers around the world learn these skills from her.

I know now that I don't want to be famous. Freedom is far too important to me. Yet

I do aspire to make a significant impact. However, the immense reward I get from being part of influencing one person's life for the better, better in the sense of them being more fulfilled and happier with who they are, drives me today.

Kristina Zumpolle Flodin

Founder of Zumflow, Leadership Development

Kristina, 43, was born and raised just north of Stockholm. She moved to California when she was 16 and attended her junior and senior years of high school there. She obtained a Bachelor of Arts degree with honors in International Business Studies from the European Business School (EBS) in London, where she lived and worked for several years. In 2003, Kristina relocated to the Netherlands and, in 2009, founded her company, Zumflow. She speaks Swedish, English, and Dutch. Enthusiastic and no-nonsense, Kristina works as a leadership consultant and develops and facilitates leadership programs across a variety of industries and countries. Her broad cultural and professional experiences shape her expansive and inspirational style. Her mission is to help people realize their full potential. Kristina continuously works to develop herself to be able to support the development of others. As her business and children, now 9, 12 and 13, are growing so fast, Kristina feels she is on the cusp of a new phase of her life: an exciting time with plentiful opportunities. Although she admits to sometimes feeling overwhelmed by how fast it's all moving, she is determined to stay curious and courageous – and enjoy the journey.

kristina.zumpolle@oxfordleadership.com

www.zumflow.com
www.linkedin.com/in/kristinazumpolle

Lead With Your Heart

by Lasse Wrennmark

For the last 20 years, I pondered more deeply on my own purpose. My observation is that it´s very simple and very deep. Simple in a way that it is not complicated and thinking that my experience will help others find their purpose. Deep in the sense that my understanding of my purpose has shifted over the years but the purpose is the same. I believe we can search for our purpose for our whole life and just understand it more deeply. For me, it´s a spiritual dimension of being human, a source, a power, positive energy that in some way connects us as humans.

Unconsciously, my quest for meaning and purpose has been there since I was a child. Maybe unconsciously, it´s that way for most of us. We are all looking for meaning and on that life journey, we sometimes forget what is important to us. Then a crisis shows up in our lives and we become more aware of our purpose again. We start asking the "why?" questions. How do I find meaning in this turmoil?

When I now reflect on my life and think of how purpose has been a driver, I can see that most of my life has been driven by my heart. I have let my passion, or heart, be a guide for me. Every time I have a misalignment with my purpose and values, the outcome is always inner disharmony. I learned this is a good indicator if you´re aligned with your purpose and values or if you are true to yourself. Do you have inner harmony or disharmony?

All the great leaders I've met during the last 20 years have a common denominator. All of them are driven from the inside out. When I ask them about their purpose, they normally say they don't have a clue about what it is, but they have a deep knowing that they are making choices from the inside. There is some kind of internal compass or intuition that they are connecting to and that guides them in life.

My purpose is to be a guide to new perspectives. When I observe my life, I can see that it has always been the same purpose. My understanding of my purpose has shifted and how I have expressed it has shifted too.

With this story, I want to share with you how that purpose has evolved and manifested itself during different stages of my life. I believe our purpose and values are expressed every day in small interactions; that is when you are your best self. I have learned that being more conscious about the journey is key for a more fulfilling and happy life.

Childhood

Before I wrote this piece, I talked to my mother and asked her what her memory of me was when I was a child. She reflected that I was a happy and quite odd kid spending time with myself and not wanting to go out. Instead, I´d prefer to sit in and reflect. That worried Mom and Dad so they bought me pets and thought that would help. Well, it didn't. Exploring my inner world started early for me and still today I feel very comfortable spending time with myself.

I have a memory of me starting to question my dad when I was around 9 or 10. During dinners we often got into an argument. My dad, with a left brain and an engineering mindset, was always reasoning with me. I was much more emotionally driven, always went crazy, and I thought my dad was to the right of Genghis Khan. That became a pattern in our relationship.

When I grew up and had my own family, every time we came to Gothenburg for a visit, the first day everything was fine. The second day, all fine, and then the third day, "HOW CAN YOU THINK LIKE THAT?"

A few years back, I was with my family for a visit and we had dinner together with my two brothers and their families. After dinner my mom asked if anyone was up for an evening walk? My brothers and I were not up for it and my dad stood up and said, "I will take you for a walk dear."

Fifteen minutes later, my mom came running into the kitchen breathing heavily, screaming that Dad had fallen.

My brothers and I were out of the door in a second and when we came around a corner about 100 meters away, I saw my dad lying in the middle of the street.

When I came up closer, I saw a pool of blood coming out of Dad's head. It was quite dramatic for me and my brothers but he was conscious. He couldn't move at all and was almost paralyzed. I leaned over him and asked, "Dad, how are you doing?" He slowly bent his head towards me and smiled and said, "I am totally fine."

Well, he was not. We had to carry him home and get him to a doctor. That started a deep process in me around my relationship with my father. This was the first time that I needed to help my father when he was helpless. He always helped me in his gentle way and now I realized it had an ending. Even if your parents are old you take them for granted.

My vision was clear, I wanted an adult relationship with my father, not a parent-child relationship. With my mother, it was like that since I was 18 but not with my father. I started to reflect on my purpose and realized that I had always lived my purpose with my father. I was always trying to give another perspective to my father. The question was how did I do it?

When I reflected on my values, I knew that when I was at my best, I tapped into the quality of acceptance, both for myself and others. I never applied that value in my relationship with my father. Now, I decided to do just that. The last five years, we spent a week at our summer place, where he grew up, with some good food and good wine. No more agitated conversation and I dared to ask those questions that I never asked before. When he passed away, it was both sad and beautiful. There was a feeling of completion.

It´s very powerful when your purpose, values, and vision are aligned. It changes the world and relationships for the better.

Punk rocker

During my time in school I drove my teachers nuts by always asking the why question. All my teachers called my mom and complained that I was disturbing the class with my questions. Today I can see that it was a way for me to understand and create meaning for my life.

Rarely could the teachers answer those why questions and I built a resistance to school. When I moved to a small town in mid-Sweden during the late '70s, the punk rock movement came. I became the only punk rocker in town, and despite the big risk of getting beaten up, I walked around with my earring, spiky hair and jeans with big holes in them, feeling great. The energy, the creativity and the freedom to start a band, playing without perfection, triggered a deep sense of meaning in me. I think these are different ways that your purpose can be expressed, and these moments of bliss, a deep sense of meaning, happiness, inner harmony, are when you are aligned with your purpose.

Look for these moments in your life and see if you can find any common denominators. It will inform you of your own purpose.

A young man with his purpose

After my military service, I moved to Stockholm and started work at H&M. Selling suits was not my cup of tea. It was not that cool to sell suits as a former punk rocker. For me, it was a wonderful time, especially when someone came in and said, "I´m going to a party and don't know what to wear." I was always so engaged and my purpose to give a new perspective was activated.

A few years later, I became a tour and ski guide. Every week, new guests arrived, and for me, it was a new opportunity to show a new perspective. I got feedback from guests "How I could be so engaged week after week?" My answer, "New week, new guests that haven't seen the slopes or the tours." Having a leading role and the opportunity to show people what they hadn't seen before became a deeply motivating for me.

After a few years as a guide, I moved back home and started working at the office for a travel agency. In that environment, it was really difficult for me to live my purpose and I entered a period of disharmony. That period of disharmony started a new chapter for me. I started my first company. Taking people out in the forest, doing survival courses, I climbed and slept in tents. I became very interested in group dynamics and leadership and a couple of years later, I meet my mentor, PeÅ Schörling. He was head of the leadership department at the National Defense School. At that time, it was one of the best places to study leadership and group dynamics.

This was a moment when I met someone who had theories, thought through ideas around something that I only had felt and it was cutting-edge knowledge. My purpose was activated again.

Peå also introduced me to Brian Bacon. This was 1999, and for the second time, I met a person who was able to articulate something that resonated deeply within me. That meeting became the first time in my life when I started to reflect on my purpose and values. A sense of purpose is much more important than a statement of purpose. At the same time, I think it´s rare to meet leaders who can articulate what their purpose is and how it manifests in all their relationships.

The meeting with Brian formed a new direction in my life and a deeper quest for purpose. It was about and how to help leaders find that source of power that we all possess. For almost 20 years this is my livelihood.

Now

When reflecting on my life, I truly believe purpose is about finding a deeper sense of meaning that operates from love and giving, not from fear and control. Now at 57 I have two adult children. One way of expressing my purpose with them is through learning journeys. We go and experience a new thing we haven't done before so we learn something new and build that adult relationship that I wanted to have with my father. Your purpose can be expressed in so many ways. The question is how does your purpose manifest in all your relationships?

I have been married to Eva for almost 30 years. We´ve had mostly good times and some hardship. I can see that both good times and bad times have forged our relationship into a deep loving bond with a lot of support, compassion, freedom, and acceptance. Eva is one of the most value-driven persons I know. I think the key to a long-lasting relationship is when you can be your authentic self and mostly operate from your purpose and values.

Future

I think the paradox of being unique yet one with all is one of life's deep truths. We are all unique in how we express our purpose or truth. When we stand up for our truth, we also stand up for the truth of others. This is why Greta Thunberg can create a movement so fast. She is only following her truth yet it also connects to many other peoples´ truths. It´s the same with leaders all over the world. If they start operating more from their own purpose and truth instead of operating out of expectations of others, we will see a lot of positive things happen in the world. Here are some examples.

- A higher level of engagement
- A higher level of ethics
- Less stress and more relaxation
- Easier to make good choices faster
- Coping with change better
- More compassionate
- More energized
- More focused
- A deeper sense of meaning
- A sense of direction even if there is a lot of uncertainty
- Building resilience
- Building stronger and more authentic relationships

Humanity is standing in the crossroads and I don't think that purpose is the solution for everything. I think it should be the starting point for everything. A higher level of consciousness and more purpose-driven humans are the keys for building a better future for all life.

Maybe my way of expressing my purpose today is shifting to be a guide for meaning and consciousness. It´s a bold purpose statement that drives me to develop myself first. At the age of 57, I can say that I have never been so curious about my own and others' inner worlds.

I try out new things. I have my own highly conscious coach, go on silent retreats, meditate every morning, explore what a shaman can bring to my development and of course take learning journeys with my kids.

Stepping out of my comfort zone is key to my development, and that is something I strongly recommend to all.

Meet and have a conversation with a shaman, a nun or someone who sees life differently than you. Engage yourself in conversation with people who have walked longer on their life path than you. It will benefit your growth and the more you grow the more you can give.

Today we have built so many things in the outer world that have served us well. Now I believe it's high time to start developing and building the inner world. I think this is where the solution lies for humanity going forward. When we become more driven from the inside, the outcome of that will be better for humans, nature, and animals. When we connect deeply to ourselves, we also connect to others. Sadhguru expresses it beautifully, "The only way out is in." We are just at the beginning of building a more purpose-driven world and that is very encouraging.

My question now is, how can we increase the level of consciousness and purpose in humanity so more can access that source, power, and positive energy field and transform this world for good?

Lasse Wrennmark

Founding Trustee, Oxford Leadership, Purpose-Driven Leadership

Lasse is the founding trustee and partner of Oxford Leadership LTD. He lives in Stockholm with his wife and has two grown children. Lasse started six companies. For almost 20 years, he is dedicated to bringing purpose-driven leadership into big global companies.

lasse.wrennmark@oxfordleadership.com

Two Good Reasons

by Dr. Marion Bourgeois

My first life ended on November 24, 2006.

I had spent the morning at school, where I had been doing a legal clerkship as a teacher for half a year, and I was looking forward to the evening. The graduation ceremony of my old girls' school was on the agenda. After twenty years, we would all finally meet again. I had been reminiscing about the stories of those days spent with the companions of my youth, and I asked myself, "What has become of one or the other?"

Only a few meters, one last bend, and I could see the house where we had been living for a few months. And I could see my husband's dark blue BMW parked by my front door. Just as it was when I left in the morning.

As I drove up the hill, a queasy feeling crept up on me, and this feeling got stronger as I parked my car, got out, and walked through the garden toward the front door. I put the key into the lock, opened the door, took a step into the hallway. At that moment, my two boys, one dark like me, the other almost platinum blonde, one four and one five, come crying, their eyes wide open with screams on their lips: „Mummy, Mummy, Daddy is lying there!" They point toward the bathroom.

I fell against the door, almost tripped over my own feet, and found my husband lying on the floor in our bathroom. He didn't move. I reached for my mobile phone and called the emergency doctor. But even as I awaited his arrival, I knew I had to accept the hard truth: My husband is dead.

A world came to an end for me. My husband, my best friend, my sparring partner, my buddy, my hero, my port -- and so much more -- THE FATHER OF MY CHILDREN - was gone.

I didn't understand what was happening. I acted like a machine, setting everything in motion that had to happen. His family was informed: first, his brother so that together we could tell his mother, my parents, friends, the company. I even managed to cancel my children's afternoon play date.

I acted calmly and thoughtfully. I was even happy about such banalities as when the man from the funeral parlor told me that he had rarely seen such a prudent person. So, I organized the funeral service and called all our friends in the next days. A good friend came and stayed with me for the first week; I don't know how I could have done it without her help.

Somehow, I worked. I had to -- at least externally. But inwardly -- inwardly -- I died that day. Inside, I found no more drive. Every new day, I asked myself, "Why does the sun rise? Why does the earth continue to turn? How can it be that all the others can simply continue to live their lives like normal, something not granted to both of us, the four of us, as a family?"

Two good reasons

But there was a reason for my continuing. Yes, not just one, but two good reasons.

The two of them flew around in our living room. They crawled onto my lap and let themselves be comforted when they were sad. They wanted to have something read to them. And when they were hungry, they had to be taken care of. So, not being able to continue was simply not an option.

The question did not arise for me -- as justified as it would have been after such a heavy loss: "Why should you even get up in the morning?" Or "Why should you shop and why should you cook?" I had no other alternative! I had to act and function. And even if I hate these terms -- then as now -- this time brought me personally, retrospectively, infinitely further. I was forced to deal not only with my grief and despair but also with who I actually was and who I wanted to be. But above all, I also needed to decide what kind of life I wanted to lead at that moment -- and in the future.

I was not the only one who had to fight day after day; my two boys also suffered. Children take what is given for granted, and they normalize things, unlike us adults, who are attached to what was. We tend to mourn the beautiful past and keep asking ourselves what would have happened if this or that hadn't happened, or to worry about the future. I had to take care of our family alone now and think about the future, while my children lived uncompromisingly in the here and now. That helped me a lot. So, I matured more and more with my two boys.

The question of guilt

I remember a moment when I realized that my husband's heart attack was not his company's fault, but that it was up to each and every one of us to say "No." "No," if it becomes too much for us. "No," if we can't or don't want to manage this one small task.

But as painful at the time as those realizations were, especially since they had their origins in the unimaginable events and upheavals in my life, they also led me exactly to where I am now and to what I stand for today. I want to share this knowledge with others. For me, it is an important concern. In part, it is also my daily driving force: on the one hand, to bring people into self-responsibility, and on the other hand, to establish a management culture and working atmosphere in which a „No" is not only permitted but desired.

But let's go back once again to the time when my life was reshaped bit by bit. After the terrible event, I kept on struggling. From day to day, from week to week, from month to month. I learned what it means to survive the first year without a partner. In Germany, we call it the year of mourning. The first snowfall. The first time when the children, their eyes shining, build a slide out of the snow in the garden. The first snowman without Daddy. In this first year, without my husband and the father of our children, there were, of course, countless such moments and scenes, which were imprinted in my mind. The first Christmas for the three of us. The first birthday. The first holiday without him.

A lot happened during this time, which made me what I am today: a successful businesswoman who stands in the middle of life, who likes to be a role model for other women, who wants to shout to them: „Trust yourselves!" But not only women. I want to shout it out into the world: "Trust youself! Take responsibility for yourselves and your lives. Do not do what others expect of you. Go your own way and begin to say 'NO' for yourselves. Please create working environments in which 'NO' is not only heard but also accepted."

I want to tell you about an event that happened five days after Patrick's death. I decided to go to his company to pick up his personal things. At the reception, I had some trouble gaining admission because I was not registered. Finally, a longtime colleague of my husband came to pick me up and accompany me through the long corridors. Even today, I remember the bright walls, the bright lights, and the smell of the bamboo parquet. He led me into Patrick's office, and I froze.

SOMEONE WAS SITTING IN HIS PLACE!

His pictures of the children and me were lovelessly put aside. His notes, already edited and used. The signs of his presence over many years simply wiped away.

I couldn't believe it. After all, he had been so committed to the company and its employees. On more than one occasion, he had completely exhausted himself. For one and a half years, he had tried to set up a department with six people. And every time he had failed in some way. Sometimes, it was the employee figures that were „frozen." Sometimes, it was the Human Resources Department that didn't get its part done. Sometimes, the boss blocked the desired development and preferred other departments. Or, or, or ... I was pissed off! After all, these circumstances were the reason that my husband had so little free time, had worked so much, and had now -- forever -- left us. I cried quietly, took all of his things, and hastily left this place where my husband was so quickly forgotten. It was unbelievable to me that this company that had forgotten Patrick so quickly -- much too quickly -- asked me to come in for a talk a few weeks later, and then actually offered me a job.

Unfortunately, there was so little one could do for me because my husband died of a heart attack, and therefore, no insurance would cover it. But maybe it could be a help for my family and me if I could earn money there. Far more money, by the way, than I could ever have earned with my dream to become a teacher.

That I didn't wring the neck of the dear HR lady at that time! I blamed these very people for my husband's death. I owe it only to my mother, who managed to educate me at least so well that I knew that strangling someone was not appropriate.

So, I sat there, thanked myself for being well-behaved, and asked for time to think about it. I needed time to finish my education. Did I need to become me? Time to decide what I wanted. Should my path lead me back? Should I really follow this path quite independently of the company?

Suddenly, I thought back to my school days: I grew up at a girls' grammar school and really wanted to take a physics course. When it didn't happen, I fought to make it work. Where there is a will, there is a way. I was already convinced of that at the time. And obviously, I was so convincing that I was able to win over our director to my idea. He finally agreed on a cooperation agreement with the nearby school, so that ten boys came to study on our campus, and the physics course was secured for me and a few other girls. Everything was perfect, until the first exam. We girls in the advanced course were above average in the beginning. But as soon as the boys were there, we fell apart completely at the first exam. Our grades were in a much worse range. That was a drastic experience that shaped me for the rest of my life.

Most of the girls said after our poor exam performance: „Well, the boys just do that better. Of course, physics is not for girls!" Some even changed their advanced courses. A friend and I reacted differently. We wanted to know why the boys scored so much better than we did. We asked them: „Why are you so much better at this than we are?"

The answer was simple: they had three times as many physics' lessons in junior high as we did in our girls' high school.

I still remember as if this happened yesterday. My girlfriend and I were sitting on my bed, and I said to her, „Okay, what do we do now?" Instead of giving up like many of our classmates, we decided to go on. That wasn't easy, of course, because we had a lot of stuff to catch up on. But we sat down, spent days studying, and at the next, well maybe not the very next, but on another exam, we were again in first place.

Even later, when I made my career in the industry, this point always came out again: If someone approaches something with the attitude that the biggest part of succeeding is preparation THEN, it works out. But if you go in with the attitude of „This won't work," then it won't work out.

A network that catches you

And so, after my husband's death, I was convinced that I needed that same attitude again. The weeks went by. Months passed. I was perfect. I went to school and attended my seminars. In the afternoon, I spent my time with the children. Fortunately, I had the greatest nanny in the world, who, by the way, is still with us today and has become a kind of surrogate mother for my boys over the years. And I had friends who caught me, who were just there, who accompanied me in the hard hours. And those hours, sometimes even whole days, were dark and made me doubt whether I was really up to the whole thing. They came again and again, even if the distances between them became bigger and bigger.

When I look back on this time today, I realize that countless people saved me after I had lost the most important person in my life. The network of these people literally caught me. They prevented me from crashing, going crazy, or drowning in despair.

It started with two people, who were still quite small at that time, my incomparable boys, of whom I am infinitely proud, and who showed me every day anew that life must go on. Then, of course, there were my family and close friends. And last but not least, people who were completely unknown to me until then. We had just moved more or less freshly to the village, and I didn't know anybody in the surrounding area, let alone on our street. Suddenly, these people, whom I didn't know, stood at our door and offered their help. Some of them are now my best friends.

Years later, I asked them once: "Tell me, why were you standing at my front door at the time?" The answer was and still is as simple as it is impressive: „Well, because you needed help and because I liked you. That's it."

Even today, I still try to pass this on, to give something back from what was positive for me at the worst moment of my life. I don't look away in crises like grief, even it is easier to do so. Conversely, an exchange with like-minded people is valuable for me; when people move something together, they have the same curiosity and thus give each other energy.

Even today, it is extremely important for me to know people in my environment on whom I can rely and who do me good. And vice versa, of course. It probably has something to do with the positive experiences at that time that I have no problem with giving my trust to unknown people, without thinking about what it brings me or what I get back for it. I love to connect people whom I believe will benefit from one another. And especially lately, I have noticed that people are recommended to me again and again whose strength or talent I need exactly at the moment.

At that time, one of those people, whom I undoubtedly needed urgently, was a very dear friend who had just moved to Atlanta with her husband. They would have certainly thought about the distance -- not feasible -- but exactly the opposite was the case: That was really great. Because of the time difference, when my day was over and I was often at the end of my rope, she had just had lunch, and we could talk. Without her and our almost daily conversations, I would not have survived that first year after the death of my husband. Because we had moved several times, many people from our network of friends were not nearby. But even if they were sitting in Hamburg and Munich, in France, or even in the United States, they were always there for me.

The conversations did me good, and, yes, somehow everything went on. I, too, was almost perfect -- at least to the outside world. I fulfilled the role of the loving mother and did everything that had to be done in the general German image of a loving mother. But I felt nothing. Nothing at all. No joy. No love. No pain. And I had no more dreams, either.

I functioned on one side, and on the other, I felt like a leaf in the wind. I had turned my back on the industry and was on my way to the second state examination. Despite all the imponderables, I was sure that for me, or better, for all three of us, with a teaching position in math and physics, the world could not really end. I was convinced that this combination of subjects would always provide me with a job.

Time passed. I passed my second state examination and finally could teach mathematics and physics at German grammar schools, but somehow I didn't know what to do. I had always been good at making plans, and I knew that something had to happen now.

During the passing weeks and months, I had learned to accept support and help. I'm still convinced today that if we can't succeed on our own, we'll have to get help. We are simply not able to ask ourselves the right questions, like we can when it comes to helping our friends with their problems.

Others helped me, or rather, they found me. Coincidences, which as you know do not exist, occurred. I was in the sauna with a friend when I was offered a trial date for floating. Rebekka was the name of the fairy godmother, who simply moved me back and forth in the water as I floated to the sounds of dolphins underwater, until I finally started to cry and let out all my pain. We worked together, with the body, not with the mind. With emotions, not with thoughts, and certainly not with old, outdated norms or values.

And something else happened little by little. My children were my best feedback system. I learned that we were only doing well together when I was doing well. I didn't want to admit that for a long time. But again, and again, some situations showed me exactly that. And I decided to take more care of myself. Very slowly, we became a family again.

This was accompanied by the question: "WHAT exactly do I want to do?" This question was not new to me; I had asked myself this question several times in the past years.

As a woman in a leading role

As a woman in the business world, I had to experience with sorrow how different systems tick when you become pregnant and are working in a leading role. The first boss was spontaneously happy with me, and his only question was: "Marion, how do you imagine this with a child?" He fully supported my part-time work, and I enjoyed returning to work relatively quickly after my pregnancy. To see my old colleagues. To do a good job.

But when I came back after the second pregnancy, someone else was suddenly there. A former management consultant. He also had two children and a wife. But she, also a management consultant, stayed at home with an au pair and two children. A completely different role model. He couldn't handle my way at all. Interesting things happened that I couldn't understand at first. Or maybe I didn't want to see. But at some point, I had to find out and admit it to myself: He simply wanted me to get out.

That fueled my frustration. I wanted to work. I still had just as much in my head as before. Why shouldn't I still work with two children? But to be so dependent on the boss who supported a part-time job? I certainly didn't want that any longer either!

I thought for the first time about what I actually wanted to do in life. I rediscovered my girlhood dream of supporting people in their development. I decided to leave the economy in order to find my happiness at school. But was that my way? Or should I return to the economy? Where was my future? How could I take care of my family safely?

Meanwhile, the offer to work at the company where my husband had been passionately active until his end still stood. I had to make a difficult decision that I did not want to make lightly: School or business? Especially in the company, which I blamed for the death of my husband.

But wait! There was something else: Hadn't I learned in the last weeks and months that my children only feel good when I feel good myself? Hadn't I had to experience painfully that everyone is replaceable?

It slowly dawned on me: Companies will always only take, take, take. Another order here, another to-do list there. And you know what? That's good and right! A boss can't know how long someone is sitting on a task. How much time does it take to work on project A or project B? He would have to tell his employees exactly the way to go. But this is exactly what contradicts the employee's personal responsibility, his freedom to handle tasks in the way he is able, willing, and believes to be sensible.

The only one who can say "no" is me

Once again it became clear to me: The only one who can say "NO" is me. And I learned even more: The only one who could have escaped the stress would have been my husband. He was the only one who knew what he had on his desk, which tasks were piled up on his to-do list. He was the only one who knew whether he had to work hard for three weeks for the evaluation, or knew someone who had perhaps already prepared it for another context. And I suddenly became aware: If he could have said "No" maybe nothing would have happened!

This realization spread more and more within me. I was overcome by an inner peace from which I was able to see it all again from a completely different perspective, even in a completely new light.

And there was even more: I wanted -- as I had done a few weeks before -- to communicate this to everyone I met. I wanted to scream: „Take care! Take your life in your hands! And then I realized: Damn, that also applies to me!" Oops, not noticed at all.

I talked a lot, with good friends, with strangers, with psychologists, women, men, teachers, and employees, and finally found my solution: Yes, I wanted to support people in their personal development. But no, I didn't want to do this at school. I wanted to accompany adult people to find their own limits and show them. I wanted to introduce companies to a culture that is characterized by joy and trust. If there is an environment of trusting cooperation, then everyone may say "NO." Mistakes may happen, but people need not be afraid of them because mistakes are seen as learning opportunities.

My husband's company was no longer taboo for me. I started again in our former company. I went one step back, was no longer a manager. All day long, I did nothing but develop concepts for a respectful and trusting company culture. And I trained people to implement this culture and live it every day, from managers to every single employee and back again. Between departments, at all hierarchical levels, from trainee to boss.

Looking back, I can only say one thing: I was naive! I actually thought that if we were to work together on the topic of customers, if we wanted to teach others that customer orientation should be the greatest and the only means for further success, then we would have to live it! My colleagues and I worked hard. We never got tired of presenting ourselves as contact partners, of getting involved with all our heart and soul. Even on a poster about our Guiding Principles, our faces smiled at us almost everywhere from the walls. We were happy and proud. And we were happy to be able to pursue this beautiful activity.

What can I say? My career did not only go on and on. It also went steeply up relatively fast. The success proved me right once again! I was promoted and was responsible for 300 million euros. My alarm clock rang punctually at 5 am so that I could read my emails before I woke up my children. With my mobile phone in my hand at 6:30, I prepared everything for school, quickly packed my snacks, had a short breakfast together, and headed off to work. My next break was from 6 to 8 p.m. Then I worked until midnight. Five hours of sleep. And the next day everything started all over again.

A déjà-vu

I didn't see what happened. I didn't see that my life had been just as strained as my husband's had been. I did not see that my children became more and more restless, dissatisfied, and unhappy. I only noticed that I had more and more stress with them. I didn't realize what it all did to me, what it did to us.

But one day I woke up suddenly! On that day, I had a feedback meeting with my temporary CEO. He had been in the office for just six weeks and was about to restructure. I led the smallest of three areas that were to be merged.

I was sitting in his office. He offered me coffee and water, just like you do. The obligatory small talk. Suddenly, he said a sentence that should have completely disassembled me: „Mrs. Bourgeois, unfortunately, we have no more use for you."

No more use? Three words I couldn't grasp! But I had given everything. Doesn't he know what I did? That cannot be! And why at all? I was speechless and unspeakably angry. I was at a loss about what was to become of me now. But I had relied on the fact that at least my job was a constant in life. By the way, there was a lot of trouble in my life again, even if I didn't want to or couldn't see it for a long time because I needed all my strength and energy for my career. I did this with the best of intentions, wanting to secure my family. That I had almost destroyed them became clear to me only sometime later.

Fortunately, there was also now a network that I could count on, people who listened to me and helped me to process what had happened in the last few months. The realization hit me like a blow and literally put me down. I was diagnosed with pneumonia.

I was forced to spend the next few days at home on the couch. In this medically prescribed silence, I finally had time to think, to think about what had happened. Fortunately, it was just pneumonia and not a heart attack like my husband's, whom I had lost six years earlier. I was in the second big crisis of my life, but this time it was really my own health, my own life, which I had put at risk.

This time I realized that I couldn't blame anybody else. Not my company, not my family. This next deep case was on my account, and again it was the well-known trigger: I hadn't said "NO." I had taken no responsibility for myself, my body, and my life.

I treated every day as a new beginning, until the beginning comes to an abrupt end, as I had experienced years before.

I lay on the couch and reviewed what had happened in the last few weeks. My father had a stroke, my mother then went to a nursing home, blaming me for not taking care for her. She had told me that over and over again. But how could I have done otherwise with my job and two children? I had just separated from my friend after he told me he didn't like being treated like my garbage can. Somehow, I had done what I could -- at least in my perception -- but it was never enough. I had lost my job, my boys weren't happy, my parents were in bad health, and I didn't have enough time for my boyfriend either -- and the time we spent together didn't do him any good.

Regardless of all those important people around me, I had taken even less care of the most important person: ME! There wasn't much left of the realization that my boys were only doing well when I was doing well. Somehow, I had lost the knowledge on my way. Somewhere I had taken a wrong turn. Something had flattened me, and that something was me.

Self-knowledge is not easy, but it is inevitable if we want to develop further. And that's what I wanted! I decided to look forward and not back. I analyzed what had happened. Now it was time again to make a plan. To think again about what I want in life. In any case, it should not go on like this. It was just before Easter, and I decided to go skiing with my boys. In the past, the four of us liked to do that, and now I wanted to use the freedom of the mountains to gain farsightedness not only for physical activity but also for thought -- about my future, about our future.

Said, done. And what can I say: They were wonderful, incomparably beautiful days and moving for me in every respect. Even though I wasn't quite as well physically yet, I was visibly recovering. And I finally decided to start the Marion project.

A moment that changed everything once again

It was in the summer of 2012. A party at a friends' house. We celebrated with one of our football-crazy friends. He had a house with a huge barn in the back. As soon as a big public event was announced, a screen was set up and the event was loudly cheered and celebrated, while the grill was running and lots of drinks were poured.

This time, there was also a DJ from our group who heated us up after the German victory. And I danced -- for the first time in ten years -- again. You must know, dancing was a great passion for me as a child. At that time, there was nothing bigger, nothing more important for me. Like so many little girls, I started ballet early. Later, I was a semiprofessional Latin American dancer. And there Gunnar sat. I only knew him because he worked for the local electrician and installed a television for me. A mountain from a man. Full of tattoos. Gunnar looked at me, watched me dance for a while, came up to me, and asked me: „Marion, where else is this woman? The woman who is so full of energy here. Does she shine in such a way that you can turn off the light? What are you doing with this energy?"

It was a question that changed my life.

That evening, I decided to pursue my old hobby again regularly. Also, I found myself back in my everyday life. I knew about my priorities in life. I knew that I would prioritize everything else, except that my children always would be first. I knew that dancing would energize me. But what I still didn't know for sure was this: How could I realize what I wanted to do professionally without endangering our existence? Without an employer?

A short time later, I was sitting in a seminar that would once again change my life enormously. This seminar was all about me. It was about my meaning in life. It was about my values. It was about my vision. And then the trainer asked exactly this one crucial question: „What would you do if you weren't afraid?"

And my whole house of cards fell down.
Yes, if I wasn't afraid, then I would be free. I'd be free to do things I've wanted to do for a long time. I would finally start my own business. And I would finally be able again to have a reliable, binding relationship.

The seminar was in 2012. A lot has changed since then.

Marion in happiness

On the day my husband died, I was celebrating my 20th school anniversary. If I look back on my eighteen-year-old self today, I would, to be honest, not do much differently. I would perhaps shout to my eighteen-year-old self: „Do your thing! Stay yourself! Have your own opinion and express it!" I could always express my emotions and arguments wonderfully, for others, for topics, for things, for ideas. But I couldn't do it for myself! Not for a long time. In the meantime, I have learned it and feel comfortable in my skin, in my life. Yes, this way, my way, brought me right here, so I would do differently only a little. Only to start with it earlier.

I am now Marion, fifty-two years old, a Doctor of Physics, but at some point, I realized that my heart didn't beat as much for numbers as for people. I have been involved in cultural change for twelve years and started my own business four years ago. I want to encourage people, especially in management, in companies, to be happy and successful by supporting them in taking on responsibility for themselves.

Yes, I'm fine, and I can't imagine doing anything other than what I'm doing every day right now. I have a job that inspires me. I am still curious and learn something new every day. When I work with my participants, I come back home full of energy. My two boys are developing splendidly. I am infinitely proud of them. And I've been remarried for three years and live in Cologne. Our wedding rings say: „Zo levve e levve lang."

For us, this means: „Enjoy every day. Enjoy every single moment. And try to see beautiful moments every day." I am convinced that you are what you are saying. If you only ever tell yourself -- and others -- negative things, then you and others will think: You are the unluckiest person! But the opposite is also true. Telling yourself -- and others -- the happy things you experience, the things you meet, then you feel like the happiest person ever. And I am Marion in happiness.
At some point, it fell like scales from my eyes:

My second life started on November 24, 2006.

Dr. Marion Bourgeois

Excellence Coach and Top-Speaker

At twenty-eight, a doctorate in physics; at thirty-three, mother of two boys; at thirty-nine, a widow. Returning to her own strengths. At forty-three, senior management within a DAX company. Member of the Supervisory Board. Renewed focus on personal values. Independent at forty-nine. As a certified business coach, mediator, and moderator, she brings people into personal responsibility and companies into cultural change with her lectures and practical training. An emphasis on the topic of women in leadership to increase the quota by exclusive coaching and not by setting a number legally. Dr. Marion Bourgeois. Her slogan is „for life arrange, for success train and chances see" because „Success is if perception meets readiness. "

marion.bourgeois@oxfordleadership.com

A Drawing Of A Tree

by Michele Scott

Pinpointing the start of one's journey is never going to be easy. Life is full of starts. Some things stick and some don't. Some things only click much later. The seasonality of this journey is part of shaping who you are. I believe that it isn't about finding yourself, rather it is about making yourself.

I'll begin this story with trees. Well, a drawing of a tree to be exact. A few years ago, I was invited to attend a leadership programme and during one of the group sessions, we were asked to draw a tree. The leaves of the tree were to represent our perceived "personal barriers" in life and the roots of the tree symbolised the perceived root causes of these barriers, the things that hold us back from achieving our goals. I was paired with a lovely Polish lady, Anna, and we were tasked to each draw our tree and then use these drawings to explore what we felt illustrated our barriers.

I come from a very artistic family. My mother and brother (and extended family) would no doubt do a fantastic job at it. I could imagine them around the workbench producing fantastic oil paintings, mosaics or large stained-glass trees. Me, on the other hand, not so much. I knew a few of my strengths and had my achievements, but I was well aware that I possessed not a single artistic bone in my body. So drawing a tree was quite a challenge and after spending a considerable amount of time listening to my partner talking about her barriers, I looked down at my very simply drawn tree and saw nothing in it at all. I mumbled something about not having any barriers.

"Of course, you do," said Anna. I looked at her, seeing how her session had affected her, how a simple drawing of a tree and a conversation with this stranger about the things that held her back had brought her to tears. I wanted her to continue. I'd much rather have listened to her but she pushed me on, pointing at my pathetic tree. "It's your turn. What are your barriers?"

I mumbled some nonsense, made small talk, even attempted a joke. Yet, quite quickly this seemingly simple exercise sounded ridiculous to me. I felt myself become rather frustrated and sat tapping my pen at my little stick-figure tree. She continued to stare at me in silence. I kept thinking "I don't have barriers?" I had already been through a lot, suffered losses and enjoyed many adventures. In my mind, I flicked through a range of life events including, leading a large-scale brand launch for over 5,000 attendees; designing bespoke female-only financial training in Saudi Arabia; developing a regional respite care programme for families with members who have mental health issues; achieving the highest individual sales record for an award-winning London-based media company; and once achieving a personal best for swimming 6 hours straight in Malaysia. I had a loving, supportive family and had much personal freedom though, of course, I had dealt with my share of ageism, classism, sexism, and xenophobia. I had failed many times so I was no longer afraid of that. I was not scared of change. Living on three different continents can do that to you.

Anna stared at me. My tree stared at me. She pressed on: "What are your barriers?" Laughing, I replied, "Money. I could do with a couple of million pounds." No response from Anna. The truth is, I honestly felt I had no barriers, but what then? I looked at the page quietly saying, "What do you do if you have no barriers?" After some time of this, she stood up, looked at me with her kind eyes and said, "You just don't get it." and walked away.

For the next hour, I sat thinking, "What could she mean?" After all, I can't help it if I don't have any barriers. It was she that didn't get it. Then suddenly it hit me like a splash of cold water. I got it. I looked at the simple drawing of my tree. Straight trunk, fork-like roots and a cloud-like head for leaves. There was nothing to it. I had no barriers and nothing was holding me back. I knew I could be whoever I wanted. I could absolutely go for it! I was elated, dancing and whooping. I raced to find Anna and gave her a huge hug.

This kick-started a whole new chapter for me. I decided to go for every opportunity I could get my hands on. I brushed up on information technology and systems, took online courses in finance, organisational development, and leadership theory. I put my hand up to manage every local and international training event I could. Outside of work, I contributed to a local town planning project to build a more sustainable traffic system with a focus on improving air quality. I raised thousands of pounds for various local community projects and even kick-started two grassroots initiatives.

The first for mental health issues offering evening and weekend activities for those suffering from long-term illness. The second was a "guerrilla gardening" initiative where you find a run-down piece of land and make it beautiful for the community.

If that wasn't enough, I decided I needed to go back to university and enrolled to do a master's degree in business administration (MBA). Self-financed and with a child under a year old, it was a risk, but I was determined to take advantage of my opportunities. In my application interview, the dean said to me, "The MBA is going to be unquestionably hard. Why do you think it is worth the bother?" I replied, as straight and simple as the tree I had drawn. "I want to add value in every way I can. I want to do more. For me, there is no plateau."

Of course, the dean was right. The MBA was unquestionably hard, and it took a personal, physical and psychological sacrifice. I continued to embrace everything fully and made the most of my MBA, helping start five small IT businesses, giving Women Leadership talks, and running Information Operating systems webinars, including one project with a nuclear scientist on a new privatised transportation system. I felt entirely out of my league but loved every minute of it.

It is fair to say that this way of living, or should I say "way of operating," was not sustainable. I felt pushed and pulled in many directions, not fulfilling my original intention of adding value. I may be giving my time to various initiatives but not offering any true value.

I began reflecting again on the little stick-figure tree that I had drawn three years earlier. It had stood so simply, proud but in some way not altogether truthful. Trees, like all of us, are far more intricate.

Kenrokuen

On the west coast of Japan, about four hours from Tokyo on a bullet train that takes you through the Japanese Alps sits the small town of Kanazawa, my home for several years. My Japanese life started as an English language instructor but quickly within a few months I became the Group Area Manager running training and sales programmes across many branches. The Japanese have a strong work ethic and life is calculated by the minute. During my free time, I spent my hours exploring the local landscape.

Kanazawa is famous for its wonderfully nurtured and landscaped gardens with perfectly manicured trees and expertly-maintained ponds. One garden in particular that captivated me was Kenrokuen. Like much of Japan, the region is also famous for its very clear seasonal changes and, on that side of the Japanese Alps, its heavy snowfall. And so here these trees need a little help.

These are not stick-figure trees, standing straight and simple, but deeply rooted, carefully managed trees, propped up when they mature and supported in the preparation of the snowfall. I must have visited these gardens over a hundred times across the seasons, and I never grew tired of them, particularly as they changed through the seasons. I loved watching the garden team prune, clean and support the trees. It takes such dedication and effort to maintain such a finely-balanced garden over all those years.

To support the trees as they grow and to allow them to branch out in any direction, teams of gardeners rig up wooden support pillars. As these branches expand, small micro-ecosystems sprout beneath the trees as they shade areas and make way for new life to grow. Though their roots went deep, and they were otherwise strong, they could not stand on their own without this support.

Over time, I have learnt I did not need to know everything, to do everything. I needed to root myself into what I knew best. Yes, I felt I did not have any barriers, nothing was holding me back, but what I understood now, looking back on those trees in Japan, was that so much more could be done with support, compassion, care, diligence, and generosity. Generosity with my time, with my skills and knowledge, generous in spirit, with dedicating myself to taking the time to see what the tree needs, in whatever season I find it, and doing what is necessary. This way, I aimed to influence and support change. Wherever I could and wherever it counted, I brought love.

It is never that simple

Living a life dedicated to compassion, generosity, care, and love can be pretty tough. I do my best, and this has been an important learning too. Be honest with me. Be honest with those around me. Show vulnerability and admit knowledge gaps and mistakes.

Picture this. The phone rings, it is the vice president of a global semiconductor company. I have been waiting for hours for his call. We are about to take 236 of their top senior executives into the Arctic wilderness on a Leadership Journey. Huge risk. Huge stakes. No room for error. At this very moment in time, it is 5.45 p.m., and I am on a bus with my hungry and tired toddler, who has not seen me in days. The phone is ringing, the window of opportunity to take the call is closing fast. I have many senior stakeholders expecting an immediate report back from the outcome of this call. What to do? I answer politely, take a deep breath and explain that I have been eagerly waiting for the call but at this point, my young son is in my arms. Knowing the potential ramifications, my heart is aching with concern that I will lose my window to speak with him. At the risk of being vulnerable, I state that I believe I would bring more value to this call if we postpone it until later in the evening, as my priority now is to be a mum. Can you imagine? Telling the VP of a multi-billion-dollar company that he is NOT my priority but rather my little 3-year-old is and risking losing the contract?

To my surprise, he calmly acknowledged that the timing was not right. He opened up and said he would take the time to actually eat something and that we would both be more effective after taking care of what is important. We hung up. I burst into tears and squeezed my little, grumpy toddler. I was honest, loving and authentic. And, yes, we did win the contract. We did take a couple of hundred of their executives into the Arctic wilderness to explore their own personal purposes and it was a great success.

Some experiences, as we all know, do not have fairy-tale endings. During such times, I have two guiding principles. The first is the much-loved Afrikaans expression "'n boer maak 'n plan". The direct translation is "a farmer makes a plan" and it is used widely to encourage oneself to improvise when faced with a problem. The second is the Japanese word "ganbatte", which means "do your best".

Seasons

Trees change with the seasons and they take the landscape with them into full-bodied summer or the stark beauty of winter. It is one of my greatest pleasures to watch the subtle changes of the landscape as the weather turns and, as they move out of winter, the bare trees start to show hints of purple, then the greens of moss and lichen before the first buds. Seasonal change is a natural part of the cycle but throughout it, all the tree remains the same, even in that highly-managed and curated garden in Japan the landscape the tree sits in is a constant and it is the seasonal dressing that changes.

I believe I am no different, but it can be easy to forget that. With multi-faceted jobs, it can be easy to switch character, role, performance to find myself asking, "Which hat am I wearing now?" I still tend to take on too much, jumping at the opportunity to support tech start-ups, facilitate high-performance meetings, mentor young entrepreneurs, and drive numerous non-profit initiatives. It's easy to forget.

I recently had to remind myself that, just as the tree is still the same tree irrespective of the demands of the season, it needs to be the same me showing up and doing so with love, authenticity, and honesty to be able to enjoy my story.

Michele Scott

Client Services Director at Oxford Leadership

Michele Scott has lived on three different continents, worked on thousands of events, education and training programs, as well as leadership initiatives. She believes every conversation, moment of frustration and all the belly-aching laughter have collectively contributed to the whole landscape nonetheless, and she will share a few of these experiences. Michele has had the privilege of nurturing global communities and working with experts across over 40 different countries. This role brings elements of exploration, creative pathfinding with enriched with refreshing moments. It holds moments of excitement and, of course, not to forget moments of grit and perseverance. All the while, filling her with energy and expanding her horizons and reaching huge summits (literal and physical) with views that take your breath away. Based in Oxford, she plays league netball and does half marathons.

michele.scott@oxfordleadership.com
www.linkedin.com/in/michele-scott-a4958015

The Magic Of Life-Changing Encounters

by Mikaela Nyström

Can it be a coincidence that most of my life-changing moments have taken place in cafés?

Over a cup of tea, I have been incredibly fortunate to meet amazing, inspiring people who have significantly altered my life journey in the most positive ways. Simply put, they have guided me on paths I could not have traveled on my own.

One of the first major turning points in my career took place in a café on an October afternoon in 2009, when I met with my colleague and friend Helena Åhman at Nokia headquarters in Espoo, Finland. At the time, I worked for Nokia.

Helena and I had just finished facilitating a very successful management team-development session, and we were feeling incredibly happy and energized. As we sat chatting over tea and debriefing, she asked me a question that ended up changing my life.

"Have you ever thought of starting your own consultancy and coaching company?" she asked, adding that it would be empowering to work together. As I started considering what she was saying, I felt a huge shift taking place within me.

The power of friendship

At the time, I was Helena's client, and she was our consultant. Later she became my mentor, and now we are good friends.

Helena is one of the few people who really knows me from the inside out.

I have even confided in her about my upbringing, which was rather unconventional. My father is an artist, who worked as an art director, and my parents divorced when I was six years old in 1971. My younger brother and I lived with my father, an unusual arrangement at the time, because my mother was an alcoholic and couldn't take care of us.

As a result of feeling abandoned at a young age, my survival strategy and sense of self were largely based on performing well in order to be liked by other people. My great fear of rejection and the sense that I was unloved and unlovable was formed during my childhood, and it's a feeling that I've struggled with throughout my life.

Growing up, I strived to be the good girl, and this worked for me in my studies and later in numerous high-performing leadership positions at Nokia, during the golden heyday years when Nokia was the world's mobile phone leader. At the time, the company's work environment was all about innovation and opportunities. It was a blissful place, and we often danced in the halls. Practicing joy has always been one of my key values, together with honesty and integrity.

But then things changed. As a model employee relying on the survival strategies that had previously worked for me, I took on too much. Around 2006, I was traveling about 150 days a year, and I had started to feel very tired and stressed. I was crying a lot and felt unhappy at work. I no longer believed that my work was meaningful or that my values matched my role or the company's values.

Around the same time, I started to feel as though I wasn't present in my life and that I wasn't doing a good job as a wife or as a mother; I had three school-age children at the time. I often felt as though I lacked the energy to truly be part of my family's daily life or the ability to enjoy the moment, whether I was at home or at work. I often also felt a strong sense of guilt. I knew something had to change.

Turning points

On a dark, rainy day in October 2009, I was sitting with Helena Åhman. We had just facilitated a management team session with great success. We were really feeling energized. At that time, I was Helena's client at Nokia, and she was our consultant. Our cooperation was so inspiring that we were already role- modeling collaborative leadership. As I already mentioned earlier, this was the question that shifted my perspective and led to a big decision.

"Miksu, have you thought of establishing your own consultancy and coaching company? Shouldn´t we work together since we had such fun today and made an impact together?"

The question sparked a totally new way of thinking.

Helena inspired me to leave my job because she believed in me and encouraged me, which was very important because I felt I hadn't received that kind of support from anyone during my formative years.

One major shift in mindset for me has been the realization that I don't need to be negative. I can choose to be positive. I can make a choice about how I approach life. I can choose to live my purpose and balance love and lightness with work and in my personal life.

My husband backed my decision to leave my full-time job. His unconditional support to jump into the unknown is something that I have always sought from another person, along with his love.

Several months later, in May 2010, my company, 4L.com, was formally established, and I resigned from Nokia.

Now ten years later, I feel so grateful that I had the guts to take the step into the unknown and have had the opportunity to work with and have great long-term relationships with my clients.

Love at first sight

Six years later, another meaningful encounter in a café also significantly altered me and marked the start of a lifelong friendship.

When I first met Lasse Wrennmark, a founding trustee of Oxford Leadership, it was to get to know one another and to negotiate my becoming the first accredited Finnish partner for the Oxford Leadership.

It was a sunny day in May 2015, and at a Stockholm café over tea, Lasse quickly became my close friend and Oxford Leadership partner. It was love at first sight, just as if we had met at an airport and were hoping that our flight would be delayed so that we could spend more time together. As my purpose is "Love and Lightness," I realized that there are many forms of love and nuances of shadow and lightness.

At the time I had been running my own business for five years and was looking for a partner. But it was not until I met Lasse and Oxford Leadership that I felt I had found a soul mate whose values matched my own and who shared the same philosophy of working in the spirit of service. Intuitively, on the spot, we agreed to work together.

As we bonded and spent the afternoon in the old and picturesque area of Gamla Stan, one of the things that Lasse said to me during our first encounter was: "Think lightly about yourself and deeply about the world."

His words have guided me since that day as a motto for how to live.

Now I have been working four years with Oxford Leadership as a fellow, and I have been enjoying every moment. Having a great community with like-minded, purpose-driven fellows and inspiring people around you to guide yourself and others into new perspectives and growth is such a joy. Working together on something you believe in and makes a difference -- I just love it!

Love, light, nature, and family

On Högsåra Island in the Finnish Archipelago, my husband and I are building our home. The island is gorgeous, with wild nature in lush patches of pine- and birch-treed forest and stretches of sand and rock.

My husband has always encouraged me to follow my dreams, and one of our favorite places on Högsåra Island is Farmors Café, about a ten-minute walk from the harbor.

Though we have had our share of ups and downs over the years of our marriage, we are committed to one another, and when we sit at our island café to take a break from working on our cottage, I feel as though we're building our dreams together. With my husband and my three adult children – Joakim, Janina, and Anton – by my side, I feel incredibly loved and fortunate.

I recently started painting again. I drew and painted a lot as a child, but that fell away as I sought out my profession with studies, career, and everything that followed. Painting is a creative part of me that I lost and only recently rediscovered again.
On our island, my eyes have opened to seeing the world in a different light. For example, earlier I might have walked through the forest and not paid much attention to my surroundings.

Now, I stop to look at the raindrops on a spider web and want to take a photograph or even paint them.

One of the conscious choices I made when I established my own company happened when I went from being an internal employee to an external one, and I noticed how some people treated me differently. I decided to consider myself an internal-external, meaning that I work with people as part of the team, not as an outsider. I want to co-create with love and lightness.

That means in the future, when our cottage is ready, I want to hold Self Leadership retreats on our island. This is not only because I love working within the Oxford

Leadership community, but also because I feel so strongly that being in nature brings out the authentic, vulnerable self, which is so important for any type of relationship to fully bloom.

With the wild open sea on one side and a calm bay on the other side, our island represents the balance of opposites that I believe all of us hold within ourselves.

And just like in a café, when people meet in nature, they go to a deeper, more reflective and mindful place together. Magic happens together.

Mikaela Nyström

Managing Director and Owner of 4L.com

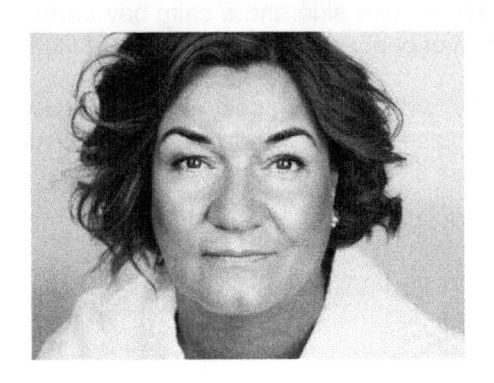

Mikaela "Miksu" Nyström was raised in Helsinki, where she lives with her husband and is planning to move to Högsåra, an island in the archipelago of western Finland. The mother of three adult children, Miksu is celebrating the tenth anniversary of her one-woman coaching and consultancy company, 4L.com, which stands for "Live, Love, Lead, and Learn." She is the first accredited Finnish partner for Oxford Leadership.

In her spare time, she loves to paint, take long walks in the woods, and Latin dance. You can follow her on Facebook and LinkedIn.

mikaela.nystrom@oxfordleadership.com
www.4l-consulting.com

Advisory Board member in the David Clutterbuck Foundation to create five million school-age coaches and mentors globally.

The Calling Of The Heart

by Monika Jankowska

It was the year of my fortieth birthday. In this moment of their lives, people usually reflect on how much they have managed to achieve. They measure their success and wonder what is still ahead of them. Today, I see the significance of that threshold, but at that time of my birthday, I was unaware of the natural cycles of life. I was living in a constant rush, almost unable to catch my breath. Being a mother of four children (ages sixteen, thirteen, four, and one), living on the border of Warsaw in a forest, and having a full-time corporate job was taking my full attention. There was no space to think, not to mention reflect. I lived on autopilot, running from one duty to another, trying to be a perfect mother and wife, a perfect house „manager," and a perfect leader. Having support from others, I became a master of delegation, both at work and at home, but the speed of my life was exhausting.

A few years before, I felt I had it all. I would have laughed with some arrogance if somebody had come to me with the idea of growth and development. I had been the expert, knowing perfectly well how to be a leader, how to raise children and manage life in general. At work, it had been expected of me to have the knowledge and to give answers and solutions. I wasn't supposed to have doubts, and if they had come, I would have stepped straight into task-and-solution mode to resolve issues. I was applying that also at home. Even when one of my sons got sick with diabetes, I cried for only one day, and then, together with my husband, moved on to organizing our family life as smoothly and efficiently as usual.

So here I was, sitting in the office and working on yet another annual budget when the thought came to me -- I could not stand it anymore. I realized that my job was not only boring me but also draining my energy. Was this how my life was going to be? Torn between the job I once had liked and the family I loved, but not feeling joy or satisfaction in either? Stuck in an obvious scenario, having a husband, having children, having a job in a company that was paying my monthly salary, I felt suffocated. Even my dreams started to mirror my state. I was waking up in the middle of the night sitting straight up and gasping for air. A tsunami was coming at me, and I couldn't move, being aware that in a second, it would cover me and I would drown. I knew I shouldn't have complained. I was lucky -- my husband loved me, my kids and the house were taken care of for me, and my corporate career was on a good track. I could not figure out what was bothering me. I was just beginning to wonder: Was I living according to my own scenario, or according to something that I believed was expected of me by society? I now see that what was missing was my own purpose, the feeling of the greater sense in my life.

This new awareness was building up in me, but I did not really know where it was leading. Should I change my job, change companies? If so, wouldn't I be complaining about the same in a year's time? I started looking around with more curiosity and observing how other people lived their lives, how they worked. I picked up books and newspapers that I had never bought before. I was looking for inspiration, and most of all, I was looking for what might be calling me. I was waiting for a faster beat of my heart.

In that research, I came across a training program on coaching. It was a new topic for me, the program was led by a major American coaching school, and its next edition was soon to begin in Warsaw. I decided to check it out. The course was designed around the Co-Active coaching model, teaching the participants the art of coaching with the idea behind it that the skills acquired there could be used anywhere, in personal issues, management development, career planning, and more. To my surprise, already after the first module, I knew that was what I wanted to start doing! I didn't know how or when. Deep in my heart, I just knew I wanted to finish this course and become a coach. For the next half a year, I was learning and practicing new skills. I was observing the impact of that approach on the people who had agreed to be my coaching clients (coachees), and I was thrilled. Our coaching conversations were having an immediate and visible influence on how people felt and what they were deciding to do differently. I was feeling great satisfaction from these conversations and was happy to be a part of these changes.

Moreover, during the coaching training program, I was going through my own internal awareness-building process. I didn't remember any time before when I spent this amount of time reflecting on my values, strong and weak sides, vision, purpose, and my own needs. By the end of the training, I knew I had found my new path. I just didn't know how to follow it. I felt both the excitement connected to it and the fear of moving into the unknown. I was declaring I would become a coach and start my own business, yet I wasn't even planning on going to register it. The voice in my head was murmuring constantly how difficult it must be to set up a business, or that one should only do it after finding a perfect name for one's company. This voice was almost shouting that it was not safe to leave the corporate life and hope to earn the living on my own. I was creating obstacles like: I had never had a private car, computer or a phone – how would I take care of them, without any help desk? My strategy was: Let's wait and see. Somehow, I would figure it out. Maybe the following month…

And then somebody gave me the challenge: "Set up your business by the end of the year." It was November 2007. There was little time to dwell on it. I was offered some guidance in the legal aspects of starting my own business, I was recommended an accountant who could take care of the financials, and as simple as that, I registered a company called Phenomenon.

Of course, doing that turned out to be much easier than I had imagined. The difficult part was to quit my corporate job and focus on my new business. My husband, who had been supporting me constantly during this decision-making process, asked me a relevant question that, unfortunately, had stopped me for weeks: „Did you make a business plan?" I didn't do it, I didn't know how to do it, and it terrified me! Thinking about money was pulling me away from becoming an entrepreneur. I wanted to be a coach; I didn't want to be a business owner. It seemed to me, though, that I had no other way. I felt so much excitement and satisfaction when coaching that I couldn't stand coming to the office anymore. My heart was shouting: Take the leap! Yet, the saboteur inside my head was saying: "You are not ready!"

Luckily, life itself took the lead. My company was reducing the headcount, and as a consequence, I was supposed to lay off my co-worker and do a bigger scope of work myself, including topics I really did not like. I took it as a sign and decided to terminate my own contract. After several weeks of negotiating the conditions of the termination, I found myself sheepishly smiling over the letter with the final offer. Apart from the financial parachute, I agreed with my employer that for half a year after I left the company, I would be supporting them as a coach. That made my landing in self-employment much softer, as I could look out for my new business clients with some security net from my previous work.

After starting my own business, I swayed from the state of ecstasy to panic. It felt amazing when I realized I was stepping on a totally new path that felt just right. It was much worse when my beliefs about work were breaking through this great feeling. In my head, work was connected to certain rules: work should be hard; work had to be done from morning to evening (at least 9 am to 5 pm); salaries were paid regularly (a bank account got larger at the end of every month, and the amount of money one received was predictable). In my new business, none of that was true. My calendar was not full, so I probably wasn't working hard enough. I did not issue a lot of large invoices every month, so my bank account was not filling up quickly enough. I felt guilty, when I started my working day at 10 am, after indulging myself with a breakfast at the table, with a good book.

To survive in this state of uncertainty, I started to learn. I was reading every book, listening to every lecture and attending every course that offered the upgrade of my skills or could build my awareness of living this new life. Anything that would help me deal with feeling uncomfortable when nobody was calling or when a potential client was choosing another coach. How to grow stronger, when I believed I was getting smaller? I could go through this period, thanks to my belief that I was on the right path and that I found the work I was happy to be doing. All I needed was practice, so I was searching for every opportunity to coach individuals and teams. At that time my life was far from perfect, yet, deep inside, I felt the power to move through all obstacles.

As a task-oriented person, I decided to treat this stage of my business life as a case to solve. One of the ideas was that doing something that strengthens me, even for free, was better than doing nothing at all. Also, doing it together with a partner, who needed practice and clients just as I did, made me feel that I was not alone in this dark time. Therefore, I paired up with a coach who had completed the same coaching education as I, and together, we started offering our services and sharing our knowledge in different places. We prepared a two-hour workshop on the topic of New Year's goal-setting for the local chapter of a coaching organization. We asked an organization bringing together professional women whether their members would benefit from a workshop on career-progress planning. Wherever possible, we were delivering short workshops, offering valuable support to the participants, but not earning any money. We called it sowing, with the hope of harvesting the results sometime in the future. Actually, it paid off: one contact returned to me even two years later, and we had fruitful cooperation after that. I was involved in several individual and team coaching processes in her company.

I never considered myself very creative. Yet, in the need to design my own job, I was eager to try anything connected with my new skills. Talking with my coaching partner about what was exciting for us, we decided it was supporting women. As a result, we developed -- created! -- a workshop that we called „The Alchemy of Change for Women." We led women through five two-hour meetings filled with activities that allowed the participants to experience and reflect on their beliefs, dreams, and plans related to the change they wanted to have in their lives. We ran several editions of this workshop, and the work gave us not only satisfaction but also confidence that we could develop something from scratch and make a difference through what we did. I was getting practice and, as a result, self-confidence.

Slowing down in order to speed up

Several years passed, and I was growing my belief in my abilities, my new skills, and the value of my work. My business was growing, new clients were calling, interesting projects were coming my way. I was engaged with multinational companies, coaching their leaders and teams. I could observe my progress, and I was proud of it. I had the opportunity to begin a cooperation with an international consulting company that was focused on developing leaders. Its founders believed that in order to become an authentic and powerful leader, one must start from building awareness about self. I fully agreed with that and therefore continued my own learning. Life was full of challenges, full of activities, and full of work. I wanted it all. I was hungry for new experiences, new projects, and new adventures. All of a sudden, I realized, I was running again. I was doing what I loved, but in every conversation, I was complaining about how busy I was. As a self-employed person, my assumption was that my responsibility was not only for working but also for taking bigger care of my family. I was often working at home, so for my children, it meant I was more available. It was my duty to be at their disposal, to drive them, to help them when they needed something for school, or to take care of some house duties. In my opinion, just because I didn't have a 9-to-5 job, meant that I was the one to serve others in the role of „doing it all." It very quickly led to situations when I would work late in the evenings because I was busy doing other duties during the day. My husband was asking me whether this was not a sign of workaholism. In my opinion, I was simply not devoting enough time to work during the day! I was back to the state when I couldn't catch my breath. I realized something was wrong when I stopped reading books, the activity that I loved most of all. Even the coaching work began to lose its freshness, and I started doubting whether I was on the right path.

And then one month came when my calendar was empty. There were no meetings with potential clients, no workshops, no coaching sessions. Nothing. I had been so busy with the current business that I had not noticed that the pipeline was getting empty. It was December, almost the perfect time to slow down. I could use this time to reflect on the passing year, to prepare for Christmas, spend some time at home, and finally read books that had piled up over time. I was looking at that month with curiosity, saying aloud: "I am not issuing any invoices this month!" That was a weird feeling, almost scary. I was taking a perverse pleasure in announcing to everybody that this month was empty. When I was asked to run a half-day of team coaching at the end of the month, I moved it to January, just to be able to say: no business for one month!

December, being a special month, passed quickly, and when my calendar remained almost empty in January and February, I started to feel uncomfortable. I was beginning to feel desperate for work, wondering whom I should call, what I should do, where I should turn. I was getting tense, both physically and mentally. Rationally, I had money, I was safe, nobody expected me to deliver. Yet, in my eyes, I wasn't doing anything important! I wasn't earning any money (a vital element in my life), I wasn't bringing any value to clients, I actually wasn't doing anything I would consider valuable. I just could not enjoy the time for my pleasure, as I started to worry that the world would forget about me if I were not active and visible out there. I was beginning to feel worthless, like I wasn't needed in the business area. I wasn't desperately needed at home, either (everything was arranged in the house to be taken care of so that my husband and I could work). Actually, my responsibility was to take care of myself, to drive kids home from school, and to look for new clients. I realized that I was measuring my success and my self-worth with the number of clients I had and with the number of invoices I issued every month. Here I was at home, taking on the duties I did not like, or consider valuable, and missing being busy with work. I could almost hear the Universe giggling at me and whispering, "You wanted more time for reading, so here you are – enjoy! You were not sure whether coaching is your path, so here you are. This is your time to think what is!" Still, instead of accepting the time "offered" to me by the Universe, I was seeing this period as a test of my ability to be successful on my terms!

I was pretending to be taking it lightly, but the panic was slowly crawling up my back. I had the memory of that feeling from several years back when I had just started my own business. The uncertainty of getting new clients, the feelings of rejection when not being chosen for a project. Generally, feeling powerless. I thought I was over this stage the last time. It seemed like I needed to find new sense in what I was doing in my life.

It all led me to the Emergency Room one day in February, with the diagnosis of coronary disease. After spending a week in a hospital, among patients in their 80s, I returned home with a surprised expression on my face. I was not invincible! Nothing in my earlier medical checkups presaged that. My test results were always perfect! This incident forced me to stop and look at myself from a new perspective. I started asking myself new questions: What was my body telling me? Why did I end up in the hospital? I noticed that the answers to these questions were much clearer to me when I was in nature, so during daily walks with my dog in "my" forest, I started my conversations with the Universe. Soon I realized what the lesson that I was getting through this event in my life was about. First, I needed to slow down both physically and mentally. Every day I was focusing on walking slower, on breathing deeper, on observing my surroundings, listening to the sounds. Most of all, I was reflecting on my self-worth without the connection to my business and, especially, without the comparison to businesses that others were creating. We live in a society that has some rules, some expectations. I wanted to clearly define which of the rules that I lived by were mine and which were society´s. I started questioning those that I realized did not serve me. Surprisingly, the world did not turn against me! In all of that, I was lucky to always have the full support, love, and acceptance of my husband, my children, and my parents.

I believe that learning is not a linear process. It is more like a spiral: our life lessons return to us time after time, but they come at a different level. It is as if the Universe is testing us and asking, "Have you really got that lesson?" Sometimes, when we believe we have, our life takes an unexpected turn and we face the same situation, but in a new disguise. In my case, I had to go through surgery to hear my heart calling again. I realized I had been running to fulfill my ego's wish for success -- plenty of clients and invoices -- pushed by the fear that without them, I would not be considered worthy. My heart forced me to slow down so that I could start with a bigger speed from a new level of awareness.

Living my dream, dreaming my life

I looked at my work with curiosity. I wanted to check again what was giving me joy and satisfaction. I really wanted to phrase my purpose, my soul mission, a statement that would remind me why I was doing what I chose to do. I participated in trainings (some of them, like writing or painting, out of the coaching field); I read books (more in the topic of spirituality); I listened to lectures. I was taking inspiration from others, but I also realized that I needed to listen to myself on a deeper level. It took me almost a year to capture the statement that felt true to my soul. When I said it aloud, I felt my heart expanding and shivers going through my body. I just knew that I was here to Bring the Best Out of People.

The simplicity of this purpose struck me. I realized that if I followed my purpose fully, my life would be truly meaningful. My purpose was not to grow my business; it was to bring the best out of my clients. It was not to issue invoices for team coaching processes; it was to bring the best out of the members of these teams so that their work was easier and more fulfilling. My purpose was not to show my value to my business partners; it was to bring the best out of them in our co-operation. My purpose was not to bring my children up but to relate to them in a way that would bring the best out of them and prepare them to bravely step into their adulthood. And, finally, my purpose was not to prove that I was right when talking to my husband but to bring the best out of him in our love and home.

I learned to ask myself questions that were leading to answers I needed to get in order to grow. More importantly, I learned to slow down in order to hear the responses. Questions like: "When would I allow myself to live slower? What would I love to be doing in my free time? What would I need to achieve in order to feel I deserved this free time? And most of all – what were my dreams for work, free time, and generally life?"

What is different now? I don't struggle. I don't fight. When I see the issue or I encounter a problem, I manage not to get emotionally sucked in by it. I look at it from a perspective, as if from a balcony. I check what is there, what is bothering me, which values are being stepped on. I wonder what I am frustrated about and check my inner feeling, which allows me later to address the issue with the parties involved. I consider my emotions my companion in making good decisions about what I choose as important for me in the way I live my life.

I am now said to be a good salesperson of my projects. When I meet my clients, I concentrate on their needs, worries, and dreams. When I do that, the sale just happens because it is not about selling anymore. It is about support, about seeing whether I am the person who is the best for them at this moment. At the beginning of my self-employment, I was concentrated on myself, on how I talk, what I say, whether they choose me. Now it is about them.

On the other hand, I check with myself whether a project is good for me. When I do not feel the excitement, or I cannot see how I could bring the best out of potential clients, I help the client find a partner that would suit them better. This means that I take on projects that are in line with my dreams of developing powerful leaders and teams who want to excel, as well as teaching coaching skills. Therefore, more projects like that come to me, as if I were attracting them.

I am grateful for my life. All highs and lows were crucial in creating me the way I am at today. I fully embrace the saying, "You never know what is good and what is bad," as I see now how many good things in my life emerged after what I considered a difficult time. What seemed to be the painfully slow period of my life, actually was the time that prepared me for moving forward with the new understanding of the meaning of my life. Life had to get slower for me to notice subtle signs of my heart beating faster at what excited me.

Most of the time, I am peaceful with myself; I consider myself happy -- not ecstatic, but stable, fulfilled, excited about what is unknown ahead of me. It means doing what I love doing, as well as accepting doing what needs to be done, being able to look for new experience, developing new areas of business, growing professionally and spiritually.

The lesson of living a life without being constantly busy returns to me now and then, as if the Universe is testing me. I still catch myself at filling my calendar to the limits and later being frustrated about it. I also notice that I compare my business activities to the activities of other coaches and coaching companies. When I see their successful projects, interesting articles, or valuable initiatives, I sometimes wonder, why I haven't done things like that. Was it lack of courage, or maybe laziness? I hope I will have enough opportunities in my life to go through these lessons and do my homework!

As for life purpose, stating it is not a one-time exercise. There were moments of small enlightenments in my life when I was noticing elements of it. Every new form of my purpose was forming on something I had learned before. What I call my purpose now may not be its final version, and I need to stay alert to new versions that might be showing up. That requires listening from the heart and being courageous to step into new paths that are unfolding. In my case, this courage comes from following my heart.

Monika Jankowska

Leadership Coach at Lead InNow

Monika Jankowska is an executive and a team coach passionate about growing leaders.

She works with clients who want to transition from transactional to transformational management style in response to the challenges of the changing market. She combines her business experience (seventeen years in international organizations) with knowledge of up-to-date trends in leadership development (Leadership 4.0). Her coaching is aimed at building the self-awareness of leaders who as a result make courageous choices in their businesses and lives.

Monika started her company called Phenomenon in 2007. Since 2014 she has also been a Fellow in Oxford Leadership, a consultancy company focusing on aligning people to strategy in organizations. With them, she leads leadership journeys based on the Self Managing Leadership model. As an Associate with Heidrick Consulting, she co-leads leadership and coaching programs. Monika is involved in Up2You, a start-up organization providing personalized online coaching processes designed to grow self-aware leaders.

monika.jankowska@oxfordleadership.com
monika.jankowska@phenomenon.com.pl

From Cell To Soul – From A Molecular Scientist To A Psychologist And Leadership Coach

by Shuntian Yao

You never know when a life-changing moment is approaching.

From an outsider's point of view, I was at the top of the world in 1994. After graduating from Beijing University, one of the best universities in China, with a bachelor of science degree in biochemistry and working in the university as a teacher for two years, I was admitted to Harvard University's School of Public Health as a major in molecular and cellular toxicology. Harvard waived my tuition (which was enormous) and even gave me a stipend for five and a half years to focus on my PhD studies. I had survived an extreme "ordeal" of heavy-duty study, lab experiments and papers, and so forth, and I had settled down in school. I thought I would go on with my dream to be a scientist, discovering the secrets of human cells and making changes in human history as my childhood role model Madame Curie had done. I was working with ovarian cancer genes and trying to find new solutions.

Suddenly a new light dawned on me

I used to be very interested in Zen back in China, and at the beginning of 1994, I was thinking of doing some Zen meditation to clear my mind and have more self-reflection and insights. So, in the Boston Yellow Pages I found an organization teaching meditation for free: Brahma Kumaris Meditation Center. In the first class, they told me, "You are a soul, eternal, and originally perfect." That hit home suddenly.

For every drastic change, there is a foreshadowing

I remembered the first time I encountered death in the family. I was still a teenager when my grandmother passed away. I remember going to the crematorium for the first time, watching the smoke coming out of the chimney from the incinerator. The young me had this big puzzle in my mind: "All humans will die one day! I cannot believe it. I am so young and happy and enjoying life now, but also one day, I will totally disappear from this world!" I didn't tell anybody about my thoughts at that time, but I knew that experience had a big impact on me. I remember I used to study very well at school, and one teacher invited me to share with her students why I was always top in the class. I said to her students, "You know why? Because one day, I will die! I have to study well before that!"

Another thing is that whenever people used to ask me about the aim of my life, I would always answer, "Perfection, Eternity, and Harmony." Some people would say, "How can all of that be possible?!" I wouldn't even try to explain to such people, I would just say in my heart, "I don't care about you, I know it's possible."

The "aha" moment

In a small room at the BK meditation center on Beacon Street in Brookline, Massachusetts, I heard, "You are an eternal soul, and originally you are perfect!" It echoed in my heart, and every wish suddenly became clear! "Yes, I am an eternal soul, the body dies, but the soul is eternal and will never die, it will just change costumes as an actor changes costumes or a driver changes a car." Then, those teenaged thoughts about me disappearing from the world suddenly cleared out. And, originally, it was perfect! That's why I was feeling it, wanting it before, and I will definitely reach it someday! At that moment, I felt all my yearnings and pursuits made sense; even the future became clear! I was so thirsty for spiritual study that, except for my scientific studies at Harvard, I spent all my time in more spiritual exploration and practice.

Back to the source

I remember my father, who teaches at the Beijing University of Aeronautics and Astronautics, and who was one of the first people to study missiles in China. He used to tell me about how missiles would be accurately launched into space at extremely accurate times, down to microseconds. Human beings had mastered the vastness of space at such a macrolevel!

I was studying genetic engineering in the 1990s and was trying to find the specific genes for ovarian cancer, working to create an antibody to it. The plan was to attach medicine to the gene and target and kill specific cancer cells. Human beings have also mastered the human body at such a microlevel!

I said to myself, "Ultimately, the only thing that human beings cannot master would be themselves! Science, technology, arts, and so on, are all created by human beings. Ultimately, we will come back to ourselves, the creator! So, I should definitely work on human souls instead of human cells!"

By the time I reached my third year at Harvard, I was totally mesmerized by the beauty of the soul, and I was doing meditation to experiment with the different aspects of the soul as if a scientist were doing scientific research. Gradually, I found I no longer had any interest and passion in studying cells and genes in the lab anymore.

The drastic change

By 1996, I couldn't bear reading scientific papers and doing experiments in labs anymore. I made a decision to quit Harvard and change my area to study human beings! My spiritual teacher, Dadi Janki (who was 103 years old in 2019), advised me that if not a PhD, at least get a master's degree instead of quitting totally as I wanted. (It turned out that an MS degree from Harvard would become extremely useful and helpful for my later career.) So, I got my master's degree, left Harvard, and worked at Dana Farber Cancer Institute and a genetic engineering company afterward. In May 1999, I decide to go back to China.

From "somebody" to "nobody"

Yes! I was back in Beijing for my dream! It is one thing to be heated and make a decision, yet totally another thing to carry on and make it a reality! The cost of that decision is that I had to start all over again at thirty years of age. All my past pride for going to Harvard, studying top science, and so forth were useless. I had to start in a totally new area. It was really an experience of "from somebody to nobody!" I wanted to work on human souls, but my spiritual study and practice took time, and all its services to the community are free of charge. I didn't even know how I could earn a living.

I finally settled on my new profession, but it took ten years! In between, I was working as assistant general manager and in e-commerce at a friend's company. (Not really e-commerce like now, the Internet just emerged then; I was there just because my English was good.) I have worked in Women Manners School; been a human resources manager in a media company, and a trainer and consultant for a US company and foreign enterprise, and so forth. I tried to have every possible opportunity to support myself.

What's even harder is that none of my parents, friends, relatives, and former classmates understood me and supported me with this big change. They all thought I was crazy to quit the Harvard PhD program and drop the Green Card application that was already in the Immigration Bureau, and then to start to do something with the intangible "soul"! I still remember how my father, who had so much hope in me and saved money for me to get a ticket to the United States in 1992, tried in every way to persuade me not to leave the United States. When he knew he couldn't convince me, he even hit his own head with his fist because he was so worried; he loved me so much. That was a nightmare, and the hardest thing that I had to endure during this change because on the one hand I love them, and on the other hand, I felt my mission calling me.

I remember one day after I went back to China, I was feeling really frustrated, not knowing where to go and what to do next. After staying at home for a long time, I decided to go out for a walk. And I saw some big yulan (magnolia) flowers coming out of the dry branches. I almost had tears in my eyes. I told myself, "In winter, they only have dry branches, and there is no sign of blossom at all. But it knows it's yulan, and it will blossom one day. I myself am the same. It might seem that I have nothing right now, but I know what I am and what I have, and one day, I will also blossom!"

The long journey up to today

To cut a long story short, for the next ten years, I was trying to find a new way out. I received training in Transformational Leadership: Advanced Executive Coaching from the Satir Institute of the Pacific & The Satir Learning & Development Center of China, certified as an NLP practitioner by Hong Kong Professional Effective Management Institute, and certified for 4D-system trainer and coach for executive and team development. I also went everywhere I could: the UK, Canada, Italy, Spain, Russia, Belgium, India, Germany, France, Holland, and so on, to learn self-managing leadership, leadership journey, psychology, relationship counseling, family constellation, organizational constellation, body-mind healing, energy work, touch therapy, spiritual practice, and other skills.

Gradually, I found myself well settled in developing leaders and organizations through psychology/leadership training and coaching. I have worked with many top-level international companies and amazing Chinese companies, including Ericsson China, Akzo Nobel, Infiniti, Embraco, Bank of China, Sino Steel, China Unicom, China Film Group, MSC, TUV, Schneider, Servier, Novo Nordisk, Lufthansa, L'Oreal, Fiskars, cTrip, Baidu, Sina, Haier, Levono, Alibaba, JD, Innovation Works, etc.

I also do workshops in personal growth, family therapy, relationships, healing, energy adjustment, and meditation. With all this background and training, I hope to support leaders to be whole and complete, so that they don't just have success in work but are also healthy in body and happy in relationships. Over twenty years of continuous learning, practicing, and experiencing have given me special depth and width to work with different people at different levels of needs and introducing deep transformation.

Happy ever after

Many friends have asked me, "Have you ever regretted that you quit Harvard, changed your area of study and started working with human beings?"

- Never ever. I felt proud of my courage and persistence. And nothing rewards me more than doing the things I love and believe in, every single day of my life.

Some friends also asked, "Then whatever you studied at Beijing University and Harvard University were all wasted."

- Not at all. The science training I had before gave me a strong mind in logic, reasoning, and systematic thinking. But meditation practice and deep understanding of human emotions, relationship lineages, and energy helped me to understand "emotional logic" and the more intangible part of me. I feel complete with both sides, and I feel so free to be able to switch to either world.

I have been back in China for exactly twenty years. Yesterday, I happened to pass by the first apartment I lived in after I returned to China in 1999, and all the past memories and feelings came back. I remembered the yulan tree that inspired me. I can see my flower blossoming now.

I will end my story with a poem that I wrote when I first began the spiritual study in 1994, which expressed the ecstasy that I was experiencing at that time. I am glad that I decided to work with the most amazing creator of the world: human beings. All energies spent on the source will never get wasted.

The Beautiful Source of Life （美丽的生命之源）
美丽的生命之源
美丽的生命之泉
我创造，我舞蹈
我歌唱，我欢笑
所有的快乐在这里
所有的欣喜在这里

The beautiful source of life
The beautiful fountain of life
I create, I dance
I sing, I laugh
Here is all the happiness
And all the bliss

Heartfelt appreciation and gratitude

I contribute this story to my dearest parents, who raised me with such love and trust, who tolerated my unbelievable "craziness." About ten years after I changed my profession, they started to see how happy and joyful I was doing the work I love and how many were benefiting because of me. Now I work internationally, and I hope my father, who has since passed away, and my elderly mother are settled with happiness that their daughter made the right decision, and this will benefit both her and many others in the world.

I also feel deeply grateful to all my teachers, friends, close ones, and amazing colleagues at Oxford Leadership who supported me, loved me, cared about me, and nurtured me along this journey, plus all of my clients and working companions who gave me the chance to progress and contribute, who opened their hearts to allow me to enter and to leave a tiny impact in a deeper space.

Finally, I thank myself. I couldn't believe that I made such a huge decision in such a clear and determined way, that I never wavered, but just cultivated my dream until it blossomed. I feel so blessed to be able to merge that passion and bliss in every moment of my life.

Shuntian Yao

*Co-Founder and Chief Trainer at
Beijing Soulight Cultural Communication Ltd. Co.*

Ms. Yao provides training and coaching to empower leaders/teams to reach a high level of awareness, energy, alignment, and excellence. She also provides services in personal growth, family therapy, relationship workshops, body-mind healing workshops, energy adjustment, and meditation as a holistic approach for different people with different levels of needs and enables deep transformation and integration. Besides working with famous Chinese enterprises, she has also trained and coached high-level executives/teams from many APAC and European countries. Seeing everyone connecting to their core and shining to the best extent possible gives her great joy and satisfaction. Ms. Yao is bilingual (English and native mandarin).

WeChat China: 天光Sakash.
shuntian.yao@oxfordleadership.com

River Of Life

by Simone Alz

My story is like a river with many bends and turns, little ones and big ones. Sometimes, my life has felt like wild water rafting, sometimes like surfing in a flow and synchronicity, sometimes like drowning or paddling against currents, trying to catch my breath.

I learned how to swim, at least. Floating with the stream makes it easier. Going against it is hard. Yet how does one figure out what is with, and what against?

I didn't experience some kind of awakening, a big bang, one striking midlife crisis. I didn't all of a sudden wake up with the question, "What is my purpose?"

Rather the question for me was, "Why do I do what I do?" This was ingrained in my life and my decisions ever since I can remember.

Kids don't stop asking, "Why?" and I have never stopped asking, even today.

So, here is my story:

I actually have to start when I was a teenager. I had that dream in those days. Whenever I was running, when I was walking, whenever I had a moment to dream, I saw myself sitting at a big round table with politicians signing a peace agreement. It could have been politicians from Palestine and Israel in that picture, or Russia and the United States during the Cold War: those were the days. I was sitting with them at the table while they signed, and it felt great. I wasn't really aware of what my role was, perhaps something around mediation, or something about being a bridge between the conflicting partners at the time. At that young age, already I was looking for meaning. Something that would be meaningful to me and give me a feeling of joy, peace, love, being here for something bigger than myself.

There were no big choices to make during my school years; life felt safe and easy with good friends, parties, and sports. The first real decision to make was what to study after graduation. I went for medicine. It seemed like a good idea, and in particular, my parents thought it was a great idea. I wonder if that was actually the main influence. Nevertheless, I believed it was meaningful to study medicine: you can work anywhere on the planet, you can do something good for people, and helping people means reducing suffering. The reality was that during the first semesters of studying medicine, I realized that the style of learning didn't resonate with me. All input was mere facts: information about biochemistry, physics, anatomy, and so on, not connected, and my ingrained need of answering the question of "Why" wasn't satisfied at all. Of course, that changed later during my studies and for sure would be different working as a medical doctor. Yet during the first semesters, I had to push hard, and my frustration increased. The prospect of helping people felt eons away.

Working in hospitals didn't change my experience for the better. The sense and smell of physical pain got to me; I couldn't handle it well. Instead of feeling empowered to help, I felt helpless.

Watching my fellow students, my feeling of being in the wrong place increased. They seemed to be more at ease, more confident, prouder to be there. It was the first time I thought about the concept of "place of best use." No matter if I rationally think it is a great job, is it the place of best use for me? Can I be and give my best? Can others do a better job?

The answer -- "this is not for me" -- got clearer and clearer.

The magic moments I take from these days are witnessing babies being born. So beautiful. Magic, indeed. When a doctor said, "Welcome to the world," it brought tears to my eyes. Pure life at its best.
So, what now? What is my place of best use?

We had one psychology class that really resonated with me. I loved that particular course. The analysis of psychological illnesses was pretty basic then, yet it lit a spark of curiosity and engagement in me.

I made a choice: I left medical studies and switched over to psychology. Some people thought I was crazy (especially my parents). The reputation of psychology was still somewhat negative, less worthy for sure than medicine, and with a connotation of "only weird people study that." Against all odds, I did it.

Some years later, I received my master's degree in psychology. There wasn't a day of regret in all those years. It was the right choice. The way of thinking, of asking questions, of analyzing in the field of psychology is so me. I could ask, "Why?" all along the way.

I majored in work and clinical psychology, not completely clear about where I would end up with it. Yet, I didn't really have to think that through because toward the second half of my studies, I got a call from a friend who was working as an executive assistant in an IT consultant firm. My friend said, "Hey, we are hiring talented people and there's a program called 'Get the Best.' Why don't you apply? And if they take you, I get money."

I wondered if she believed I had talent, or if she was up only for the money. Even more so, I was wondering why on earth I should be an IT consultant. In those days, I was still bathing in the "saving the planet" arrogance, and being a consultant seemed a remote aspiration from that.

She put forth a lot of arguments: "It's good money, good learning, a cool experience, and I will write your CV and take care of all the paperwork." I guess the learning and no hassle with the process convinced me to say "Yes." Not long afterward, I found myself in an assessment center in Frankfurt wearing the first of many business suits to come.

I passed and ended up with a really attractive contract in my hand. Baffled, I asked the hiring manager why they wanted me in their company. After all, I was a hippie type, the wanting-to-save-the-world kind of person. Besides I didn't even know what the World Wide Web was, I had no computer, no IT skills... and to become an IT consultant?

He didn't bother much with the answer: "We can train you." I said "Yes." It was tempting to be trained in something about which I had no clue. Learning and personal growth were and are very high on my list of what gives meaning to me.

The start was hilarious. During the first week, I ruined a computer by putting a floppy disk in the CD ROM slot (young people reading this might wonder what I am talking about). So funny. My learning curve was steep. It was great to have so many talented people around me. A totally new world. Flying around. Meeting zillions of people. Learning and learning.

During a training in Chicago, I went to a bar with my peers, and I shared my dreams of having a positive impact on the world, wanting to make this world a better place. We were laughing (and drinking). They called me "Recruiting Error" -- a hippie in the business world. We ended the night by betting on me being a United Nations employee on a mission by 2004. I couldn't think of any other organization more in line with my ethics, values, and dreams. I won the bet, but that comes later.

After a couple of years, my learning curve flattened. Similar projects, processes, topics. The repetition caused a voice in my head to become louder: "Move on!"

The economic crisis hit and led me to an easy way out. We were offered to take a flexible leave: we could take off three to twelve months, still getting one-third of our salary. The only obligation: we had to come back within twenty-four hours if we were needed. I think I was the first one who called human resources to go for the twelve-month option.

I put all my stuff in storage. Packed my backpack and left for Central America with my best friend. Up for: Freedom. Adventure. Independence. Self-determination.

We were so happy, excited to have months ahead with no restrictions, no fixed agenda. Our plan was to start in Mexico City and make our way down to Costa Rica, and we promised ourselves to not miss a single beautiful beach along the way. Paradise.

We had no fixed agendas, yet I had a hidden one: Not to come back.

Plan A was to look out for social projects along the way. Maybe there would be options for me to engage in. Plan B was to make a living as a diving instructor (with the little detail of not being qualified yet). And there was the thought of combining A and B: Making a living at the beach and engaging in meaningful projects alongside.

We found the perfect place to go for the missing diving training: Roatan, an island of Honduras. I convinced my friend to stay long enough for me to sign up for the rescue and master diving classes. So far, so good.

Until the river of life showed me otherwise. I had a diving accident. In a rescue training setup, I dislocated my shoulder. Being under water, in a wetsuit and far away from help, it took hours to rescue me from the situation. The shoulder was ruined. Plan A, Plan B, and my hidden agenda to not come back were ruined with it. And the end of diving, surfing, beach volleyball… I ended up having surgery back home and needed months of recovery to use my arm again.

While recovering, I got a note from a friend. He had seen an ad by the foreign ministry looking for young professionals to be sent to the United Nations. I applied, of course.

I remember sitting in the garden with my mom saying, "If I get the job, I will be the happiest person on the planet." I got it, and I was indeed the happiest person on the planet.

A few months later, I sat on a plane to New York to start my job as Associate Expert with the Department of Economic and Social Affairs. The next adventure.

And I won the bet. It was in 2002. Who would have guessed?

To me, it felt like meaning was inherent in that organization. Wasn't the whole UN created to make this world a better place? I loved it. My learning curve was high again. I met fantastic people. And we had tons of fun in Manhattan. What a gift to be part of this world. My day-to-day job turned out to be somewhat bureaucratic, though. Despite the overarching meaning of the whole organization, I didn't feel in the best spot to apply my skills. The question "Am I in the place of best use?" came up again.

When the opportunity arose after a couple of years to move to Rome and work for the World Food Programme (WFP), I took it. One of the best decisions in my life, I would say.

WFP is a front-end, emergency agency of the UN family. It felt much faster. On the spot. Its purpose right in front of me. I remember one magic moment flying in a helicopter across the Sudan. Looking down onto the savanna with tears in my eyes, deeply touched. What a gift to be able to work here. To be paid for a job that is so close to my heart. To be paid to travel to all these places. It didn't feel like a job. It truly felt like being on a mission. No doubt about purpose. Inherent. In my face.

Another important learning happened during the same mission.

I was assigned to visit a UN camp in South Sudan where living conditions were almost humanly unbearable. Landing in the middle of nowhere, it became apparent to me that we had no place to sleep, the little clay houses being unusable since they were besieged by thousands of bats. What to do? The two emergency workers on the ground proved their flexibility, setting up beds under the open sky, covered by mosquito nets only.

The night approaching, I started to feel more and more uneasy. After all, I was in the desert with two men I had never met before plus two local guards walking around with guns to protect us. Not to forget there was a brutal war going on just outside of the wooden fence of the camp.

I lied down on the bed, seeing only shadows of the guards circling around me in the pitch dark, sometimes their flashlights checking out the camp area.

I took a deep breath while looking at the limitless sky. The most beautiful sky I have ever seen. No cloud in the way and no electric light disturbing the vastness of the universe.

I told myself there was nothing, absolutely nothing I can do. I had no control over that situation. That very moment I just decided to feel safe and protected. By the men around me. By the fence across from me. By the stars above me. I realized and felt that trusting can be a choice -- independent of the circumstances. I slept deeply and soundly.

Life got even better during this period of time. I fell in love. I met a German lawyer on one of my home visits, and we became a couple. He moved in with me, and life was perfect. Rome was followed by New York again, where I had another assignment.

While we were living in Manhattan together, he got a call, a job offer in Munich. A great opportunity for his career.

That moment I probably took the most untypical and radical decision ever; I left my career to follow him. Several values were driving that choice. Fairness: He supported my career, so I will support his. Family and friends: I would be closer to loved ones at home. Our intention to have a family of our own. The timing was perfect. In my mind, it was the absolute right decision. Strangely, it didn't feel right, which I stubbornly ignored.

We didn't last long back in our home country. We were a good couple in my world. We were not good together in his. The breakup was bad. Very bad. I was too exhausted to leave and resume my old life. The river of life had carried me here, so I stayed. I was lucky to find a great job as head of people and organizational development in a semiconductor company. Kind of back to the roots. Back to business. It helped me to pull myself back together. It was my first global leadership position, and I loved being responsible for an international team, being in charge of the learning and development of the company.

Before I could become complacent or ask myself my favorite question again, if I was still in "the place of best use," the company went bankrupt. No decision to make. I learned what it meant to close a company and let go of thousands of employees. Huge learning that I hope I don't need to experience again.

A completely different thought came up during that time. I could hear my dad's voice in my head. He kept saying, "You can't work for anyone. You never did and will never do what others say." Well, yes. They were poor supervisors who had to cope with me.

In 2009, I created my own business and have worked as a leadership coach and consultant ever since. I was introduced to Oxford Leadership the same year, and I joined this great network of passionate people. What a gift. I can choose what I do; each and every day is a free choice. Accompanying leaders on parts of their life's journey and asking them about their "Why?" is meaningful and fulfilling to me. It feels like I do what I always loved: being in conversations with people. My friends used to say, "Give her a chair and a person to talk to, then she is happy." So true. Deep conversations absorb me; I love to listen to people's stories, motives, dreams, aspirations, I love to stay with them wondering, laughing, crying, and creating. With curiosity and in the spirit of exploration, time and time again, I am fascinated.

I have to admit that a hidden agenda is driving me also: I believe that leaders who are connected to their purpose can make a huge difference, purpose guiding them to use their power wisely. I am in the second row now, serving my clients, supporting the creation of healthy teams, striking strategies, working for sustainable solutions, and fulfilling lives.

This kind of work also demands a lot of me. It takes energy to "swing" with the clients, stay focused 100%, and hold a container for people in which they can create. Yet, it doesn't feel like a job. It is part of me, part of my life.

I sometimes question my concept of "place of best use" nowadays. Is it still valid? Or is it rather a matter of who do I choose to be? With an emphasis on being, rather than doing?

As of today, I cannot describe this chapter from a real metalevel perspective. There are no retrospective conclusions yet since it is NOW. My assumption is that this is the path I will stay on. Who knows?

And yet the story doesn't end here. The river of life had one radical turn for me along the way: I was very sick during this last decade. It would go beyond the scope of this chapter to share the details of the illness. But I intend to write a book about my insights at a later stage. It gives me peace to think that someone else might benefit from my experience.

The question of "Why?" almost drove me nuts while being sick. There was no straightforward diagnosis, all very complex, and I just couldn't figure it out. Life slowed down during this time, and I had even more time to think and learn. I spent months researching, looking for answers, and healing in the fields of medicine, psychology, and spirituality. I was wondering what comes first - body, mind, or spirit -- and I tested any healing method I came across. It wasn't one method that helped me recover. Folders of diagnostics and analyses, great experts in their fields, much trial and error and patience, time and time again, led to improvement.

Bound to home a lot, I embarked on another rewarding journey, writing my first book together with a friend and colleague: "The Golden View: The Key to Self-realization and Becoming Conscious." Honestly, I underestimated the time and energy it would need. But we did it and proudly published the book in German in 2014 and in English a couple of years later.

All medical indicators look pretty positive as of today. I should be amazingly happy and relieved about it. Yes, I feel less fear, less tension. Yet I am still searching for humility and gratitude inside me after that rollercoaster. It has been a slow recovery. Not one "eureka" moment. It felt like hard work, and I wasn't able to accept this part of the river fully, I went against it often in my mind. The struggle left some traces, which I am still trying to overwrite. Some days, it feels like waking up after a nightmare with a racing heart, still sweating. Like fog lifting, trying to orient myself.

I wanted to run always, not walk. Travel, not stay. Laugh, not cry. I wanted to conquer the world, and I didn't. My ego was screaming loud. I climbed uphill and am on my way downhill now. Which is great. I made it. I am wondering if I am wearing the right shoes for this part of the path.

It dawned on me during those years that I might not be the center of the universe. I couldn't pretend anymore that I was en route to having a tremendous impact on the world. My ego hated to tap into my own insignificance, and I didn't figure out how this could be liberating as some people claim. I wish I could say I am wiser, calmer, and enlightened now, after all. Oh well.

Peace is emerging in me only recently. My ego is quieter most of the time.

I love my friends, my animals, nature, my work. I feel more connected to all around me. Less searching for "kicks" (well, a little less). The river didn't flow as I wanted. Surprise. Yet, I am still here and curious to see where it will lead me next.

I see us all in one boat on this river of life. Only together can we overcome any challenges ahead of us.

Regardless of how impactful my life will be in the end, no matter what is still to come, I will base my decisions on answering the question "Why?" And my intuition has to go along with the answer: "It just has to feel right."

Simone Alz

Coaching and Management Consulting, Psychologist, CPCC

Simone Alz holds a degree in psychology and is a qualified coach (CPCC). She has nearly two decades of international experience working with a variety of global companies and organizations.

Having begun her career in a renowned management consulting company as a human performance and change management consultant, she then worked for the United Nations in both New York and Rome. As Associate Expert for the UN Department of Economics and Social Affairs, her remit included strategic personnel allocation and staff delegation and development. In her role as a staff counselor for the UN World Food Program, she not only worked as a psychological advisor but also provided crisis intervention and training for staff at headquarters and on WFP missions. She then went on to develop crisis intervention programs for the UN Department of Safety and Security.

Within the private sector, she has led international teams and held executive responsibility for the departments of People and Organization Development, Leadership Development, and HR Strategy and Change Management.

From her base in Munich, Simone Alz currently works as an independent consultant to senior executives, and she coaches team, personality, and consciousness development for multinational clients. Alongside mediation and conflict-management expertise, she also provides coaching and facilitation training. Her work is characterized by her strategic way of thinking and her distinctive talent for facilitating transitions with intuition and clarity.

Simone published her first book The Golden View in 2014.

simone.alz@oxfordleadership.com
www.linkedin.com/in/simone-alz

Be The Change

by Xavier Bertrand

I was born and grew up in the mid-1970s, as the first child of my family. My brother came four years later. Both of us were born in Paris, though our parents were from the central western part of France near Poitiers, between Paris and Bordeaux. They both grew up on farms in the countryside and moved to Paris in their early thirties. I spent most of my early childhood holidays in fields of that countryside. I have vivid memories of looking after my greataunt's goats with her and her dog, enjoying simple and free moments under the sun and the wide, open skies.

School was fine for me, as I have always been eager to learn, with an open and curious mind, and I was a rather social child. But there is a wound I carried from the age of five. I had not yet started primary school. My mother was a working mum. She worked hard for forty years as a molecular biology scientist who took part in research teams that identified significant genes. My dad had started his journey in the army before becoming an engineer. On Wednesdays, there was no school, and I was looked after by a nanny at her place. My first nanny was a gem with kids of her own, but she moved to the South of France as I turned five, and I was then placed with a different family for a year. I did not like that second house. There were two grown-up teenagers who stayed on Wednesdays. On several occasions, I was abused by the younger one, who made me swear never to divulge anything of "our play." So, I shut up. I shut myself. I was so scared. Every time it happened, I mentally cut myself off from my body to cope, as it was my only escape since the room was closed and I was threatened. As if erased from my memory, I grew up never mentioning these events, until twenty years later.

I had left home by then. My self-esteem was especially affected in my teenage years. This hidden wound prevented me from flourishing and becoming my true self. I felt ashamed, yet I could not find courage or comfort at home to confide what had happened to me. So, I kept my secret and grew up with it, uncomfortably. I found solace in books, studies, and music, and I had an angry, rebellious mind, very sensitive to injustice in the world, influenced as I was by my painful wound. I was searching for something to soothe my soul, and I left home at eighteen, to pursue higher studies in management. I was on a deep quest for meaning, trying to reconcile business school studies with being involved in social activities. Unable to find true inspiration in France, I decided to seize the opportunity of studying abroad to leave for India, eager to experience a different culture, where tradition and values might hold society together.

Awakening to the world and myself in India

Living and working in India for sixteen years between 1996 and 2012 was a defining period during which I grew to become a conscious human being and a responsible leader. Reading The Paths of Wisdom by the French author Arnaud Desjardins, who had met remarkable beings such as Ma Ananda Mayi, Swami Sivananda, His Holiness the Dalai Lama, Kyabje Kangyur Rinpoche, and some pirs in then Sufi Afghanistan, had reignited a sincere spiritual questioning in me before I became a postgraduate student at the Indian Institute of Management in Ahmedabad, the I-I-M-A. Ahmedabad is the city where Gandhi settled on his return for good from South Africa, and I discovered his life and Satyagraha (or "search for Truth") spending much time at his Sabarmati Ashram. From being largely ignorant about India, I became filled with its colors, smells, contrasts, and genuinely intrigued by its spiritual customs and traditions; all its diverse living and buzzing realities stimulated me tremendously! Although far away from home, I felt free and eager to embrace life anew!

Studying at IIMA along with some of the brightest minds of India enriched me deeply. Seeing my intense interest in Indian culture and spirituality, one fellow student who has remained a dear friend gave me a copy of his preferred book: Autobiography of a Yogi. The story of Yogananda pursuing the path of Indian sages inspired me to travel to many parts of India to visit ashrams and places he or Arnaud Desjardins mentioned in their writings. Beyond reading and traveling, I started realizing the depth of self-discovery through first-hand practice, as I was initiated to yoga and the yogic science of breathing -- pranayama and kriyas -- which I practiced daily for years.

This led me to experience a turning point. After my studies, I was able to find work, initially in Chennai, for a waste management firm, while pursuing my research thesis on climate-change economics. Then in Mumbai, as a junior diplomat of the Ministry of Finance, at the Consulate General of France, facilitating entry into the Indian market for French companies, and assisting senior diplomats in trade negotiations. I was able to sustain myself well with work in Mumbai, and I also enjoyed dedicating my free time to visiting local women's associations to learn how microcredit could foster social change. I also pursued spiritual practices with Indian friends who shared that interest. Every week, we gathered for long Sudarshan kriya sessions. I practiced long kriyas regularly, as I felt this practice helped me cleanse emotional blocks and allowed me to let go of my past childhood abuse experiences. That turning point came on two occasions, each time at the same moment of a long kriya.

This may sound weird, but I experienced leaving my body on those two occasions, each time toward the end of the kriya process, as one relaxes, lying down, closed eyes, listening to sacred mantras. The first time, I was taken by surprise by the experience, and I could not completely fathom what had happened. But when it occurred again in similar conditions several weeks later, I grasped what I experienced: I vividly recall that I could see and feel myself as if floating above my body... my whole sense of being pervading the full room I was in as if liberated from my physical body boundaries. That experience contradicted all the beliefs about myself, and in fact, the whole sense of who I thought I was. It stunned me. Yet, I could reconcile with the truth of the experience and all it truly meant after I experienced it again. This showed me that life is much more than I thought it was, and it anchored in my cells the veracity that I am, beyond my body and my mind. Beyond my little sense of self, this part of me that says "I" -- my ego. I continued growing through my journey in India with this deep realization embedded inside me.

In the early 2000s in Mumbai, I was very fulfilled with work, serving my country as a diplomat, contributing to enhanced relations with the country I had decided to live in, which I loved. I worked closely with ministers and even heads of state during two presidential visits. I realized, however, that pursuing diplomacy as a career would have meant leaving India for other geographies. But I had promised myself I would not leave without discovering the authentic traditional wisdom of the Vedic culture, that I could see still cemented Indian society so strongly, despite modern foreign influences. I had begun studying Vedanta, the Indian teaching tradition underlying the system of yogas and Vedas, and I regularly attended classes and retreats to study scriptures such as the Upanishads or Bhagavad Gita. I was so inclined to Vedanta that when an offer came to head the newly set up Indian subsidiary of a famous French luxury house I had helped prospecting, I felt torn between accepting this golden opportunity and studying Vedanta full time. It was not an easy decision.

When the offer came a second time a few months later, I seized it and became, at the age of thirty, the youngest CEO of that prestigious company. It was a big ego boost! Because of the image of that French luxury house, it was in a way like continuing to represent France in India -- and starting a new business. Everything needed to be done from scratch, and this experience opened my world even further. I feel grateful I learned so much in those years, from 2005 to 2010. Initially, I could hardly sleep due to my anxiety to succeed and do things well. I was entrusted with such great responsibilities for the first time: What if I failed? Focusing on me did not help, however, and I realized what I needed was to humbly focus on work. I assembled a team and engaged with clients. I felt more comfortable as I led a collective. I started trusting myself as the business grew. From my little ego to building a whole ecosystem, and acknowledging what is, I learned to become a responsible leader. The culturally diverse environment and state of inequalities made a challenging context. To connect with India, we created a local nonprofit foundation to invest in socially responsible projects aiming at training young women, empowering populations living close to precious natural resources or acknowledging the rich local hand-craftmanship.

We invented innovative strategies with my team to create a profitable path in the nascent Indian market for western luxury. It took longer than expected and my bosses started putting pressure on me to deliver faster. I worked hard, believing we were on the right path. I continued being inspired by India and spent time in retreats, trying to balance a not-so-healthy CEO lifestyle. Working very intensely had stressed me and brought me twice to hospital interventions that had been warnings. In parallel with the busy life of a CEO running a new business, I set up a trust with friends to foster microfinance development in India and Nepal through capacity building and technical assistance. I then shared my life with an older Indian woman, with whom I had a strong spiritual companionship. My sincere pursuit of a study led me to an authentic Vedanta teacher, Swami Dayananda, thanks to Surya and Neema, two dear Indian friends who had been his students for years.

In 2010, I was forced to cut costs to turn our Indian subsidiary into profits, asked to send excellent people off, and to wind down our foundation. I learned how business can be a matter of fact, which was challenging for me to reconcile fully with as we were in a particular market context. However, I reacted by committing to deliver on business and also to outplace the concerned people to better jobs. I was also relieved our socially responsible projects could initiate a new project that would become a global corporate foundation. I suggested to my president to integrate our relatively small Indian business under the very profitable Middle East region and proposed to train my peer in Dubai to handle my responsibilities before I left to become an independent entrepreneur in India. The corporation did not choose to reinvest in India to sustain its efforts. As a result, my team slowly left the ship one by one after I did. Being in good terms with my employer, I could be coached for the first time to prepare my next chapter. I had decided to join hands with Sanjeev, a dear friend from South India, to develop an independent advisory business he had created in Bangalore. As we organized several learning journeys from Europe into India, I traveled back to France more regularly to train and become a facilitator and a coach.

Coming home to become a family man

A seven-year period of transition began for me in 2010. Not only was I to leave a well-paid corporate CEO job. I also separated from my companion, feeling confused about how we could grow old together. She had two boys who were grown adults. I was unsure whether I wanted to marry and have children of my own, but it was not an option with her.

Early in the year, I went to Nepal to visit Matthieu Ricard, a French Buddhist monk with whom I shared the connection of Arnaud Desjardins. Matthieu had invited me to the Schechen monastery to attend the 100th birth anniversary of Dilgo Khyentse Rinpoche, his second spiritual teacher who had also been a teacher to His Holiness the Dalai Lama. I attended the celebrations honoring the soul of that great teacher and took some time to visit the activities of the Karuna Schechen foundation. Later in April, I had again joined Matthieu in Zurich to attend the annual symposium of Mind & Life with His Holiness the Dalai Lama on "Altruism and Compassion in Economic Systems: A Dialogue at the Interface of Economics, Neuroscience, and Contemplative Sciences." I decided my next chapter would have to do with impact work that could reconcile my interest in meditation and wisdom teachings. Matthieu has been a great source of inspiration. He introduced me to a Belgian friend Charles-Antoine Janssen, with whom I started a conversation on how to make this a concrete move.

June 2011 is when I met Claire for the first time in Paris, at a coaching seminar with Robert Dilts on "Going Beyond Your Limiting Beliefs to Achieve Your Dreams!" We shared lunch with her associates. A few days later, she decided to join me for a retreat to which Matthieu invited me to the South West of France. We then spent most of that summer together, and she visited me in India afterward. Sanjeev, who had lived in France for several years and returned to India with a French wife named Claire, helped me realize time had come for me to settle. In fact, it was during a retreat on 11/11/11 in Rishi Kesh with him and our two Claires that I decided to make a conscious choice to leave India and move back to France to live with Claire. Moving to India was not easy for her since her family is deeply rooted in the South West of France for over ten generations. After a few months of sharing a place in Toulouse, traveling back and forth to India where I still worked, I asked her whether she wanted to become my life companion. She accepted, and I took her to South India, to the ashram where I was retreating and Surya and Neema were studying Vedanta, in the jungle of the Nilgiris, to call for auspicious times in our life union through prayers. Swami Dayananda was so kind as to bless our vows and requested the temple priests to perform rituals for a proper Vedic wedding ceremony, on May 12, 2013. We subsequently got married officially in France in Claire's family region on July 5, 2014, surrounded by our families and friends from various parts of the world, many of whom were Indians. Claire invited my close friends three days earlier, to celebrate my fortieth birthday.

It was a period full of transitions. From Mumbai to Toulouse and a small village of the rural South West. Being able to walk in the fields at sunrise or sunset when I was home helped me ground me back in France. Though I would still travel to India regularly, living in rural France helped me focus on what was essential in our life at such a transition time. Work called back quickly, however. Claire aspired to find a job in larger organizations to grow her skills and experience. I regularly traveled to Paris for a client of mine who had asked me to become their CEO. She came with me once and quickly found a good job in digital learning.

We decided to move to Paris at the end of 2014 to prioritize our work. I took over as CEO of a global nonprofit founded and chaired by an influential public figure in France, who had created this NGO with a focus on microfinance to alleviate poverty. The project was inspired by his friend Dr. Muhammad Yunus, who was our supervisory board chairman. That began a very busy working period for us both in Paris. I was extremely tied up with work, passionate about making an impact, traveling extensively to many new countries in Africa or Asia, working with governments, development finance institutions, UN agencies, local civil society organizations and other NGOs like ours. I realized soon, however, why my predecessor had left: after six months, seven of the eight direct reports in my executive committee decided to leave, mainly after long tenures that had brought them close to burnout. Our work environment generated exhaustion, but our workaholic chairman was adamant about letting go of such culture that, among other aspects, prevented the organization from transforming for good. We persevered in more of the same even though it was not sustainable. I entered a period of a real struggle, trying to turn our organization around into a more balanced one, but I faced a failing system as well as my limitations. I had wanted us to be coached as a whole organization, but again, our overpowering chairman objected. I dared not confront him. Despite long hours and much effort to try and find a way, including restructuring, new strategy, even changing the name of the organization and its governance, we were stuck with a failing business model that was too grant-based instead of being driven by impact monitoring and propelled by hybrid financing. I came close to burnout myself, and my saving grace was Claire becoming pregnant. My beautiful wife tried to warn me of my unhelpful patterns getting too deeply committed at work without sufficient awareness and care for our essential needs. It took me months of her being pregnant to wake up! One night, I dreamt of a soothing baby girl's presence caring for us. I knew intuitively Claire expected a daughter.

On November 14, 2015, I suddenly woke up at 1 am, which was unusual. I had gone to bed at 9 pm, after coming back from a trip. I looked at my phone and figured I had received messages from friends all over the world, asking if we were safe. I did not understand. With a weird feeling inside, I turned on the TV and watched the tragedy that had happened in Paris, just after I had fallen asleep. I was torn, shattered to pieces. Terrorism had again struck reawakening what I had experienced in Mumbai seven years before on November 26, 2008, with terrorist attacks that had killed a couple of friends. Shocked again by so much barbary, I cried deeply that night. Claire found me silent in front of the TV in our living room in the early morning hours, and we sat together as she discovered the tragedy too. We received friends at home the next day and were happy to enjoy the joyful presence of their children. The atmosphere was one of mourning, which remained so for weeks in Paris. As I resumed work, we gathered our employees to observe a solemn moment together and remind ourselves our activities to alleviate inequalities were one of the things we could do to prevent such barbary from breeding on poverty.

Five days later, Claire called me at work to bring her to the maternity clinic. Eva Ananda was born on November 18, 2015, ten days before the due date. She brought us light after darkness, and we let space to live again with a sense of relief. Welcoming our daughter home helped me regain balance at work, too. I pushed again for our organization to be coached, but my efforts were in vain. I wish I had been able to be both a CEO and a coach to facilitate our transformation process, but instead, I faced my own limitations to address wider systemic issues. I decided to learn systemic change later and focused on changing myself before changing the world.

Becoming a father allowed me to get rid of some of my masks, be more authentic and truer to myself. When I am with our little girl, there is no veil. I was initially awed by her presence and easiness to connect to what is. Fatherhood has been revealing in many ways. It helped transcend aspects of my family history, with a lineage of misunderstandings between fathers and sons that prevented them from feeling comfortable in daring to show and express love. On my mum's side, the sudden demise of a great man figure, my grandfather Michel, who had departed in a tragic car accident while in service as a peace guardian, marked my mother's life and affected me as well. I always searched for a grounding reference of authority before realizing I needed to ground my own inner authority instead, to become who I really wanted to be.

In June 2016 I met with my chairman to inform him I initially thought could be a dream job but ended being a rather nightmarish experience, albeit one from which I learned a lot. I regained sufficient time for another transition. I later learned I was replaced by three senior managers, which made me realize how hard I had been working, despite my not being able to land our transformation process. The day after packing off my office, I left for Brussels to attend the annual Symposium of Mind & Life, where Matthieu and Charles-Antoine had kindly invited me. Those three inspiring days on "Power & Care," with a community of 2,000 like-minded people, made me feel very hopeful for our collective capacity to bring about real change. During that symposium, I discussed concrete steps with Charles-Antoine to work together with Kois Invest, his impact investment fund. That symposium is also where I had a seminal meeting with the person who would become my spiritual teacher for the coming years. I connected with Thierry Janssen in a way that reminded me of what Yogananda had written in his autobiography: when the student is ready, the teacher will appear! Thierry invited me to join the initiation school he had just founded in Brussels, which offered a three-year path to initiate doctors and health practitioners to "Therapeutic Presence." There could begin my last transition towards embracing my true purpose at work: "Accompany leaders through a conscious metamorphosis to heal and transform the organizations they lead and in turn bring about systems change and societal impact."

Embracing my true purpose

From the first session at the School of Therapeutic Presence, I knew I was in the right place at the right time for me. Working on myself amidst a group of health practitioners allowed a profound self-healing transformation that would empower my work as a coach. The deep inner work Thierry led us through during the first year made me aware of my wounds as a human being, and how my neurotic behaviors helped me adapt and build my personality to create a sense of myself. I needed to deconstruct that to become my true authentic self. This psycho-spiritual work I embraced at the time of becoming a father was exactly what I had wished for to offer a better self to our daughter Eva. Like all parents, Claire and I focused on providing her with the best attention and love we could give for her initial growth. We were awed at how fast she developed and started communicating and how comfortable she has always felt with other beings. She truly became the new light in our lives.

In parallel to this deeply transformative work, I had started working with Kois Invest to lead impact projects that linked responsible investors with social entrepreneurs to create coalitions for good to address UN Sustainable Development Goals such as access to health or access to education. With the help of Thierry, I soon saw myself repeating patterns of working intensely, without listening to my essential needs or the ones of my family. Claire was disturbed by my frequent travels and found it difficult to handle Eva alone, even if we had a nanny come to our home every day. So, when Kois offered me to become a partner, although I loved the quality of the work and its people, I took time to reflect and eventually said no, in order to say yes to myself and my family. My choice was to focus on human potential to enable conscious change and transformation, rather than structuring capital to finance impact projects. I completed the executive coach program I had started, along with other certifications in Human Element to learn about high performing teams, and Theory U to learn awareness-based systems change. I even pursued new studies in medicine, meditation, and neuroscience. In May 2019, I completed my three-year initiation at the School of Therapeutic Presence. This involving group work helped me transform and reconnect with myself like none before. I acknowledge my sensitivity and rely on my intuitive self. I learned to pause in silence and create a space where one can let emerge a reconnection with one's deeper self, which can foster healing. Claire and I had also traveled to South India with Thierry, which enabled me to reconcile this work with my initial spiritual journey with traditional Indian wisdom. All this, along with pursuing work with a trustworthy supervisor, gave me the confidence to embrace becoming a coach and facilitator. I connected with Lasse and Cyril who co-head Oxford Leadership and joined our collaborative network in early 2017, inspired by the renewed focus on aiming to "Transform Leaders for Good."

A last defining transition is actually happening as I finish writing these lines. Claire and I experienced difficult times since the end of 2018 after she left a job she loved at a leading natural cosmetic company due to moral harassment from her boss. She has been looking for a new employer who recognizes her talent and capabilities. Living in Paris without an opportunity to truly flourish proved stressful for her as a mother, and this, added to my regular travels, affected our balance as a couple and as a family. It made me worry whether we could succeed in creating a balanced life staying in Paris, as our relationship had become tense and we were no longer available for one another. Eva's presence in our life already compelled us to readjust our balance. Bringing her in the center possibly made us forget ourselves as a couple. We had to learn how to listen to each other and reconnect more deeply, to be able to express our essential needs to one another in the wake of such difficulties. We did not find Paris and its "agitated" environment conducive for a harmonious living for us and Eva, especially since we both aspire to live close to nature. Despite daily morning walks in the woods opposite our home across the Seine River, my inner work had made me too sensitive not to be affected by such agitation. I listened to myself and heard a deep desire for a more peaceful pace of life and talked to Claire. We decided to leave Paris where we had been living for five years, to settle back in the southwest of France, where her roots lie. Earlier in spring, we had traveled several times to Bordeaux and Arcachon, where we had enjoyed walking on the ocean shore. That allowed us to reconnect with a desire for a simpler life, less agitated and closer to nature. I had a vivid vision of myself being able to enjoy walking on the ocean shore daily before I turn fifty, and it reignited me inwardly. We moved to Bordeaux last August as a choice to embrace a more "ecological" life, in a smaller city, more suitable for us and Eva, and get closer to our dream to live close to the ocean. Workwise, this brought me closer to Cyril, with whom we set up a new base for Oxford Leadership in Bordeaux with colleagues. This move is driven by a deep need for inner coherence, hearing a call for a more peaceful, conscious and harmonious family living.

It truly inspires me to continuously learn how we humans can reach our best selves. Self-realization has been my key driver for a purpose. In a work context, it translated to a focus on how to foster high performance in a way that is ecological and sustainable, for teams working together. And in a broader sense, to how we can grow our conscious best selves as humankind, and integrate wisdom to live a more peaceful, harmonious life. What is our fate as a species? What are we to become, on this beautiful, living planet? We have become so powerful, impacting our environment so drastically, yet remain so fragile, and still largely unaware of who we truly are, as we forgot we are nature and belong to the living realm. We live in a period where human consciousness is emerging; there is an awakening, and a reason to rejoice, yet it is truly time. Eva Ananda will be eighty-five in 2100. When she will then turn back on her own life's journey, I wonder what kind of world she will have witnessed and evolved in. How can I bring my best contribution during the coming fifteen to twenty years of my life, to let emerge a more peaceful transition towards a stable and sustainable world for all to thrive and flourish as conscious human beings, in harmony with other living beings? Nurturing such deep questions regularly helps me keep perspective and cultivate a humble yet meaningful purpose for my actions, especially at work.

My purpose has been to help leaders become better human beings, so they can offer their best, perform better in a way that is also more ecological for them and others, and the system they belong to. We are all leaders of our own lives. Learning to grow more conscious has been a key driver since my twenties, and I got to discover the world through India and the lens of its ancient art of living wisdom. I have been inspired by such ancient traditions that remain alive, which coupled with modern scientific advancements might help us live a more conscious transition, provided we remain humble enough, respecting who we truly are, of what life and living are.

In my favorite movie Contact by Robert Zemeckis, which is dedicated to Carl Sagan, the lead actress Jodie Foster is asked by a jury gathered to select the best scientist to experience a journey through time and space. „If you were to meet extra-terrestrial beings, what question would you ask them?" Her answer is: "How did you do it? How did you evolve? How did you survive your technological adolescence without destroying yourself?" I find this question so relevant at the stage of our evolution. We will soon reach a singular point wherefrom machines and technology conceived by humans will surpass some of our forms of intelligence. What can we possibly do to evolve consciously? My humble answer is to strive to know ourselves better and redefine what it means for us to be human beings. I try to know myself better, to become more whole as a person, and to keep growing. So, I can offer my best self to people I love and people I live and work with. Having studied Gandhi's life quite closely when I lived in Ahmedabad, I have been inspired by his "mantra" "Be the change you want to see in the world." Reading his autobiography My Experiments with Truth was an initial inspiration to link inner transformation with organizational evolution and societal change, to let emerge conscious sustainable living.

I recently experienced two weeks of work with Oxford Leadership colleagues in Asia and Europe and had the impression to have rediscovered soulmates with whom I had already worked to transform and heal human souls. It feels uplifting to share a common purpose to heal and empower organizations' change by enabling people to express their full being through leadership as a way of being. Embracing my self-transformation through our work fills me with sheer joy.

After our move to Bordeaux, Claire became pregnant again. She carries our second daughter, who is due around the end of May 2020. I am so happy life seems to acknowledge our conscious choice toward harmony. This is a truly new beginning for me as a father, husband, and colleague. I hope that our community at Oxford Leadership can contribute to reintegrate wisdom to leadership for our transitions to happen peacefully.

Last year, I was invited by a friend to join her for a meeting at the Elysée Palace, the French Republic President's office, to present a collective project consisting of organizing a civil society Forum of World Wisdoms that could take place in Paris. I was then invited to the Paris Peace Forum to interact with stakeholders of the international community, where I could approach luminaries like maestro cellist and UN Messenger of Peace Yo-Yo Ma. I felt so inspired by his projects to enable peace through music. May such a project emerge through global collective work and intelligence. My wish is this: May peace arise on Earth through a heightened human consciousness that can Transform Leaders for Good.

Xavier Bertrand

Founder Nayanam SAS, Core Group Partner

Xavier is forty-five and lives with wife Claire and daughter Eva Ananda in Bordeaux, near the Atlantic Ocean, in the southwest of France. He joined Oxford Leadership in early 2017 and believes in their endeavor to "Transform Leaders for Good." Through coaching and awareness-based systems change, he enables positive and healthy transformations in large organizations for a more conscious work environment. In his journey, Xavier led teams in diverse cultural contexts, as a trade diplomat, as CEO of a French company in India, and as CEO of a global nonprofit based in Paris, working in thirty countries. Initially trained as an MBA and MPhil in France, working in India for sixteen years profoundly impacted his journey. Discovering meditation, yoga, and Vedanta, the ancient wisdom tradition of India, drove him to focus on conscious human transformation within organizations authentically involved in driving the sustainability agenda to bring a more harmonious living.

His motto is: BE THE CHANGE YOU WANT TO SEE IN THE WORLD

xavier.bertrand@oxfordleadership.com

www.linkedin.com/in/xavier-bertrand-8a98036
www.twitter.com/xbinindia

Conclusion

by Cyril Legrand

When my colleague Eve Simon inspired me to develop a book about purpose, it was a foregone conclusion. There is nothing more natural for our network of leadership practitioners than to extend our cooperation by sharing our "intrinsic motivation" with more people. So, what differentiates our unique, collaborative Oxford Leadership community in the universe of leadership consulting? It is living passionately our raison d'être. And we have successfully done so for more than twenty years.

We are a sharing community that helps large organizations accelerate the sustainable growth of their leaders, teams, and bottom line through high-impact and transformational leadership and organizational culture interventions. We help leaders and their teams find deeper meaning in their work by connecting individual purpose to the higher purpose of the company. We have been constantly growing since the late 1090s, building a global network that is today recognized worldwide. The network has reinvented and transformed itself by going through the ups and downs of all entrepreneurial adventures and establishing strong partnerships with its clients. We share at least two fundamental things as a community.

The first is that we are all completely committed to the same purpose: "Transforming Leaders for Good." We strive to be consistent and aligned in this ambition which inspires us, guides us, and completes us. It is a strong link that transcends our egos and our differences to bring us back to what is fundamental: Why are we together? Why do we exist? What do we have to offer?

The second is that, before preaching to our clients and partners about the power of "meaning," we have all, without exception, done deep personal work on our individual raison d'être. This is an essential and founding element. How could we be credible and have an impact on our sector if we did not do thorough work? We have explored the twists and turns of self-awareness.

We have committed to a marvelous quest in search of what makes sense for each of us. It was certainly a foregone conclusion, a flash, one of those moments of realization which marks a before and after. For others, it was (and still is) an iterative journey, an enigmatic puzzle that makes us explore with introspection our path through life. It allows us to collect these conclusions that clarify for everyone what is essential, what inspires us, what gives us contagious energy.

We have institutionalized in Oxford Leadership the regular sharing of our lifelines. This is an excellent method to constantly get to know each other better and create this intimacy which feeds our social and operational unity. It is also a good exercise to benevolently share our strengths and weaknesses, to exchange our motivational levers, our aspirations and that which makes us better and more alive. It is never easy to give of oneself, to deliver oneself to others without masks. It is an act of courage and trust which cements our relations.

Personally, I have always found it fascinating and enriching to listen to these slices of life. They allow me to think about mine. They give me thought processes and make me work on my humility and detachment. They are often a source of inspiration and development.

Consequently, if we are together, how could we not propose to our colleagues that they share their experiences? How did they navigate their quests for meaning, live their purpose and create a capacity for sharing their learnings? Neither conceptual nor theoretical elements were shared, just slices of life, a part of them that they want to offer beyond our community.

I am excited to see the results coming together, and I know it's a work from the heart. It is representative of our mindset and the values that motivate it.

This reminds me of a commentary from one of our clients (the chief human resources officer of a leading global retailer) responding to someone who asked what made our community different from others. His response is representative and echoes what many others will say about us: "On paper, many things can seem similar in terms of offers and services, but these leadership alchemists have a particular energy that emanates from them and an indescribable magnetism that greatly contributes to the success of their services. They create transformational experiences and have unique authenticity that is the result of humility and generosity that is rarely found elsewhere. They are exemplary. They walk their talk. It is not only about what they do, but it is also all about who they are."

I am convinced that our collective commitment and personal work on meaning contributes to this difference. I am proud to belong to this community and to contribute to its development.

I will share a story that is a perfect illustration of what makes me resonate in my work and which gives meaning to my everyday life.

We had the chance to contribute to the in-depth work of a company that is a world leader in their sector. We worked on their raison d'être and especially how to make them live this every day for all of their collaborators.

The company's purpose which was the result of veritable work on collective intelligence was expressed by a strong, inspiring and engaging slogan: "Adding Colors to People's Lives."

This message certainly generated many promotional and commercial initiatives to become a reality for the company's clients. However, this needed to be especially transformational and mobilizing for all the internal teams no matter their role and function.

I thus went to India where I worked for several weeks with the board of directors on the project for the deployment of the company purpose. We decided on a series of leadership development programs based on meaning and values. It would be accessible to all the levels of seniority, and all the employees would benefit from it.

To give more substance to the initiative, we decided that, for each group that participated in a program, it would be possible for them to nominate a community or association that they want to support in the name „Adding Color to People's Lives."

Thus, the day before the program, the group would go to the community of their choice and share a moment with them and repaint their facilities (which would have been prepared beforehand) to make good on their promise.

May arrived on the plains of Mumbai. In a small remote town, we committed to connect an isolated community to the periphery. We arrived before a group of small buildings whose colors were faded over time in a community that welcomed all those for whom no one is able nor wants to care. There were old people, people with special needs, orphans, and AIDS sufferers.

The fifteen people from our group were received with respect. We were given a presentation and a tour by those responsible; they were nuns belonging to an order with which I am not familiar. The residents sat in a line inside the buildings. As we passed by, a heavy silence was palpable. We passed through places and received many glances, sometimes empty, sometimes inquiring and curious. It was difficult to establish contact because a world truly separated us.

We started working, giving color to the living spaces and exterior equipment. The colors were chosen by the residents. We felt useful and gave meaning to our actions.

We were about to leave and thank our hosts when they approached me and suggested that I ask the group to please stay a little while longer. Around the exterior equipment that we had just partly restored, the nuns installed audio equipment. They invited us to sit down and informed us that the community wished to share with us. We sat down on the ground in a semi-circle with the residents across from us. There were around ten individuals with special needs. Typically, Bollywoodesque music started to play, and those individuals began dancing with the support of their helpers. Their gaze shined and the music transported them. They looked at us intently. This deep eye contact was touching and deeply affected our group, as it was a way of thanking us.

Despite their disabilities, they approached us and each one of them invited one of us to share in the music and dancing. They took us by the hand and took communion. I saw the emotion overcome our participants. Their eyes got teary; nobody spoke. A highly symbolic moment.

The contrast between this suspended and magical moment and our first contact during the presentation of the community was striking even if it did not last for more than five minutes. The images, emotions, and sensations were unforgettable. We got on the bus and everyone became quiet. Each one of them lived and incarnated what "Adding Colors to People's Lives" means. The raison d'être was no longer an abstract concept but rather an emotional reality full of meaning. We had just consolidated its foundations.

This is why I love my work and I fulfill myself through it. I feel great happiness, thanks to being able to share these magic moments which contribute to developing an authentic, truly humanistic leadership approach based on meaning and strong values.

The workplace needs to actively contribute to this. I always separated private and professional domains, but I also maintained the deep conviction that the organization should be a place for self-realization. Only then can the workplace truly become a meaningful, healthy and even healing habitat.

My professional experience was a determining factor in my quest for meaning. At first, the purpose was purely intuitive and very kinesthetic for me. I felt what was good for me, especially during transitional moments. In fact, it was only later on that I worked on this notion of raison d'être. For a long time, this was simply focused on a deep sentiment, a deep feeling, an intimate conviction of fully living in the moment. I had the feeling that I was there, where I should be and that I needed to get as many benefits out of it as possible.

This meant a certain clarity in my choices and decisions without me being able to explain why. It was all in my capacity to live in the moment and be connected to my feelings. Then the feeling of elevation arrived. I put painful events and moments of intense happiness in order and added meaning to them, thus getting an overview. Things fell into place. The events contributed to something very rewarding, a consciousness accelerator and a realization. I was aligned and congruent.

People have often asked me if purpose is something that is unchanged, or if it is something that develops. For me, it is a dynamic to be explored. It is only found at the fringes of our experiences. However, it is only by observation and reflection on these experiences that the meaning appears. Only by connecting the different elements can a coherent and -- for me -- really transcendent purpose emerge.

I hope that our book will not only provide you with a deeper understanding and feeling about the Oxford Leadership community but will inspire you to embark on or pursue your own rewarding quest for meaning.

Bon voyage ...

Cyril Legrand

Founding Trustee and Chief Executive Officer at Oxford Leadership

Cyril is one of the Founding Trustees and the Chief Executive Officer of Oxford Leadership.

Before Oxford Leadership, he held senior management positions in the consumer-goods sector for over fifteen years, especially in Asia. Experienced with business operations in complex multicultural and multidisciplinary environments, he is a recognized global C-Suite consultant and executive coach on organization transformation and executive teams' transition and performance.

His purpose is to support top executives and top teams to find their X-factor to care, dare, and share with maximum impact, transforming business for good. He has built a unique approach in supporting and sustaining leaders and their teams to quickly shift mindset and behaviors, transform relationships and conversations for peak and sustainable performances.

He is an alumnus of HEC Paris and Oxford Saïd Business School and is still pursuing his doctoral research in the fields of team coaching, collective intuition, and leadership innovation.

cyril.legrand@oxfordleadership.com
www.oxfordleadership.com

A Higher Cause

Our mission is to make the world a better place by inspiring leaders to transform themselves and their entities into a force for good.

This book was not intended to be a profit source for us, but to share our stories, our path and beliefs to inspire you.

Therefore, the profit of this book will go to a non-profit which plants trees for an environmental impact such as reforesting the Amazon.

We believe in the urgency of major forest restoration effort. Trees provide so many benefits to our everyday lives. They filter clean air, provide fresh drinking water, help curb climate change, and create homes for thousands of species of plants and animals around the globe.

Planting trees will help save the Earth. We know we can do it by inspiring you one book at a time.

Enjoy the journey to finding your purpose.

Acknowledgment

Writing a full-length book is an act of commitment and faith over multiple months. Having 22 authors, every one busy with life and career, and with different levels of experience in writing, we are thankful to have had someone on board to lead and support us on this amazing journey.

We want to thank Doris Gross, Founder of Fempress Media, and her team, who helped us not only to assemble the vast amount of life experience and emotions but also supported us with a lot of expert insights forming the backbone of this book and helping us spread the word about this wonderful topic on purpose. Her help and patience throughout the whole manuscript development have been very valuable and appreciated.

While we made an effort to write about our valuable experiences and what made us to the humans we became, Doris and her team showed us how to frame our experiences in a book, which is valuable for our readers and to shine a light on the things that shaped us in the past and still do nowadays. There is so much more to writing a book than to just actually write it. Doris and her team took on the enormous amount of project management and organization behind the scenes, graphic design, layout, editing and also PR and marketing. With her holding all strings together we are so excited about presenting you a book, we are all very proud of.

We greatly appreciate the motivation and understanding for our crazy life and business schedules. With her help and support, we have been able to complete this book.

Learn more about Doris and Fempress Media and their expertise in self-publishing for single authors and community book projects here:

www.fempressmedia.com

„Talking about purpose is easy. Sure, we all want it – but how do we actually find ours? Be inspired by the 22 deeply personal stories of how finding a purpose transformed the authors' lives. Find yourself in their stories. Read this gem of a book, and you will instantly look at your own purpose through a fresh lens. Powerful!"

Achim Nowack,
Author/Business Thinker/C-Suite Success Coach

„We climb highest when we have let go of what we do not need. From these authors' examples, we learn how to discard our misconceptions, travel light and reach our goal."

Michael Pockley,
Zen priest, Head of Religious Studies, Devon

„Where is the energy coming from to do the extraordinary? To lead your team to reach the targets and go further when things get challenging? I've learned what a powerful enabler purpose is. This book allows you to see the multitude of solutions, showcased by various viewpoints and experiences."

Roland Meyer,
Managing Director, Germany

„PURPOSE is a refreshing book containing resonating stories – illuminating thought-provoking and heartfelt transformative experiences around reaching that place where one can align core beliefs with the workplace for a better fit and emotional happiness. Moreover, it reminds us as leaders to be conscious of those around us to ensure they're able to be in that place as well."

Russell Corvese,
Silicon Valley Executive

„This book is full of honest, heart-revealing, and powerful stories about people who have found gifts to share out of their own personal challenges and grief. I am so grateful that I listened in to their voices. As a writer, I will reflect on their wisdom and courage for a long time to come."

Alexandria Giardino,
Translator and author of books for children, including Ode to an Onion (Ode à un oignon), The Good Song, and Me + Tree.

„Where is the energy coming from to do the extraordinary? To lead your team to reach the targets and go further when things get challenging? I've learned what a powerful enabler purpose is. This book allows you to see the multitude of solutions, showcased by various viewpoints and experiences."

Dietmar Bochert,
Senior Vice President Corporate Communications at Franz Haniel & Cie. GmbH, Germany